Election 2005

Jon Smith is Political Editor of the Press Association, the national news agency whose wire service supplies every daily newspaper and broadcasting organisation in the country. He was previously a political correspondent and industrial editor on the *Sun*.

For my family

Election
2005

Jon Smith

POLITICO'S

in association with

The Press Assocation

First published in 2005
Politico's Publishing, an imprint of
Methuen Publishing Limited
11–12 Buckingham Gate
London SW1E 6LB

Printed and bound in Great Britain by Bookmarque

Methuen Publishing Limited Reg. No. 3543167

A CIP catalogue record for this book is available from the British Library

ISBN 1 84275 142 5

10 9 8 7 6 5 4 3 2 1

Contents

Foreword

'I just woke up this morning and thought, thank God it's under way.'
So said the Prime Minister, the Rt Hon. Tony Blair, on the afternoon
of Tuesday 5 April. He was chatting after his first campaign stop of
election 2005, and his relief was palpably genuine. Not only had the
death of Pope John Paul II caused him to delay his announcement of
polling day for 24 hours, but this was the moment, this election, that
New Labour had always dreamed of. A third successive term in office
had never been achieved by the party; it would be the ultimate justification for the Blair project. And now the only thing that stood
between it and victory was a Conservative Party, led by a man Labour
considered tarred with the brush of Tory governments of the past,
which itself would need an unprecedented electoral swing to win.

This was always going to be an historic election; this is its instant
history. Blair said the campaign battle was being fought
constituency by constituency. This is the day-by-day story of how
that battle unfolded. The entries are all contemporaneous; none
were completed more than 24 hours after the events they describe.

Access to the Blair campaign was more tightly restricted than
ever before in a general election, partly reflecting the bleak security
environment following September 11. The Conservatives, too,
decided to limit access to Michael Howard. But as the independent
national news agency for the UK, serving all the country's broadcasters and daily newspapers, the Press Association provided the
wire service pool reporting coverage for the nation's media, and
travelled to every location with the two leaders as they criss-crossed
the country by train, plane and helicopter. The Liberal Democrats

welcomed all-comers with open arms and the PA accompanied Charles Kennedy, too, on his battle bus.

Elections are profound expressions of democracy. Mercifully, in this country they can sometimes be very funny, too. And they can still, even in the days of focus groups and multiple opinion polls, spring surprises. After all, this one did.

Jon Smith,
Westminster, 7 May 2005

Acknowledgements

This book would not have been possible without the immense contributions of the Press Association's team of dedicated and professional reporters and photographers, who worked tirelessly across the country throughout the campaign. Special thanks are due to: John Deane and Andy Woodcock who travelled with Tony Blair; James Lyons who travelled with Michael Howard; and Jamie Lyons (no relation) who travelled with Charles Kennedy. And to photographers Stefan Rousseau and Kirsty Wigglesworth (Blair); Andrew Parsons and Gareth Copley (Howard); Gareth Fuller (Kennedy). Thanks also to Westminster colleagues Gavin Cordon, Trevor Mason, Joe Churcher and Viv Morgan; specialist correspondent colleagues Alan Jones, David Barrett, Peter Woodman, Tim Ross and Nick Allen and Elections Editor Chris Mead. Any errors, however, are mine and mine alone.

Sean Magee and Emma Musgrave at Politico's were immensely supportive, patient, kind and great fun to work with.

Finally, thanks are due to my Editor-in-Chief at PA Paul Potts and Editor Jonathan Grun for their help and support, not just with this book but over the years.

1

It's the election, stupid

At 11.52 a.m. on Wednesday 2 March, the fax machine in Tony Blair's private office, down a little corridor behind the Speaker's chair in the House of Commons, spluttered into life. Following a phone call from Conservative Campaign Headquarters – which sparked enough alarm in itself – a sheaf of documents relating to an NHS patient, Margaret Dixon, 69, from Penketh, near Warrington, began tumbling out, detailing the seven times her life-threatening operation to rebuild her shoulder had been postponed. Michael Howard had observed the cruel courtesy of informing Blair he was about to launch the 'War of Margaret's Shoulder' and, with it, the general election campaign of 2005.

Blair is always nervous before public appearances, believing it's necessary for him, if he's to do a good job, and never more so than at Prime Minister's Questions, which was about to begin at noon. He now had plenty of time to worry about just what he was to face from the Rt Hon. Michael Howard, QC over the Despatch Box.

Blair's suite of offices in the Commons includes a replica – almost – of the Cabinet table, with green-backed portcullis chairs. The Prime Minister often sits there alone, tapping his fingers and running through likely questions and answers he may have to give at PMQs. Usually, the Labour questions he knows, the others, he doesn't. The Tory leader's routine questions will normally have been predicted by Blair's own political aides, and the premier would have gone through his own answers, mumbling to himself the jibes, affirmations of government policy, and repetitive rhetoric designed to get the backbenchers cheering, until the moment when he pockets his spectacles and walks into the chamber itself.

But today was different.

Blair had one, initial, loyal questioner, asking about women's rights at work, before Hansard records the following exchange:

Mr Michael Howard (Folkestone and Hythe) (Con): 'Margaret Dixon is a 69-year-old pensioner who lives just outside Warrington. She is in constant pain and desperately needs an operation. Because she has a weak heart, she has been told that her chance of surviving that operation is less than 50:50. On seven separate occasions, she has been given a date for the operation, been prepared for it and said goodbye to her family in case she did not survive. On each of those seven occasions, her operation has been cancelled. She has praised the doctors and the nurses; but can the Prime Minister explain how, after eight years of his government, all the money they have spent on the NHS and all the promises they have made, that can happen in Britain today?'

The Prime Minister: I have to look into the details of the particular case the right hon. and learned gentleman mentions. It is true that, literally seven or eight minutes before Prime Minister's Questions, he faxed me some of the letters about this case, but obviously I have not had the opportunity to look into it. If it is as described, it is completely unacceptable, but I do not know the details of it. Frankly, probably neither does he at the moment. However, I think that it is wrong to take a case which, if true, is unacceptable, and to try to make what I believe to be an exception into a rule for the National Health Service.

The fact is that the vast majority of people treated by the NHS – a million every 36 hours – are treated extremely well. Let me remind the right hon. and learned gentleman that when he was a

Cabinet Minister waiting lists went up by 400,000. They have fallen by more than 300,000 under this government.

Mr Howard: Mrs Dixon's is not an isolated case. Last year, 67,000 people had their operations cancelled – an increase of 10,000 compared with five years ago. On five of the seven occasions when Mrs Dixon's operations were cancelled she was actually in hospital being prepared for the operation. Will the Prime Minister tell us why he thinks so many operations like Mrs Dixon's are cancelled in that appalling way, causing such trauma not just to the patients and their families, but to the doctors and nurses who are involved as well?

Within minutes, the Tories had Mrs Dixon on air, live on the *World at One* on BBC Radio 4, and Labour had begun letting slip her medical details. Walsingham Road in Penketh was turned into an instant media village, all of which meant – it's the election campaign at last.

The phoney war had been started weeks before by Labour, unveiling their election campaign slogan: 'Forward not back', in a tasteful red and lime green logo. A letter-writer to the *Daily Telegraph* wryly remarked it was similar to the old German Democratic Republic's slogan: '*Vorwarts immer; ruchwarts nimmer*' – Forwards for ever, backwards never.

Alastair Campbell had already swaggered back into Labour's new campaign HQ at 39 Victoria Street, a couple of hundred yards from parliament, and just down the road from the Conservative HQ at No. 25. There, the party's new Australian media guru Lynton Crosby was installed. Labour had also already unveiled its six election pledges:

1. Your family better off
2. Your family treated better and faster
3. Your child achieving more

4. Your country's borders protected
5. Your community safer
6. Your children with the best start

The feast was set, the guests were met. The exchanges at PMQs began the party.

It was the start of an extraordinary pre-election campaign, a kaleidoscopic period of shifting fortunes, which was to feature the death of Pope John Paul II, a royal wedding, a constitutional showdown sparking rumours of a snap election, an act of breathtaking political ruthlessness and, to cap it all, there was even a bit part for the Chinese President Hu Jintao. But for the moment, it was Margaret Dixon centre stage.

The day after PMQs her family travelled to London for tea with Howard and his ex-model wife Sandra. Health Secretary John Reid took the opposite route and went to Warrington for a long-standing engagement, but toured the hospital in question. He refused a poignant handwritten invitation to visit Mrs Dixon, saying he would not be part of a Tory publicity stunt.

The normal law of election gravity says that if you throw an individual case into the headlines it merely falls back down on you with a thump. The War of Margaret's Shoulder defied the rules, and Labour were rattled.

Reid accused Mr Howard – who also championed the cause of Maria Hutchings, a mother who had confronted Blair on television over the lack of provision for special needs children such as her ten-year-old autistic son John Paul – of using people as 'human shields'.

Mr Howard simply retorted that Margaret Dixon was not a human shield, she was a human being.

By Friday 4 March, 48 hours after PMQs, Blair was at Labour's Scottish Conference in Dundee, flaying Howard who he said had 'used the case of someone in pain and tried to make it a symbol of today's NHS'. He went on: 'Today as I speak to you about this, I feel real anger.'

But Blair was in no doubt the battle was on in earnest. He began his speech: 'The fight is on. It is a fight for the future of Britain. A fight between us and them – Labour and Tory. That is the choice in the end.'

The success of the Margaret Dixon affair galvanised the Tories. They were getting the rub of the green again. Issues popped up as irritating to Labour as moles on a bowling green, and as fast as they sought to stamp on one, another raised its head.

The government announced the start of new powers for councils to get 'stop orders' designed to help thwart temporary unauthorised travellers' or gypsy encampments. But the same powers also required councils to provide more sites, if they were deemed insufficient. Headlines abounded of the dangers to suburban tranquillity of Labour's enforced gypsy sites; the unspoken fears of Middle England subtly awakened.

The Chief Constable of Nottinghamshire, Steve Green, surfaced, telling the *Sunday Telegraph* his force could not cope with serious crime. His comments were later mollified, and weeks later Her Majesty's Inspector of Constabulary criticised the force – but the Conservatives rolled with the story.

In comments made weeks earlier to *Cosmopolitan* magazine, a difference of view emerged between Howard and Blair on abortion: Howard favoured reducing the time limit for terminations; not a policy, but a view. But again it chimed with headlines and there was even speculation the issue could become a major election factor.

While all these irritants swirled around Blair, his election co-ordinator Alan Milburn, Campbell and his media machine, the Prime Minister faced a potentially far more serious threat the week after the War of Margaret's Shoulder; a threat which even saw talk of a snap election sweeping aside the carefully laid plans for 5 May.

In December 2004 the Law Lords had ruled that the government's policy of detaining foreign terrorist suspects without trial was incompatible with human rights legislation. The policy discriminated against foreign nationals and was disproportionate. The government was bound to find an alternative. But security was also a touchstone for Blair. Having argued for so long and so passionately that the terror threat facing the nation was so grave, any new measures had to reflect that gravity. The measures Home Secretary Charles Clarke announced amounted, in the most extreme cases, to house arrest. Lesser regimes involved electronic tagging or denial of communications equipment, from a mobile phone to the internet. What is more, the 'control order' was to be imposed on the say-so of Clarke himself, before a judge would later become involved.

There was outrage as the measure proceeded through parliament, compromises and amendments dangling from the legislation like so many tins on a wedding car. Finally on Thursday 10 March came the showdown in the House of Lords. Such had been the opposition to various aspects there, that had not a single Conservative peer voted, Labour would still have lost.

But time was running out. The existing legislation expired at midnight on Sunday 13 March. The Bill ping-ponged between the Commons and the Lords. The Tories were demanding a 'sunset clause' in the legislation, meaning it would automatically lapse in November, allowing time for more measured scrutiny and drafting. The government would not give way. The Tories, buoyed by recent events, were in no mood to back down either.

Thus you will search in vain for the Hansard record of parliamentary proceedings for Friday 11 March. For in parliament, the calendar does not change until the House rises. On Thursday, the House did not rise. The Bill went back and forth for 30 hours. Opposition peers could barely contain their excitement at the constitutional standoff. And opponents of the legislation included among their number such luminaries as the former Lord Chancellor and Blair mentor Lord Irvine of Lairg.

If some of the scandalous gossip that inevitably accompanies such late-night shenanigans is to be believed, some legislators did indeed not contain their excitement. Through it all, the current Lord Chancellor Lord Falconer battled bravely on, defying calls for a sunset clause.

At 5 a.m. on Friday, Falconer was on his feet again, pleading the Government's constitutional case. He began with characteristic drollery:

Sunset clause, my Lords. It will soon be sunrise!

We all know that the purpose and role of the House is to scruti-nise legislation; not to block it. On the three issues that I have identified the Liberal Democrats and the Conservatives in this House will not engage. On a significant number of major issues in relation to the Bill the government have listened and proposed substantial changes in another place. I went through the examples on the previous occasion. Perhaps as many as 80 per cent of this House's requests have been met.

But now we are in a different situation. In the eight years that I have been in this House I have never seen a situation where a Bill of this importance was blocked by this House on the three issues that I have identified. What has happened is that the House believes, despite the clearest possible message from the Commons, that the view this House has expressed on the three issues must be complied with.

It goes further than that. Unless agreement is reached by the Commons to those three issues, this House is saying that we will block a piece of legislation, the urgency of which is apparent to everyone and has been accepted by the Commons; and the content of which significantly affects the national interest.

Their lordships were unmoved. For 24 hours speculation had been floating that if the peers did not back down, Blair would call a snap election on the issue.

At 3.05 p.m. I rang No. 10 on a hunch that they would soon have to close the issue down, one way or another. They were just about to ring me. Could I come over for a 3.30 statement inside Downing Street by the PM? He wouldn't – would he?

I was joined at No. 10 by three broadcast colleagues, a BBC producer and a cameraman for the pooled coverage. We dumped our mobile phones in numbered pigeon holes in the entrance lobby (I always try and get No. 007 – boys will be boys) and thus said goodbye to the world before going upstairs to the Pillared Room.

So we couldn't tell anybody that the lengthy delay that occurred was not the sinister spin-doctoring and conspiracy-concocting many imagined. It was simply that unusually, and contrary to No. 10's understandable assumption, there had not been a satellite truck to hand at the rear of Downing Street. One had to be summoned, then searched and 'swept'. No. 10 were desperate to go live – but by the time the truck had been cleared, Clarke was on his feet in the Commons announcing a climbdown and the PM waited until he had finished.

By the same token, of course, we did not know at the time what Clarke was announcing, or even that he was on his feet.

Blair eventually strode to the microphone and with a sweep of the hand sideswiped 'talk of an election'. The legislation would be reviewed in a year's time. But there was no sunset clause, he maintained.

Blair insisted: 'We have a sensible way through. They should come to their senses, drop this opposition and let us get on with the business of protecting the people of this country.'

At his own press conference, Howard, however, was equally adamant: 'Our bottom line has always been the sunset clause,' he said. 'That is what we have now been given.' The Tories had accepted the deal, and, tired but happy, like so many chattering school-children, trooped off for the weekend. Things really were getting better. Blair had blinked. Howard had claimed victory.

But next week was the Budget, Labour MPs reckoned to themselves. Not for the first time, they looked to the Chancellor Gordon Brown for salvation. Brown's role in the campaign had inevitably attracted the speculation so wearisome to Blair. One minute in one headline Brown had ousted Milburn to take the tiller and rescue the so-far floundering ship. The next day, inevitably, it would be vice versa in another headline.

Undeniably, though, Wednesday 16 March, Budget Day, was meant for the Chancellor to excel at what he does best – rattle off economic triumphs faster than bullets, then list in glorious detail the investments and benefits those triumphs have procured for the British people. He did not disappoint his colleagues.

Brown rose at 3.30 p.m. and delivered a buoyant assessment of the economic outlook, boasting that the country had enjoyed 'the longest period of sustained economic growth since records began in 1701'.

He forecast economic growth of 3 per cent to 3.5 per cent in 2005 easing back to 2.5 per cent to 3 per cent in 2006, while predicting borrowing would fall from £34 billion to £22 billion over the next five years as tax revenues picked up.

While the government was on course to deliver its promised £21 billion in efficiency savings, with 12,500 civil service posts already gone, Brown insisted any further cutbacks – as the Tories, he insisted, were planning – would hit frontline services.

He then blatantly set out to woo the 'grey vote' with a promise of free bus travel for pensioners and a (one-off) £200 refund on their council tax bills. There were also carefully targeted sweeteners for families, homebuyers and savers. There would even be a memorial to the Queen Mother in the Mall.

In the Commons, Howard protested it was a 'vote now, pay later' Budget. He added: 'This Budget is not about what's good for our country. It's all about the interests of the Labour Party.'

For the Liberal Democrats, Charles Kennedy protested Brown had failed to tackle both social injustice and the 'ticking time bomb' of council tax revaluation.

Labour MPs took Howard's soundbites as a backhanded compliment. They hoped it would, indeed, be very good for the Labour Party. Older voters are statistically the group that most often votes at general elections. At least handouts were going to people who would actually turn up on polling day, in a contest where even more than usual, turnout might be crucial.

Now at last, the backbenchers sensed, their show could get on the road. A photo call was scheduled with Blair and Brown for the next day, unveiling a poster claiming the Tories planned '£35 billion in cuts'.

The Tories had earlier published detailed spending projections, and details of savings in bureaucracy they claimed could be made without hurting frontline services such as health or education. Indeed the savings from their James Review would enable them to direct the cash to the front line. Their spending graph showed a disparity between the growth in their spending and the trend growth in Labour spending of £35 billion by 2011/12. This gave Labour its '£35 billion cuts' slogan that Blair and Brown set out to lambaste the Conservatives with.

They stood proudly in front of their poster. What could go wrong? There were not even supposed to be questions from the handful of journalists who had been invited – a characteristic of Labour that was to dog them and the media throughout the campaign.

What went wrong was Nick Robinson. The combative political editor of ITV News threw a question at Blair: 'Prime Minister, can you only win by distorting your opponents' policies – you know that they don't say that they would decrease spending, but that they would increase it slower than you would increase it?' There was a grumpy exchange with Blair – and the next day's headlines were not the ones Labour had planned. Just how stupid do you think the British people are, was the tone. The Tories relished a minor triumph once again. Things really were looking up.

Labour banged on with its slogan, but for the Conservatives – if not the voters – it had lost its menace. Tory co-chairman Liam Fox asserted the government was simply 'lying' about his party's plans.

Good Friday is not normally a hectic day for political news. The House is in recess, parliament deserted. But something had stirred overnight on Thursday 24 March. That evening the Labour Party alerted the media to a story about to drop in the first edition of *The Times*, which we would normally see around 11 p.m. The MP for Arundel and South Downs – one of the safest Conservative seats in the country – Howard Flight, a deputy chairman of the party and a frontbencher responsible for liaising with the City, a former member of the party's treasury team and instrumental in devising the James Review, was on the front page for all the wrong reasons.

He had been taped at a meeting of the Thatcherite Conservative Way Forward group on the Wednesday, in the Adam Street Club in London's West End saying: 'The potential for getting better taxpayer value is a good bit greater than the James findings [which have been] "sieved" for what is politically acceptable and what is not going to lose the main argument.'

He hinted that further tax and spending cuts would be possible once the Conservatives were in power because 'everyone on our side of the fence believes passionately that it will be a continuing agenda'. Flight said after an election had been won, 'you can actually get on with what needs to be done'. Labour were cock-a-hoop. Their strategy was vindicated. The Tories had a secret agenda to slash public spending.

Flight immediately tendered his resignation from the Conservative front bench and surrendered his deputy chairmanship, complaining his remarks had been 'spun' and misinterpreted.

On Friday, Blair led the Labour charge, saying: 'The fundamental point is that the Conservative Party have not changed.' Later, at a hastily convened press conference Cabinet ministers queued up to lay into the Conservatives. Milburn, Reid and Education Secretary Ruth Kelly put the political boot in. It was too much for Howard, at home in his Folkestone constituency. He summoned a TV camera with no reporter or producer and prepared a statement for the Press Association. Broadcasters had no idea what was on the tape until they were airing it.

Howard's brutality was stunning. He said his party would be totally straight with the public:

> We will not promise one thing before an election and do something else after the election. We will not say one thing in private and another thing in public.
>
> Everyone in my party has to sign up to that. If not, they are out. Howard Flight will not be a Conservative candidate at the next election.

Flight put up some resistance but in the end bowed to the inevitable. Within minutes of Howard's statement, party HQ said its national nominating officer would not be signing Flight's election papers whatever happened. Under Electoral Commission rules, therefore, he simply could not be a Conservative candidate.

Labour's glee was unbounded. Reid said simply: 'Michael Howard ended Howard Flight's political career for the grievous crime of telling the truth. This is panic leadership driven by the headlines of the day.' Arundel eventually selected the former director of the Reform think tank Nick Herbert to fight the seat.

All Labour's spin-Googlers could pin on him was an old article warning the Tories not to adopt a secret agenda.

And so to the announcement itself of polling day, 2005. It had long been pencilled in for Monday 4 April, announcing voting on Thursday 5 May, the same day as 34 county council elections and elections for mayor in several cities and three unitary authorities. Surely nothing could go wrong. At 8.37 p.m. BST on Saturday 2 April, Pope John Paul II passed away peacefully in Rome.

Downing Street were forced to issue a statement on the Sunday saying Blair had no plans to go to Buckingham Palace on Monday to seek a dissolution of parliament, the technical process by which a general election is triggered. It had been put on hold for 24 hours.

And then there was the funeral. Vatican protocol insists the Pope's funeral is held four to six days after his death. That put Friday 8 April squarely into contention – the only problem being that Friday was also the day earmarked for the wedding of His Royal Highness the Prince of Wales and Camilla Parker Bowles. Party leaders, especially Blair, would be expected to attend both – and so, incidentally, would the Archbishop of Canterbury, who was due to preside at the service of blessing and dedication of the royal marriage at Windsor Castle.

The dilemma was solved by a 24-hour timeshift which saw the announcement of the election put back until Tuesday 5 April and the wedding to Saturday 9 April. In a final twist, the Grand National, due to be run at the same time on Saturday as the royal wedding blessing, with both events scheduled for live TV coverage, then also had to be put back on the racecard. With Monday ruled out for an announcement, Blair held talks on the Tuesday morning inside No. 10 with Lord Falconer; Baroness Amos, the Leader of the Lords; Commons Leader Peter Hain; Reid and Culture Secretary Tessa Jowell, before leaving for the palace. At 11.27 a.m. he strode from his green Jaguar on his return and approached the microphones in the street, standing on an A4 sheet of white paper secured to the requisite spot by gaffer tape, and faced the TV cameras. He said:

> I believe that Britain has a great future within our reach. We are poised to embrace that future if we have the confidence and self-belief to do it. And one of the other things that the next few weeks will allow me to do personally is to restate to people again the one thing that motivates me personally every day of my political life.
>
> A belief that we should create a country where regardless of someone's class or background or race or colour or religion they get the chance to make the most of themselves, to develop their potential to the full, and through them the country gets its chance to develop its potential.
>
> So it is a big choice. It is a big decision. The British people are the boss and they are the ones who will make it. I look forward to seeing you all out on the campaign trail.

His last remark turned out to be somewhat optimistic. The 'all' in this case on the immediate campaign visit to the Weymouth and Portland National Sailing Academy, in Labour's most marginal seat of South Dorset, where sitting MP Jim Knight enjoyed a majority of just 153 over the Tories last time round, turned out to be me, PA photographer Stefan Rousseau, Nick Robinson of ITV News, Andy Marr of the BBC, Michelle Clifford from Sky News, and three TV cameramen.

We endured the convoy to Battersea heliport from Downing Street, which travelled at a characteristically breakneck speed, before Blair climbed aboard his hired blue and white Sikorsky S76 helicopter, and we scrunched into ours which would land ahead of his. The lack of access to Blair by the media was to be a constant running sore of the campaign.

I am a notoriously bad flyer, and helicopters bring out the worst in me – but the flight was smooth and trouble-free. So was the brief visit, when Blair emphasised again the 'fundamental choice' facing voters to an audience of Labour T-shirt-wearing supporters.

Howard told a rally of party supporters in London, even before Blair's announcement, that voters indeed faced a choice: 'They can either reward Mr Blair for eight years of broken promises and vote for another five years of talk – or they can vote Conservative, to support a party that's taken a stand and is committed to action on the issues that matter to hard-working Britons.'

Kennedy went to Newcastle to start his campaign effort with a pledge to be 'positive and ambitious' for Britain. 'I am not going to spend these next few weeks going around talking Britain down,' he said. 'I am going to be addressing people's hopes, not playing on people's fears.'

The die was now cast. Campaigning proper would start on Monday 11 April. Pope John Paul's funeral on Friday and the royal wedding on Saturday would create political news exclusion zones. The parties announced they would suspend national campaigning on Friday.

Except . . . the ailing car firm MG Rover had been in talks for weeks with the Shanghai Automotive Industry Corporation. And on Thursday night, Trade and Industry Secretary Patricia Hewitt announced that MG Rover had gone into receivership after the talks had collapsed, threatening thousands of jobs in the West Midlands. Her announcement was actually premature, the board of MG Rover not confirming until the next day that the company formally appointed administrators as the company's UK factory stood at a standstill following the collapse of the talks. Workers left the company's Longbridge plant in Birmingham at lunchtime at the end of their normal Friday shift and were told to return for duty on Monday. But many said they believed they had made their last car for the company and were now focusing on any payoff they might secure.

Blair, flying straight back from the pontiff's funeral on Friday afternoon, accompanied Chancellor Gordon Brown on a visit to the area, following in the slipstream of Hewitt. Though few of the seats around the plant were likely to change hands, the loss of such a totemic industry was hardly welcome news just a few days before the Labour manifesto launch. Blair had spent 25 minutes on the phone to Chinese President Hu Jintao the night before, urging the SAIC to close the deal that would have saved the plant. The Chinese would not play ball.

Nobody could say it had been a dull phoney war.

2

Manifesto, baby, manifesto

Monday 11 April

The simple longings of the British people. That is how Michael Howard described the handwritten slogans that adorned his party's election manifesto as he held it aloft at Conservative Campaign HQ: 'More Police. Cleaner Hospitals. Lower Taxes. School Discipline. Controlled Immigration. Accountability.'

Howard expressed his own longing in a simple, personalised, appeal to voters as the Tories became the first party officially to launch its election blueprint. 'I'm 63 years old,' he said.

> I've fought many battles in my life. I battled the union bullies that once crippled our economy. I battled the judges and the legal establishment that said crime couldn't be confronted and beaten. I battled to get where I am from a state school in a small town in south Wales.
>
> So if you think I'm not determined to change our country for the better, think again. I could easily decide to hang up my boots, enjoy my retirement and spend more time with my grandchildren.

> *But I'm not going to do that. Because there's another battle I have to fight. I love my country and I know it can be a much, much better place to live than it is today. So I'm going in to battle for Britain.*

He added: 'This is our manifesto. It doesn't have a picture of me on the cover. It doesn't have anyone's picture on the cover. On the cover are the simple longings of the British people – people who feel forgotten and ignored. They don't ask for much.'

The low-key launch took place in the press briefing room of the party's campaign building just after 8 a.m. On the second floor, the unimposing room features a low-rise stage, and a backdrop for slogans bathed in blue. Reporters sit in white, hard-backed chairs with fold-down note-taking tables. Today, Howard stood behind a simple podium, gazing out both at the reporters and at two transparent autoprompt screens, one each side of him, invisible to TV viewers, that carried his script. The manifesto document itself was just 28 pages and 7,400 words long and, after the hurly-burly of the pre-election campaign which had been pock-marked with 'mini manifesto' launches by each of the parties, contained no surprises; it also contained no details of the Conservatives' promised £4 billion of tax cuts. Did that mean the party had got its sums wrong, Howard was asked. 'Absolutely not. We make our announcements at a time of our choosing and we will be announcing the remaining tax cuts very soon.' He said the manifesto was slim because he wanted people actually to read it. 'It is a very readable document.'

It committed the Tories to £12 billion of savings by cutting waste and bureaucracy – while preserving and improving frontline services – of which £8 billion would be used to reduce borrowing and £4 billion used to finance tax cuts. But where the tax axe would fall was not revealed, except for a pensioners' council tax discount.

On the first day of the campaign proper, when all three leaders began their official tours, there had already been a taste of the early morning guerrilla war so loathed by journalists, but which has become a more frequent feature of modern campaigns. The Conservatives had said all their daily London press conferences would be held at 8.45 a.m.; the Liberal Democrats at first opted for 8 a.m., then went for 7.30 a.m.; Labour kept all their options open, Alan Milburn saying simply that some days they would have a press briefing – other days they would not. So it was only on Sunday night that the line-up for this morning had been finalised: Lib Dems at 7.30 a.m., the Tories' manifesto launch at 8 a.m. . . . but Labour, in the shape of Blair, Brown and Education Secretary Ruth Kelly, sneaking in at 7.20 a.m. It is not the earliness of the hour journalists mind, although the parties smugly think so; it's just the constant chopping and changing.

Blair, Brown and Kelly seized their early bird chance to launch a pre-emptive strike at the Tories, while presenting their own economic and education pledge card.

Labour's low-ceilinged media room is bathed in pink light, and, with its rows of low-slung, red tip-up chairs, conjures images of a seedy Soho cinema club. But only, it has to be said, when it is empty.

Labour's trio strode onto the stage and quickly went on the attack. Blair whizzed through his party's economic pledge card. (An inflation target of 2 per cent and mortgages as low as possible; one million more homeowners by the end of the parliament; one million more people helped by the New Deal; 300,000 apprenticeships to be created; minimum wage to rise to £5.35 per hour; education spending to rise to £5,500 per pupil by 2008). He then wasted little time in getting his soundbite in first. He dubbed the Conservative Party general election manifesto a 'fraudulent prospectus' based on 'fundamentally flawed' economic plans.

Blair, animated and gesticulating, consonants slipping away as his voice betrayed irritation, told reporters: 'The simple point is that you cannot, as a matter of economics, spend more, tax less and borrow less – all at the same time. How do they square this economic circle? It's an economic nonsense. The whole of the manifesto is based on faulty economics. It is a fraudulent prospectus.'

Away from all this, the Lib Dems' Charles Kennedy tried to pursue the path he had commended to his party's election candidates at a meeting in London the day before: never mind the negative, accentuate the positive; talk Britain up, not down. His efforts were not entirely successful. Even he could not resist at least a token dig at Labour. He failed helplessly later in the day. But perhaps, as it turned out, the father-to-be's mind was on other things.

At his party's chosen morning press conference venue – the plain, unremarkable surroundings of Local Government House, Smith Square, also a few hundred yards from parliament – Kennedy recited his party's education policies before boarding his mustard-yellow battlebus.

He gave a commitment to provide 21,000 extra teachers to cut primary school class sizes. Kennedy said the extra teachers would mean smaller class sizes for infants, with an average of only 20 pupils per teacher – down from the current level of 25.

Class sizes for juniors would also reduce, with an average of 25 pupils per teacher – down from the existing norm of 27. The party would pay for the initiative by scrapping Labour's planned £1.5 billion Child Trust Fund scheme, which Kennedy panned as 'expensive, unnecessary and will deliver little in the way of real benefit'. He added: 'The more time a teacher can spend with a child, the better the chances for that child.'

He cut a slightly lonesome figure as he waved from the platform of his bus, which was scheduled to take him – with the help of a plane – to Totnes and Kingsbridge in Devon, by way of Godalming College in Surrey. Kennedy was the only leader to use the old style battlebus–plane formula. And his wife Sarah was supposed to give birth to their first baby in just a couple of weeks' time, meaning emergency transport had to be on hand at all times. The Lib Dem leader had promised to take time off the campaign trail when the baby was born, and, understandably, to give the health of mum and baby priority. Howard, however, was in confident mood as he left his manifesto launch to visit the Sunnyfields Day Nursery in Bromley, where he and wife Sandra played snap with the little ones, before helicopting off with his small band of reporters (The PA and three broadcasters) to launch his party's Scottish and Welsh manifestos in Glasgow and Cardiff.

Blair made more stately progress to the Airbus UK factory in Broughton in North Wales, before the bright lights of Runcorn beckoned.

Polls published this morning had given all the party leaders and their backroom maestros food for thought.

A YouGov survey for the *Daily Telegraph* put Labour and the Conservatives neck and neck on 36 per cent, ahead of the Liberal Democrats on 20 per cent, while an ICM poll for the *Daily Mirror* and GMTV gave Blair's party a comfortable five-point lead on 38 per cent, ahead of Howard's Tories on 33 per cent and Kennedy's Lib Dems on 22 per cent.

The *Telegraph* survey, meanwhile, suggested that the dreams of many of those who enthusiastically backed Mr Blair in 1997 had soured during his eight years in office, with Iraq a key cause. Some 62 per cent polled recalled being optimistic about a Blair administration in 1997, compared to just 23 per cent who were worried then about the prospect of Labour rule. And just 47 per cent of 1997 enthusiasts now reported feeling pleased with the way Labour had performed, against 34 per cent 'somewhat disappointed' and 19 per cent 'very disappointed', according to the poll. More than half of those questioned (54 per cent) said Britain and the US were wrong to take military action in Iraq, and the figure rose to 66 per cent among those who said they were disappointed with the way the Labour administration had evolved. Iraq prompted a scathing sideswipe from Kennedy as he spoke to the students at Godalming. It had been, he said, quite simply the biggest foreign policy disaster since Suez and there should be a phased withdrawal of British troops.

Howard, too, was quizzed on Iraq at his press conference, defending his position that the war had been right – but Blair wrong over intelligence. 'I do not resile one bit from what I've said,' he told reporters. 'The world is a better place without Saddam Hussein. The decision to go to war was right. It was quite wrong not to tell the truth about the reasons for going to war, in particular quite wrong to mislead people about the nature of the intelligence.'

Up in Blair's Sedgefield constituency, Reg Keys, whose Royal Military Police lance corporal son Tom, 20, died in Iraq, had announced he was standing as an anti-war independent against the Prime Minister. Responding to an assertion over the weekend from Blair's long-time agent John Burton that he would trust the Labour leader with his life, Keys issued a harsh statement today. He said: 'The families of 85 British servicemen trusted Blair with their sons' lives. They trusted that he was acting with integrity and honesty when he sent them to war on the basis of Iraqi WMDs. Their trust was misplaced; they came home in coffins, their oaths of allegiance betrayed.'

Labour's theory that Iraq was now a neutral issue for the campaign was clearly to be put to the test in the coming weeks.

There was another heffalump in the room, though, which Labour could not ignore: the continuing crisis at MG Rover. An overnight bail out following the collapse of the Chinese talks had seen the government pump in £6.5 million to stave off what would have been 5,300 redundancies announced today by administrators

PricewaterhouseCoopers (PWC). But the administrators also revealed the company's losses were running at up to £25 million a month. The same number of redundancies might have to be announced next week, they said in a televised press conference even as Mr Blair and Mr Brown were heading off to Airbus for a joint appearance designed to show how successful manufacturing could be under a Labour government.

In regional newspaper and radio interviews there, the Blair-Brown question inevitably surfaced again as the Labour leader insisted he was happy to be with his old colleague: 'Yes, it is fantastic. We have worked closely together for many, many years. We more or less put the whole project of New Labour together. The fact that Gordon and I are together I hope symbolises that joining together of the campaign for economic efficiency and that for a more just society.'

But Blair was also pressed in north Wales about the car firm and had to promise to do his 'very best' to save it.

'We have always made that clear. The important thing to emphasise today is not that everything in the economy is always good. There will be some jobs that come, some jobs that go,' he said.

Blair went on: 'The important thing is to keep the basic economy strong, growing strongly, interest rates low, inflation low, have a number of jobs in the economy so that even if people lose their job for any reason they have other jobs to go to, and then invest heavily in technology and education, and that is what we are doing.'

There were rumours then that Labour had had to scrap its planned manifesto launch, slated for Wednesday in Birmingham, for fear of Longbridge workers demonstrating outside or even infiltrating the event to inflict one of those iconic TV moments that can be so embarrassing for premiers – as Blair had found out to his cost in previous campaigns. An alternative location was being sought, according to the gossip.

Some Rover families, led by wives and partners of workers, were also threatening to protest in Downing Street on Wednesday. Liz Hanks, 41, whose husband Phil had worked in the paint shop at the plant for fifteen years, was among them.

The mother of two, from Kings Norton, said: 'We're trying to get as many women and children to support their husbands and fathers. We want the same payout as those at [the Ford plant in] Dagenham – £30,000 to £35,000 each.

'These workers are getting the minimum – £4,000 – which is not enough for any family. The government have just taken the heart out of Birmingham. We're fighting for our children and our families.'

She handed out contact details to workers at Longbridge, describing the potential closure of the site as devastating, not sparing the government that others attacked for bending over backwards to help the firm. 'They're crying tears of guilt because they didn't do enough,' she said. Gemma Cartwright, whose husband Andrew, 41, also worked in the paint shop, said she would accompany Mrs Hanks on the journey to London. The 28-year-old mother of four, also from Kings Norton, said: 'It's much more than just Longbridge. It's about the whole area. They've taken the motor show from us. They're now taking the car industry from us.'

The second visit on Blair and Brown's itinerary kept them, for the moment, though, far from Longbridge. It took them to Abergele Community College, near Colwyn Bay, on the north Wales coast. They toured the computer room and cafe at the college, which doubles as an adult learning centre. Mr Blair spoke to one long-standing Labour member who, almost on cue, said she had returned to the fold after earlier becoming disillusioned about the Iraq war.

Olwen Edwards, 89, from Colwyn Bay, said later: 'I told him frankly that I was angry about Iraq and I had even cancelled my membership. But I have since thought about it more and now I understand his decision to go in.' The pensioner said she enjoyed meeting the Prime Minister. She added: 'He looks much younger than I expected.'

The next stop on the Blair and Brown roadshow was a visit to The Heath Business and Technical Park at Runcorn in Cheshire.

The park, on the site of a shut-down ICI works – oh, cruel fate – is now home to more than 120 new businesses, and Blair and Brown had to use the long-planned excursion to highlight the importance of regenerating business and industrial areas which have fallen on hard times.

The two men were treated to a display of glass-blowing in a small business unit, before Blair addressed a meeting of employees who work on the park. He told them, in a message that might have rung hollow in Birmingham:

> *This is what the future of the UK economy is about. It is about constant change, and adaptation, it is about investment in science, technology and skills, and it is about recognising that there is no point in us saying in this new world that is developing 'Stop it, I want to get off.' That is not the way it is going to work.*
>
> *We have actually got to make it work for us. And we have got therefore to be constantly on the move; taking the country forward; making sure that, as other countries come up behind us, we are reaching up to a new and different level.*

As Blair and Brown fanned out among the audience, shaking hands with and chatting to the people gathered for their visit, the PM smiled as he insisted: 'I am doing the talking, Gordon is doing the hard work. He does the work, I get the credit, it is a good deal.'

But as the leaders continued their criss-cross of the country, another and more pressing drama erupted. Just after 2.13 p.m., PA political correspondent Jamie Lyons, travelling with Kennedy, filed the first takes of a breaking story:

> *Liberal Democrat leader Charles Kennedy cut short the first day of his election tour after his pregnant wife was taken to hospital, his official spokeswoman said today.*
>
> *Mr Kennedy had been due to fly from Farnborough airport in Hampshire to Totnes in Devon, but he drove back to London to be with his wife Sarah who is due to give birth in the next few weeks.*
>
> *Mr Kennedy's spokeswoman said: 'Sarah has gone into hospital. Charles has spoken to her and he says she is fine. He is now going back to London to be with her.'*

Sarah had accompanied Kennedy to the royal wedding on Saturday, where one guest said she had looked 'gargantuan – but gorgeous'. It was hardly, however, a rest day. Now she was in hospital – with Kennedy supposed to spearhead the launch of his party's manifesto at 7.30 a.m. the next day. The party had made contingency plans for the campaign leadership while Kennedy was off on 48-hours brief paternity leave; but the launch of the manifesto was different.

Within minutes, the party confirmed it had been postponed. Sarah was still said to be 'fine' and veteran deputy leader and foreign affairs spokesman Sir Menzies Campbell was called in to stand in Kennedy's place on visits the next day.

The other campaigns steamrollered on. Howard headed for Hampden Park in Glasgow, to launch the Tory Scottish manifesto. Unlike the document published in London, it contained not even a single picture of the Tory leader.

Replacing him on page 2 was a section headed 'Our contract with Scotland', signed by Shadow Scottish Secretary Peter Duncan, the party's lone MP north of the border, and Scottish Tory leader David McLetchie.

Mr Howard admitted that many of the policies contained within it were only in the gift of the Scottish Parliament, but said the party was looking ahead to elections north of the border as well as the nationwide contest on 5 May. He told voters:

> *No matter what you think of your local candidate, when you vote you're not just voting for someone who represents you locally – you're voting for a national government.*
>
> *So if you think that crime's too high, immigration is out of control or that Mr Blair has hit you with too many stealth taxes, then you need to send him a very clear message.*
>
> *Enough is enough. And you can't do that by voting Liberal Democrat or SNP.*

He went on to deliver a similar message at the Welsh launch in Cardiff. And Labour was still wheeling out its attack machine for a second, afternoon, bite at the Tory plans. Milburn and Kelly were joined by the Chancellor's former economic adviser Ed Balls, now himself a parliamentary candidate.

Milburn told the afternoon news conference:

> *These proposals hardly amount to a programme for govern-ment. It would be comical were it not serious. This Conservative manifesto will come to be regarded as the shortest suicide note in history, not because of its brevity, but because at its heart it contains a dangerous plan. It confirms the Conservatives have learned no lessons from their past failures. Their manifesto would take Britain back to those very same mistakes of the past.*

Blair went on to revel in some old-style New Labour campaigning at an 'interactive rally' in Oldham alongside showbiz and sports figures, featuring party supporter and Alastair Campbell's old chum Sir Alex Ferguson.

Sir Alex, 40 years a member of the Labour Party, told the enthusiastic audience: 'I think it's important to give encouragement and most importantly we have to vote, we have to get out there and make sure we are all voting, we can't be complacent and can't forget what we have achieved over the last eight years.'

Blair and Brown left the rally to cheers and applause amid the strains of U2's 'It's A Beautiful Day'. And to two eggs thrown at their Range Rover by some Fathers 4 Justice campaigners.

And while the dynamic duo were there, the nation was treated to the first shots in the party political broadcast campaign, with Labour's opening offering, designed to cement further the image of unity between the party's two major players, which will be treasured by many New Labour faithful. In a film made by a team that included Oscar-winning director Anthony Minghella, Blair and Brown were shown chatting informally about the fruits of their joint efforts.

'It's all about working as a team,' Brown told his old chum in the film. 'It's about trying to break new ground all the time. People have different attributes that they can bring to teamwork.'

Reminiscing on the birth of New Labour, Brown went on: 'It really did start from a sort of shared sense of what are the values that are important to people . . . justice and dignity and fairness, as long as the Labour Party supported enterprise and markets and business.'

And Blair, talking with his Chancellor in his Commons office about Labour's record and aims, told him: 'It's a partnership that's worked, that's done a lot for the country.'

The only reference to possible conflict between these two lifelong political pals, comrades and allies had a coy Mr Blair saying: 'I mean, you know, there is never an endless amount of money. So you might say . . .'

The film featured captions highlighting key achievements of Labour's terms of office as the two men drifted across the screen in shirts and ties – although Blair's tie strangely disappeared on occasions.

They ended up sitting across from each other at the premier's desk, where he was shown writing a list of Labour achievements.

'We have made progress but there is a massive amount still to do,' Mr Blair conceded.

The conversation, now switched to Labour's campaign HQ in central London, concluded with the Prime Minister's analysis of Labour's task:

> *How do we create a society where everybody, not just a few, get the chance to succeed? That's the basic motivation, that is why we are in the Labour Party not the Tory Party and that is why we have to build on the progress made until everyone, whatever their wealth, or their class or their background, colour or creed, get the chance to make the most of themselves. That's the Britain we want.*

The video will have been archived by more than a few supporters, well-intentioned or not, of the two men. Of such moments, for some, political memories are made.

Charles Kennedy probably didn't have time to watch it. For by then he was pacing the corridors of St Thomas' Hospital, just over Westminster Bridge from the Houses of Parliament . . .

Tuesday 12 April

Boy, some guys have all the luck. Imagine being a party leader and producing your own baby to kiss at the start of a general election campaign. Donald James Kennedy came into the world at 12.14 a.m., in St Thomas' Hospital, weighing in at six pounds and nine ounces, blissfully unaware of the political import of his arrival. The political world was equally unaware of him, until six hours later when the story hit the PA wire.

Kennedy and wife Sarah said in a statement: 'It is wonderful for us both and we are extremely grateful for the superb clinical and midwifery support which we have received. Everything went very smoothly and we are looking forward to returning home as a family in due course.'

So the hectic dash back from Farnborough had not been a wild goose chase after all; more like following the stork.

As the couple basked in newfound parenthood, the Liberal Democrat campaign chief Lord Razzall opened his party's morning news conference, saying: 'We obviously are extremely happy today that Charles Kennedy and his wife Sarah had their first baby today. We are all absolutely delighted and send our congratulations to Charles and to Sarah.'

The savvy MP Malcolm Bruce, President of the Scottish Lib Dems, was more to the point. He congratulated the couple and said the birth would not do the election campaign any harm at all. In an interview with BBC Radio Scotland he said:

It sounds as if it at all went very well and I am sure both Charles and Sarah are absolutely delighted.

The due date did suggest this could happen during the campaign because, of course, babies make their own timings and this is obviously slightly early rather than late. I think Charles will be happier as and when he gets back on the campaign trail knowing that everything's fine and that he can get back home to Sarah each night.

He had indicated that he would take some time off immediately after the baby was born and that he would organise the campaign so that he could get back to Sarah so I would imagine he would probably take two or three days.

I think the trouble is he probably doesn't know that when your first-born child arrives the sense of excitement is pretty strong, but my understanding is he will make it clear in the next few days that he will resume the campaign but no doubt will take more time off.

Bruce added:

They will be not just resting but feeling the wonderful afterglow of having a child and in many ways this is great for Charles and Sarah at this time.

It will do the campaign absolutely no harm.

It's not just women – an awful lot of men like babies too and people generally respond warmly to family pictures. It makes a point that here is a man who has a new family and I think a lot of the issues we are addressing are about families in Britain today. We are happy for any family that has an event of this kind and it is just one of those fortuitous outcomes that Charles and Sarah have had a baby at the start of an election campaign.

Even your rivals have to, figuratively speaking, kiss the little mite – or at least bestow a soundbite on him, the greatest gift, surely, any party leader has to offer, rather as the fairy godmothers line up to sprinkle stardust on baby Aurora in *Sleeping Beauty*.

Thus Blair at his morning news conference offered 'warmest congratulations' to the proud parents. 'I just wish them well and we all wish them well. It is a particular joy when you have your first baby,' he said.

Howard – who had eschewed a morning press conference to stroll in Lib Dem-held Torquay, part of the Torbay constituency – paused in his perambulations to join the congratulations club, stressing that the best wishes he sent came from his wife Sandra, too. 'It is wonderful news. I send them my warmest congratulations. I remember very well our first baby. It was the most magical, wonderful moment and I can empathise very much with them. What a wonderful moment it is.'

It was not without a certain irony, then, that Sir Menzies Campbell, deputising for Kennedy, kicked off his party's news conference on the economy by confirming his party's plans to scrap Brown's 'baby bonds' establishing a Child Trust Fund for every newborn infant. That's politics, kid.

And back in that world, economic credibility was today's touch-stone. Campbell set out to establish his party's, defending its policy of a new 50 per cent top rate of tax on income over £100,000, abol-ishing the aforementioned Child Trust Fund, introducing free personal care for the elderly and scrapping all student fees. 'We want fairer taxation and the sound investment of taxpayers' money on the priorities that matter to most people in Britain,' he said. 'We are straightforward and upfront about the cost of our policies and how we would pay for them. We will publish detailed costings of our policies in our manifesto. Today we are publishing a headline summary of our plans which shows, by policy area, how much we would spend and how much we would save. The sums add up and the books are balanced. If we want a fairer Britain, it means fairer taxation. And it means spending government money differently.'

And the public, said the party, agreed with them. In a survey for the Lib Dems, pollsters NOP asked how much people would be in favour of a new 50 per cent income tax rate on earnings over £100,000. They were told what the money would be spent on. Some 40 per cent said they would be 'very much' in favour, 35 per cent somewhat in favour, 11 per cent not much in favour and 10 per cent not at all. A further 3 per cent said they did not know.

Treasury spokesman Vince Cable, once chief economist for Shell, insisted the party's programme was rigorous and costed and denied high-earners would be punished unduly: 'People are already paying a 40 per cent top rate. There are many domains in the world where the top tax rate is 50 per cent. We do accept that you cannot have penal rates. That is why we are capping the top rate at 50 per cent. We do need a fairer system, we do think there is scope for some redistribution. But we are also realistic about the level you can have without creating significant disincentives. A balance has to be struck.'

Labour, in the shape again of that famous double-act, Blair and Brown, were intent today not so much on shoring up their own economic credibility (could anyone doubt it?) but with tearing the Tories' to shreds. 'They are an absolute mess, that's what they are,' thundered the PM at his morning news conference.

There was one small problem, though. It probably won't affect the outcome of the election. But this morning Blair donned a smart light blue shirt, tied an elegant burgundy tie and pulled on a posh dark suit. Now, just check your hair . . . Oh, no! He forgot to check his hair. It was an absolute mess, that's what it was. TV viewers sat mesmerised by a small portion of his coiffure, just behind his left ear, that appeared to have been lacquered in the 'messy' position. It just refused to lie down, but instead flapped and wobbled as Blair became more and more animated in his denunciation of the Tories.

That denunciation by Blair, Brown, and Alistair Darling – currently Transport and Scotland Secretary, a former Treasury Chief Secretary and just maybe Chancellor in waiting – took several twists. Having rounded on the Conservatives at the beginning of the campaign for planning £35 billion in spending cuts, Labour now began stressing the Tories were committed to too much spending, which would leave that galactic feature of so many campaigns, 'a multi-billion pound black hole', in the public finances. This was not, the Labour trio patiently explained, a contradiction in their critique of the Tory position. It was a contradiction inherent in that position itself. Shadow chancellor Oliver Letwin had begun by planning big overall reductions in spending, then bowed to pressure from colleagues to increase it in individual areas. 'They can't square that circle,' insisted Blair.

Brown said: 'Yesterday the Conservatives published a manifesto document of few words and fewer figures – a shopping list of promises based on sums that cannot and do not add up.' The Tories had made commitments cumulatively totalling £15 billion in additional spending, including 5,000 more police officers a year and 25,000 drug rehabilitation places.

Brown rattled on: 'Yet in his first budget, Mr Letwin is also already committed to £4 billion of tax cuts and a reduction of £8 billion in borrowing, claiming that you can cut taxes, cut borrowing and raise spending all at the same time – exactly the same mistake John Major made in 1992 when he promised tax cuts, borrowing reductions and spending rises – creating a multi-billion pound black hole.'

The Conservative plans would put pressure on interest rates – 'an economic risk to the country that would endanger economic stability and force Britain back towards the stop-go of the past.

When all plans are taken into account, Mr Letwin has a black hole of £18.9 billion in year one, £18.5 billion in year two and £14.4 billion in year three – a black hole which would require either huge spending cuts or increased borrowing and which the Bank of England would have to take into account and put pressure on interest rates.'

Brown ploughed on: 'Only the Conservatives could manage to offer the electorate the extraordinary combination of a black hole and severe public spending cuts.' He said the Tories' own figures would mean cuts starting at £8 billion in 2006–7 and rising to £35 billion five years later. He went on: 'For months the Tories' only defence has been that the £35 billion need not mean cuts in services because the James Report has found cuts in bureaucracy beyond that of the 85,000 job losses in the Gershon Report. But today we are exposing that, of the £35 billion James review savings on which Letwin is relying, the first £21 billion are already included in the Gershon review – savings already used up and allocated to the front line.'

Brown said the Tories had published a manifesto 'so threadbare that it raises more questions than it answers'. They remained 'an unchanged and unreconstructed' party that had failed to learn from the elections of 1997 and 2001.

One faction in the Tory Party has opted for opportunism, the strategy of promising spending rises, tax cuts and borrowing reductions – exactly the same John Major strategy of 1992 which led to economic disaster.

The other faction wants a commitment to full-blooded spending cuts more extreme than in the 2001 election manifesto.

Unable to reconcile these differences, the Tories claim headline spending can be lower and tax cuts are possible while still able to increase spending on all the vital services from policing and transport to hospitals and schools.

It was a tour de force.

Blair joined the attack, dubbing the Tory proposals a 'completely incoherent mess – and if you elect an economic plan that's a mess, you elect an economic risk. That's the danger with these Conservative proposals.' Just to be helpful, he offered the advice that they needed another period in opposition to sort out their ideological direction.

In the absence of a Conservative morning press conference, Letwin, knowing the line Labour would take, had to settle for getting his rebuttal in first on the *Today* programme.

'On our spending plans it will be possible for us both to reduce borrowing and avoid the tax rises that are implied by Labour's spending plans after the election and to cut taxes by £4 billion,' he insisted. He denied the Conservatives had wrongly claimed the approval of the independent Institute of Fiscal Studies for their spending plans, after the IFS warned that it could not be guaranteed that the Tories would achieve all their planned savings through cutting waste and bureaucracy.

'The approval from the Institute of Fiscal Studies is for the fact that, if we spend what we have set out we are going to spend department by department, we will be able both to reduce borrowing and avoid tax rises and cut taxes by £4 billion,' said Letwin. 'This election is not about questions of accountancy, whether you can or you can't achieve a particular change in a particular department on a particular timescale. This election is about a massive question of choice for the British public.'

When shadow chief secretary George Osborne mentioned in TV interviews that – almost self-evidently – any tax cuts in the Tories' first, post-election June Budget would not come into force until the next financial year, Brown – by then in Edinburgh for a joint visit with Blair to talk to party faithful – struck again. The Tory tax plans were 'unravelling', he confidently predicted.

Howard, meanwhile, had become tangled up in a local south coast controversy which threatened wider ripples. It was a classic election clanger.

Ed Matts, the Conservative candidate for Dorset South, the same marginal seat held by Labour by just 153 votes that Blair had visited after announcing the election, had doctored a photograph on his election literature.

The original picture showed him holding a placard with a picture of Verah Kachepa and her four children who were facing being returned to Malawi.

Alongside him, Tory former home office minister Ann Widdecombe was shown with a placard with the slogan 'Let them stay'. But in the version which appeared on Matts's campaign literature, the picture of Ms Kachepa was missing and has been replaced with the slogan 'Controlled Immigration', while Ms Widdecombe's slogan had been changed to read 'Not Chaos and Inhumanity'.

Labour, having given the seat symbolic significance with Blair's visit, pounced. And Howard was ensnared.

John Reid said if Howard failed to sack Matts as a candidate, he would be sending out a message to other candidates that they can 'do anything they like to fuel a wholly negative campaign. To pose in one picture in support of an asylum seeker, and then doctor the same picture for a political stunt is sick'.

For the Lib Dems, Campbell insisted: 'Howard Flight was sacked by the Conservatives for telling the truth. Ed Matts, the Conservative candidate in Dorset South, should be sacked for telling lies.'

Howard was duly bushwhacked in Torquay. 'It should not have been done and the candidate concerned has apologised for it – and so he should,' he said.

Should Matts go the same way as Howard Flight? 'No, no, not at all. He has apologised. He should not have done what he did but he has apologised.'

The Conservative leader insisted the incident was not a sign of wider confusion in the party:

> *We have a very, very clear message on immigration.*
>
> *We believe that immigration is out of control in Britain today. I think it is very important in order that we have good community relations, that we have a proper grip on security and on the demands of our public services that we have controlled immigration with parliament setting an annual limit. It could not be clearer.*

Matts issued a statement saying: 'I apologise for making a foolish mistake – I had no intention of causing any embarrassment. However, being involved in an individual asylum case is not inconsistent with the Conservative view that Britain's asylum system is in urgent need of attention.'

Howard went on to the more welcome attentions of local party activists as he tramped the pavements of Torquay, reducing a number of mothers to giggles as he grasped their hands and asked for their votes on the seaside town's high street. Cherie Hopkins, wife of a local party worker, was bowled over. She had been so excited he was coming to town, she said, that 'I could hardly eat my breakfast'.

But if it's not your day, in politics as in life, it just isn't your day. An Age Concern cyber cafe was Howard's next stop of the day. His visit coincided with the 70th birthday of Sheila Parks, who was brushing up her computer skills along with other pensioners. Asked if it had been a pleasant birthday surprise, she replied: 'No, I don't like cameras.'

Moving on to Rothwell, Northants, Howard addressed hundreds of supporters – and only a handful of Labour hecklers – defending his manifesto, saying:

It's great to be here in Rothwell this afternoon – out of Westminster and away from London – meeting people, listening to their concerns, addressing the challenges facing our country. Yesterday I published our manifesto – our timetable for action.

It focuses on people's priorities: school discipline; cleaner hospitals; more police; controlled immigration and lower taxes. It's short and it's simple. Why? Because I want people to break the habit of a lifetime. I actually want people to read it – that's right, read it. And when they've read it, I want them to hold me to it, because a Conservative government won't just make a difference, we'll be different.

In the real world if you screw up you risk losing your job. I don't see why politicians should be any different, do you? So in the government I lead, if ministers don't deliver on their commitments they'll go. It's as simple as that – they'll be out on their ear.

On the stump in Labour-held Kettering, third on the Conservative Party's list of target seats, crime was Howard's theme as he highlighted figures showing more than 4,500 offences committed by criminals let out on early release. Echoing a party poster put up across the country, he said: 'How would you feel if a bloke on early release attacked your daughter? It's an outrage. And under the Conservatives it will stop. There'll be no more half-time sentences for full-time crimes.'

He joined reporters on their bus, seeking to recover more ground, referring to Labour's apparent shift from accusing the Tories of planning public service cuts, to promising unaffordable spending, which aides said had delighted him. 'The truth is neither,' he told the journalists. 'Mr Blair is clearly rattled and clearly, I think, he has lost the plot. His slogan is "Forward Not Back" and he is not talking about his plans at all.' He conceded the party manifesto said: 'Within the first month our first Budget will cut wasteful government spending, stop Labour's third term tax rises and lower taxes' but insisted that was compatible with pensioners waiting until next April for the council tax rebate contained within it.

Meanwhile at the Edinburgh Corn Exchange, Brown and Blair were chatting to 60 invited guests. Reporters were kept outside, listening to snatches of conversation on loudspeakers. The two made plenty of hay at the Tories' expense, but in classic New Labour fashion they took a bit of stick as well, a strategy so well-worn over the years and called by some the 'masochism' approach. Some observers thought it was new to this campaign, when Blair began going on TV shows to be berated by audience members. I have seen him do it all over the country, taking flak from all sorts of audiences, for the last eight years. Today Brown got his share too.

William and Betty Pollock told the Chancellor that the combined increase in their pension this year was less than £5. Mrs Pollock, 73, urged him to include the annual winter fuel allowance and the one-off £200 council tax rebate for older people within the main weekly pension, to ensure these extra payments continued every year. She was worried that otherwise, the benefits might cease at his whim.

'You could stop that any time you like,' she told Brown. He replied: 'I agree, but you will continue to have your winter allowance. Please believe me, you can trust me on that.' Mrs Pollock replied: 'You don't smile enough,' – prompting loud laughter from the Chancellor. Brown replied through his grin: 'I must let you meet my young son, he smiles all the time. John is doing well. He's eighteen months now. And his favourite word is "No".'

Babies, babies.

On the Lib Dem campaign trail in Bristol, substituting for the new dad, Campbell predicted Kennedy would be back in harness within 48 hours. 'Charles will be back campaigning in the next day or two. We are dealing with this on a day-to-day basis.' He added dryly: 'It was an hour-to-hour basis.'

Then he continued:

Charles and Sarah have been anxious – and entirely rightly so – to try and preserve as much of their privacy as possible in these very special moments for them, notwithstanding that it was in the middle of a general election campaign.

There will be no running commentary. What I know is what you know, everything went well and mother and son are extremely well.

The party would probably launch its belated manifesto at the end of the week, he said, presumably to coincide with the leader's return.

Kennedy and wife Sarah left St Thomas' Hospital shortly after 5 p.m. with the wee boy, named after his paternal great grandfather, whom they described as their 'pride and joy'. Mrs Kennedy, grinning broadly, said she felt 'fantastic', adding: 'It was a good experience, Charles was a real support.'

As cameramen and TV photographers trampled each other and fell over their own kit, in time-honoured fashion, Kennedy, impersonating a daft brush as most new fathers do, said:

On behalf of all three of us – which is a wonderful feeling to leave St Thomas's as a family – first of all Sarah and myself are immensely grateful to all the clinicians, midwives and all the staff who over these past nine months and particularly the last 30 momentous hours have been so kind, so professional and so fantastic, supportive. Really from the bottoms of our hearts, our thanks to them all.

Secondly, to all the family and friends who have been pouring in messages of support – both here, at home in Scotland and across the River Thames here at national party headquarters, we are

41

immensely grateful for all the gifts and kindnesses and the expressions of goodwill. That really has been marvellous for us both.

Everything went tremendously smoothly and we are very grateful for that and we are exceptionally happy with the new Donald James Kennedy that becomes the latest addition to the clan – he's our pride and joy. After we have a bit of a private break, towards the end of the week I will be looking forward to rejoining the campaign. And I'll be rejoining with both a song in my heart and a spring in my step.

And no, he didn't kiss Donald. But after all, the campaign is still only 24 hours older than he is. Plenty of time yet for a seasoned pro.

Wednesday 13 April

London's Mermaid Theatre, located in Puddle Dock, Blackfriars, was founded by Lord Bernard Miles in 1959. The first theatre to be built in the City of London since Shakespeare's day, it now advertises itself as 'a flexible venue where service is our business and success is yours'. All about delivery, then. A suitable venue for one of the more extraordinary election manifesto launches in recent times, featuring as it did confirmation from the party leader concerned – both in person and in writing – that he would be resigning.

Just after 11 a.m., Tony Blair appeared on the stage more used to hosting Radio 2's *Friday Night is Music Night*, flanked by six Cabinet colleagues each brandishing their copies of the 112-page, 23,000-word paperback *Britain Forward Not Back* containing Labour's 250 promises to voters. For the first time since 1997 there was no picture of Blair on the cover, but a photo of him adorned the page opposite his preface.

In it he wrote: 'Our ideals are undimmed: extend opportunity to all, demand responsibilities from all, secure justice for all. Our policies are refreshed: never has a governing party proposed a more wide-ranging programme of change for the country. Our vision is clear: a country more equal in its opportunities, more secure in its communities, more confident in its future. It is our social contract: we help you, you help yourself; you benefit and the country benefits.' He added: 'So now, I fight my last election as leader of my party and Prime Minister of our country. My call is a passionate one: let's together make irreversible the positive changes that are happening in our country. Let's make the values of social justice and a fair deal for all the governing ideal of our country not just for some time but for all time. People freed from barriers of class, building a better future for themselves and for the country. Self-interest and national interest together.'

The magnificent seven ministers – Blair; Deputy Prime Minister John Prescott; Chancellor Gordon Brown; Home Secretary Charles Clarke; Education Secretary Ruth Kelly; Health Secretary John Reid and Trade and Industry Secretary Patricia Hewitt – stood behind small white podiums dwarfed by the huge arena, looking for all the world like so many hapless celebrity game show contestants. ('Who's the weakest link?' one questioner later demanded. 'There are no weak links up here,' replied Blair.)

With a palpable air of finality, Blair launched into his initial address. 'I believe this country is better, stronger and fairer than the country we inherited from the Conservatives in 1997. But we can do so much more. This manifesto is quintessentially New Labour. At its core is the traditional value that we should stand up for the many, not the few, breaking down the barriers that hold people back, allowing everyone to fulfil their potential. It's also set firmly in modern reality, in a fast-changing world. Opportunity and security for all in a world of change – that is our purpose.'

He went on: 'There is a big vision behind today's manifesto. It is that everyone, not just the few, should get the chance to succeed and make the best of the talent they have. Every line in this manifesto and the driving mission behind it is to support and help hard-working families to cope and prosper in the face of the stresses and strains and struggles of modern life. Their interests come first. Their priorities are our priorities.' The manifesto, so detailed, so thorough, reprinting page after page of Whitehall ministries' already-announced five-year plans, was clearly supposed to stamp so clear a New Labour, Blairite hallmark on the next Labour government, that, whoever became leader after him, there would be no turning back. He virtually said as much himself in his closing remarks. But first each Cabinet colleague read brief promises from the manifesto, interrupted only briefly when Clarke's mobile phone went off.

Brown went first, saying stability would be the economic watchword of a third Labour term. 'Economic stability for hard-working families is and will be the foundation of a stronger, more flexible and enterprising Britain, and the first economic pledge is that we will take no risks with stability.' A Labour government's inflation target would remain 2 per cent, he said, keeping interest and mortgage rates low.

Conscious that the eyes of so many within his party were upon him, Brown promised to 'step up the pace, scale and scope of our New Labour public sector reforms' and vowed that vested interests would not be allowed to 'stand in the way of reform'.

He went on: 'We ask the British people: are you better off than eight years ago?

'Is the British economy stronger and more stable than eight years ago? And who is best to continue the stability of growth we have achieved?' Renewing Labour's pledge not to raise the basic or top rate of income tax, he also said that VAT would not be extended to newspapers, children's clothes, transport or food. He made no commitment on National Insurances Contributions. 'Our priorities to the British people yesterday, today and tomorrow are stability and we will do nothing to put the stability and prosperity of British hard-working families and British business at risk. I believe the 1997 settlement will, in time, be seen to be as important as the 1945 settlement, enabling not corporatist or controlling government – but enterprise, markets and Labour flexibility its hallmark. An empowering, not a dependency-creating welfare state; not mono-lithic, top-down or impersonal, but personal to all. Health and education tailored to individual needs, rights matched by responsibilities, new frontiers in childcare, early learning and care of the elderly, and a new economic purpose and destiny for Britain.'

How many Labour manifestos can you have in one day?

Once all the speakers were done, Blair made his closing remarks:

The manifesto we published today is Labour's most ambitious in its goals and most radical in its means. Had we said in 1997 that we would halve child poverty, deliver a whole generation of stability and growth, achieve the highest ever level of employment, reduce maximum waiting lists from over eighteen months to eighteen weeks, we would have been called impractical dreamers.

Had we said in 1997 we would make every secondary school an independent specialist school, that we would introduce diversity in the provision of health services and give choices over where and when to be treated to every patient, people would have said we had a political death wish.

I am proud of this New Labour manifesto.

I have said this is my last election. At the election following there will be a different leader. What this manifesto shows is that when, at that election, this party is under new leadership, it will continue to be the modern progressive New Labour Party of the past ten years – one that the British people can support with confidence.

Quizzed over when precisely he would step down, Blair insisted: 'I have said I will serve a full term. That's what people are electing if they elect this government. But you can see now this is a New Labour manifesto on which everybody is agreed. The stability of that New Labour message is there, in my view, for the foreseeable future. It's there, and shared by absolutely everybody on this platform.'

My legacy is secure, whoever succeeds me; there is no going back now, would have been a briefer way of putting it.

Blair also intrigued reporters by spelling out exactly what he meant by a 'full term'. Asked if he would serve until the next parliament was dissolved and a general election called, he replied firmly: 'Yes. When I say a full third term, that's exactly what I mean.' Until dissolution, came the shout again. 'Yeah.'

There followed a fruitless hour's questioning of the Cabinet front row. Michael Howard was swiftly onto the attack, hosting a news conference within minutes of Blair closing his presentation and heading for Rushden, Northants. The Tory leader strode on stage and plunged straight in:

> Mr Blair said this morning that this is the last election he's going to fight. Well as far as the British people are concerned, he's already fought one too many.
>
> In 1997, people voted for change. In 2001, people were prepared to give Mr Blair the benefit of the doubt – not any more. People have given up on Mr Blair because they can see he has lost the plot.
>
> Mr Blair's manifesto is full of promises. But Mr Blair's had eight years! What's he been doing? It's no use making all these promises now – he's had eight years. They've heard it all before. Everyone knows it's never going to happen. But there's one thing you can be certain of – if Mr Blair gets in again, taxes will go up again.
>
> I think Mr Blair should have started by recognising how much he's let people down over the last eight years: his stealth taxes, his waste, and his endless broken promises. Instead, all we got today was more of the same: more taxes, more talk. It's obvious to everyone that Mr Blair just isn't able to get a grip on the things that matter. If he had, don't you think he would have done it by now? He's had eight years. Whatever Mr Blair says today, everyone knows that his government has got the wrong priorities and the wrong values.
>
> Instead of getting a grip on people's priorities, he pussyfoots around. Instead of taking action on the things that matter, he just

talks and talks and talks. Instead of giving taxpayers value for money, he puts up taxes by stealth, and then wastes the money on pen-pushing, political correctness and bureaucracy.

People want more police on the streets – real police – to confront crime and to enforce respect, discipline and the law. But Mr Blair's more of the same manifesto does nothing to tackle the paperwork, political correctness or lack of prison places needed to make our streets safer.

People want their children taught in disciplined schools. But Mr Blair's more of the same manifesto does nothing to give head teachers control over their classrooms or get rid of Whitehall targets. People want the security of knowing that when they go to hospital, it will be clean. But what hope of cleaner hospitals is there in Mr Blair's more of the same manifesto? Whatever he says, you know it's not going to happen unless he gives local professionals – doctors, teachers and matrons – the power to close infected wards and operating theatres.

People want to end the abuse of our country's generosity by controlling immigration properly. But Mr Blair's more of the same manifesto does nothing to limit and control immigration – Labour offer nothing but five more years of chaos, just like the last eight years of immigration chaos.

And people want lower taxes and value for money. But Mr Blair's more of the same manifesto offers precisely the opposite: higher taxes and more waste. People have got wise to Blair economics: they know that his promises not to raise taxes aren't worth the paper they're written on.

Just as Mr Blair's last manifesto meant years of stealth taxes, so today's manifesto means yet more stealth taxes for Britain's hard-working families. This morning I went to the Aylesbury estate – an estate Mr Blair visited four weeks after he was first elected. When he went there he made lots of promises – he promised there'd be 'no

*no-hope areas in New Labour's Britain'. This morning – eight
years on – I met people who told me that nothing's changed: the
promises were all talk.*

*I saw for myself how little Mr Blair has done to fulfil his
promises and help those families. People will have a clear choice
on May 5th. They can vote for a straightforward, accountable
Conservative manifesto to get a grip on the big issues that matter:
controlled immigration, more police, cleaner hospitals and lower
taxes. Or they can reward this government for eight years of
broken promises, and vote for Mr Blair's more of the same
manifesto. A manifesto that sweeps the big issues under the
carpet, with more empty promises, and yet more stealth taxes.*

*There's only one alternative to Mr Blair. If you've had enough
let-down, if you've had enough stealth taxes, if you've had enough
broken promises, you have the power and the responsibility to do
something about it. It's time for change. It's time for action.'*

The Lib Dems, meanwhile, confined their reaction to a brief
statement from deputy leader Campbell: 'All the promises and all
the pledges in this manifesto will not cure the profound sense of
distrust so many people have about Labour. On 5 May, Labour will
be judged not by what they say, but by what they have done.'

Earlier, they had launched their health policies. Campbell
confirmed the party would promise:

*A universal service, a common good funded through general
taxation; delivering good health care to all citizens; based on
need, not on what a person can afford and free at the point of
delivery.*

*It's time to reinvigorate the founding principles of fairness in the
NHS.*

Targeting the much-coveted grey vote, the party stressed its commitment to providing free personal care for the elderly and for people with long-term or debilitating illnesses.

'The principle is that personal care that is free in a hospital should be free at home or in a residential home,' Campbell said. A further reform would be free eye and dental checks at a cost of £205 million a year, with the party arguing that prevention is as important as cure and that charges discourage people from getting regular tests.

Tomorrow Kennedy would be back on the campaign trail, launching his party's own manifesto, postponed from earlier in the week by the arrival of baby Donald.

Following his manifesto launch, Blair hit the stump again after travelling to Rushden by train. Speaking without notes and clutching a copy of what was to become known as 'Blair's little red book' he told his audience of several hundred:

It is a very, very big moment for our country.

If we succeed then the Conservative Party, as they should do, will have to reconsider how they work, how they think, how they then go and win support.

Because the fact is at the moment they are an unchanged, unreformed political party. They have not changed one jot; they are the same old Conservative Party, pretty much the same leadership, and policies that are if anything somewhat more extreme than the ones they used to have.

But more important, if we manage to succeed, we can bed down in this country a progressive consensus, a settlement for our age every bit as important as that which the 1945 government achieved in the postwar years.

And from then on, instead of our position being that in a long period of Conservative government, there are intermittent periods of Labour in government, almost as if from time to time they need

*a rest and we come in to give them breathing space, we change
that.*

*So that we can keep governing. Governing with the support of
our country, governing because we had the courage to make the
changes that made this a government that can run the economy
well, invest in our public services, and create a fairer country.*

Blair argued that the election represented a choice between two
sharply contrasting sets of values.

He told his audience that everyone should remember the Tories'
eighteen-year stretch in office as a time when the 'governing philosophy' was one which said there was 'no such thing as society and
you had to choose between an economy that was prosperous and a
society that was just'.

The PM, increasingly animated, went on: 'In this last eight years,
it is not just the individual achievements that matter, it is that we
have shown that economic prosperity and social justice are not
opposites but in the modern world they should be partners in a
country where everybody – not just a few – get the chance to make
the most of themselves.'

Dropping another clear hint about Brown's future remaining in
No. 11 Downing Street, Blair told his audience:

*On 6 May, either people will see Michael Howard walking into
Downing Street, and then within a month Oliver Letwin
producing his first Budget, or we will be continuing in government,
with myself as Prime Minister, Gordon Brown as the most
successful Chancellor this country has seen for many, many years,
as Chancellor.*

He went on: 'That choice is a choice of leadership, it is a choice of
policy, it is a choice of values.'

The Prime Minister had been introduced by his travelling companion for the day, John Prescott. As he welcomed Blair, Prescott made one of his famous verbal slips. To the predictable amusement of the audience he described Blair as 'the man who has led us, the most sex – successful Labour Prime Minister we have had'.

Blair responded: 'Thank you, John, for that rousing introduction. I never knew you felt that way about me.'

After the event, a 20-year-old girl was arrested for allegedly throwing an egg at Mr Prescott's battlebus as it drove away. Police detained veterinary student Harriet Sluman.

Pro-hunt campaigners, who barracked Blair and Prescott as they arrived at and left the venue, accused the Deputy Prime Minister of taunting the 40 or so demonstrators who were kept behind barriers a hundred yards from the doors of the centre.

Video footage showed him, on the loudspeaker of his battlebus, saying to protesters: 'Thank you very much for turning out, Countryside Alliance. Thank you for coming out, lovely people, right to roam.' He added: 'Vote Labour'. They don't make 'em like that any more.

But hunting supporters were not the only ones angry with Labour on manifesto launch day. If politics is about people and their lives, some people brought their lives with them to London. Their worries about mortgage rates and bills were very real.

About 100 wives and children of MG Rover Longbridge workers descended on Westminster and Downing Street even as Labour was launching its manifesto. Carrying home-made banners and posters supporting the workers, they handed in a letter to the Prime Minister asking him to 'pull up his socks' and redouble attempts to secure a partnership deal with the Shanghai Automotive Industry Corporation. Later, they spent an hour with Hewitt who took some of them into her London office for tea and biscuits after saying: 'We are doing everything we can to save jobs. The anxiety these women are going through is dreadful.'

One of the organisers, Gemma Cartwright, said the closure of Longbridge would have 'horrendous' effects throughout British industry. She said: 'We have come here today because we need the support from the government. We want them to pull their socks up and get behind the Shanghai deal.

'Rover cannot die because the impact would not just be felt in Birmingham, it would hit people across the country.' Accompanied by her two young children, she led a group of three women into Downing Street as they handed in a letter to No. 10. It read: 'We are women working at MG Rover and wives of workers at Longbridge. We live in the local community and we know how important the Longbridge plant is to all of us in the West Midlands and beyond.'

The letter said that Longbridge workers had given everything they could to make the company a success and they had the skills and commitment to make great cars. The women said Rover needed a partner and urged the government to convince SAIC that the proposed deal could still go ahead.

It went on: 'We know that we may not be successful and that Longbridge's future is on the line. Help us defend manufacturing. Help us defend the lifeblood of the West Midlands. Please tell the Chinese government and SAIC that we are willing to take on the world with them.' The party of up to 100 included a seven-week-old baby boy and other small children in pushchairs.

Two children, Hannah Doughty, aged seven, and her three-year-old sister Brodie, held up a hand-made sign which read: 'Please don't forget about us Mr Blair.' Their father Darren had worked at Longbridge for sixteen years. Natalie Yarnall, whose father Tony had worked at Longbridge for 20 years, said the uncertainty since the partnership talks collapsed last week was badly affecting the local community around Longbridge.

Mrs Cartwright said she had received telephone calls of support from across the UK since she decided on Monday to help organise today's protest. The women brought with them a bouquet which they left at Downing Street as a gesture of thanks to everyone who had voiced support to their campaign. Another organiser, Liz Hanks, 41, said the public's response to the campaign had been 'overwhelming'. Her sons Daniel, fourteen, and Luke, aged eight, joined today's protest. Daniel, whose father Phil, has worked at Longbridge for fifteen years, said all the children who travelled to London today were hoping that the government, MG Rover and union leaders could help resurrect the partnership deal.

One of the home-made banners read: 'My husband gave 31 years to Rover. What will Rover give to my husband to survive for the next 31 years?' Hewitt had earlier been asked by reporters if the government's help for MG Rover would continue only during the election campaign. She replied: 'We are doing everything we possibly can to save jobs and to secure the future of car building at Longbridge. All of our focus, all of our work is delivering the right proposal to the Chinese. The administrator, the trade unions, the government are all focused on that work. We are monitoring the situation literally day by day.'

Politics, plans and the real world. They sometimes don't make happy bedfellows.

And our leaders got a rude awakening from the younger generation too, in a poll out today of nine to thirteen-year-olds. While 68 per cent could name Tony Blair, only 6 per cent recognised photographs of Howard, and just 1 per cent knew the identity of the Liberal Democrat leader.

The youngsters put Wayne Rooney (an England and Manchester United footballer, m'lud) as their first choice for Prime Minister, followed by fictional J. K. Rowling creation Harry Potter and former Busted (a popular Beat combo) singer Charlie Simpson.

McFly (Oh, don't bother) star Danny Jones and Tony Blair both lagged behind with 8 per cent of the vote.

But then, manifesto launches are not shown much on the Cartoon Network. Then again, perhaps they should be. Today's Labour launch will certainly be one for The History Channel in future years, with one manifesto speech from Blair swiftly followed by another from Brown.

In 1950, nine years before his Mermaid Theatre opened, Bernard Miles starred in a production at the London Palladium of *The Uncrowned King of the Chiltern Hills*. Today another uncrowned king had almost certainly graced his beloved stage. The only question is: who was it?

Thursday 14 April

Kamel Bourgass, a 31-year-old Algerian, went berserk and stabbed Special Branch Detective Constable Stephen Oake to death on 14 January 2003, when he was cornered in a flat in Manchester. Bourgass also knifed three other officers following a raid by Greater Manchester Police Special Branch. The failed asylum seeker had gone 'clandestine', or underground, when his application was rejected two years earlier, and despite being arrested for shoplifting in 2002, he had remained at large.

Manchester Special Branch stumbled on him, almost literally, when they raided the flat of another suspected terrorist and Bourgass was there. But investigations showed, following the dreadful events of that day, that Bourgass – also known as Nadir Habra – had been handpicked for training in poison-making in one of Osama bin Laden's camps in Afghanistan and that he was part of a network of hundreds of mainly Algerian terrorists which stretched across Europe and North America. The network has been linked to numerous other plots including some in the United States, France and Spain.

Detectives believed Bourgass was planning to smear ricin or other poisons on the door handles of cars and buildings in the Holloway Road area of north London. And on Wednesday 13 April 2005, he was jailed for seventeen years for conspiring to cause a public nuisance by terrorising the British public. Only then was his conviction and life sentence for murdering DC Oake revealed to the public. News organisations had been forbidden from reporting it for fear of prejudicing the poison trial.

It was a sensational case in its own right. It was also to reverberate throughout the day's election campaign – bringing together both the firecracker issue of asylum and immigration, the government's insistence on the gravity of the terror threat faced by the UK, and the Conservatives' opposition to the controversial measures Blair had insisted were needed to combat it: ID cards and the Terror Bill which had caused that 30-hour parliamentary marathon.

But first, there was the small matter of the Liberal Democrat manifesto launch to get through.

At 7.30 a.m. Charles Kennedy walked into the launch looking like a man whose wife had had a baby two days earlier and who had got up very early. The 20-page manifesto entitled *The Real Alternative* was even slimmer than the Tories' document, and was presented as a compact newspaper. He told the assembled reporters – those of whom who had arrived early enough had feasted on the bacon sandwiches, croissants and sausages provided:

> *Today the Liberal Democrats are setting out our positive programme for the government of Britain. It is a programme based on fairness and opportunity, dignity for older people, real opportunity for our children and a fair deal for families. It is a fully costed and affordable programme to create a fairer Britain. The Liberal Democrats are the real alternative at this election.*

Kennedy went on: 'Over the course of the last parliament the Liberal Democrats have been the real opposition – over issues like Iraq, student top-up fees, the council tax and compulsory ID cards – while the Conservatives have either lined up with Labour or flip-flopped. Our manifesto sets out a vision of a Britain with quality local public services – good schools and good hospitals, a strong stable economy, a Britain that celebrates diversity and provides the opportunities for each individual to make the best of their talents, a greener Britain that lives up to its responsibilities to future generations – cleaner energy and less pollution. That is why we have called this manifesto *The Real Alternative*.'

He said under its proposals a local income tax would replace the council tax. While 99 per cent of people would pay no more, the benefit would be felt by 100 per cent of people.

Kennedy repeated his opposition to the Iraq war and criticised Tony Blair's relationship with President George Bush. He said: 'We reject a foreign policy placed on "my ally right or wrong". And we say that war should always be a last resort. Many people will remember the principled and consistent Liberal Democrat opposition to the war in Iraq, representing the views of millions of our fellow citizens. Many people will remember that the Conservatives lined up with Tony Blair and George Bush.'

Kennedy called for a phased withdrawal of British forces from Iraq at the end of 2005 when the UN legal mandate expires.

He promised 21,000 extra teachers, 10,000 more police officers and an extra £100 a month pension for the over 75s. And he pledged just one tax-raising measure – a new top rate of income tax of 50p in the £1 on earnings over £100,000, to pay for free personal care for the elderly, the scrapping of tuition fees and to help keep local taxes down.

But then the questions started. And Kennedy was not at his best. He dealt with the baby ones OK. 'How much sleep have you had?' he was teased. 'Could have done with more,' he admitted. 'Having said that, it's the best feeling in the world.' But it was the detailed ones he bungled. Asked how much people would have to earn before they paid more in local income tax than council tax, he didn't know the answer. He searched for help from colleagues before almost giving the right answer. He also got confused about whether local income tax would increase the overall tax burden or be a tax-cutting measure. First he said it was tax-cutting, then he said it was neutral. The manifesto said it was tax-cutting.

Kennedy told reporters: 'Our local income tax, that will replace the unfair council tax, is a tax-cutting measure. Its overall burden will be less than the overall burden of the council tax. In every town, city and constituency, local people overall will pay less than they do today under council tax.'

He later claimed the overall tax burden would remain the same. 'The total sum that is raised under our proposals on local income tax is no more than the total sum that is presently being raised by council tax, full stop,' he said. 'But not less and we are not saying less.' The party's figures confirmed that the amount raised by the local income tax would be £2.4 billion less. The shortfall would be funded from the party's proposed new 50 per cent tax rate on incomes over £100,000.

Defending Kennedy, the party's treasury spokesman Vince Cable told reporters: 'We've had one mistake which we have acknowledged, that we failed to point out that local income tax is a tax-cutting measure. It's a tax-cutting measure and we should have made that clearer.' Challenged that Kennedy did not know his own policies, Cable said: 'He does, but that did not come across.'

But one message, eventually, came across loud and clear from the Conservatives, who were supposed to be highlighting their education policies. Howard's news conference began unremarkably enough as he outlined proposals to review the national curriculum, urge children of immigrants to learn English and give teachers more control over school discipline.

Howard launched into his script:

My driving ambition is to give people real opportunity – the opportunity to make a success of their life. And education is the key to all opportunity. I know – I come from an ordinary family. My parents ran a clothes shop in Llanelli. If the teenage Michael Howard were applying to Cambridge today, Gordon Brown would love me. My socio-economic background ticks every one of his politically correct boxes: the child of immigrants; from a small town in Wales; a family with modest means; educated in a state school. And of course, Gordon Brown would hate Tony Blair.

We didn't have any special privileges. But we were lucky enough to live in a town with a first-class state school. At Llanelli Grammar School, discipline was at a premium. Teachers were respected. We all learnt the basics. Ambition, excellence and hard work were encouraged.

But after he had finished his set piece remarks, Howard was asked about the Bourgass case. He wanted to give a detailed answer, he said, as it was a very important question. Howard appeared to be reading from his autoprompt as he began:

Our thoughts this morning are with the Oake family. Stephen Oake's family reminds us of the risks which the police take every day so that we can live in safety.

The tragedy of what happened is that Kamel Bourgass, an Al-Qaeda operative, should not have been in Britain at all. He was one of the quarter of a million failed asylum seekers living in Britain today who should have been deported. His case underlines the chaos in our asylum system – Bourgass was smuggled into this country on the back of a lorry.

His application for asylum was refused. His subsequent appeal was unsuccessful, making him liable to arrest and deportation, but he went on the run for two years. In 2002 he was arrested for shoplifting. This was drawn to the attention of the immigration authorities, but it seems no effort was made to remove him. Britain faces a genuine terrorist threat to our way of life and a threat to our liberties, but Mr Blair's government has little idea who is coming into or leaving our country.

Howard added: 'If Mr Blair had delivered the firm but fair immigration policy he promised eight years ago, Bourgass would not have been in Britain. He would not have been here to plot a ricin attack or commit murder.'

Labour Campaign HQ had been watching the Howard remarks, and had been expecting them since the previous evening when shadow Home Secretary David Davis had begun an offensive saying simply: 'This officer was killed by someone who should have been deported when his asylum application failed. Unfortunately this failure was a direct consequence of the government's chaotic asylum policy and its porous borders.' But the enormity of the crime itself had dominated news coverage. Today was the start of the political battle.

Now Labour began its counter-attack. Home Secretary Charles Clarke told the PA:

This terrorist used multiple identities to evade capture and prosecution. The police and security services say that identity cards will be a vital tool in the fight against terrorism. We agree with them. The truth is, ID cards would be law by now if the Conservative Party had not blocked them last week after nearly three years of discussion in parliament.

The question Michael Howard now has to answer is this: is the Conservative Party for ID cards, or against them? Do they want tough action against terrorism or to just continue playing politics with the issue? Labour is the only party committed to bringing in the high-tech ID cards and electronic border controls Britain needs in the fight against terrorism.

John Reid was ushered round the TV studios both to swat away the Liberal Democrat manifesto as soft on yob crime and drugs and flaky on finance, and to fight back on immigration. Reid told BBC

News 24: 'If you really want to fight terrorism, then Michael Howard should come clean on this – where is he on ID cards? Yesterday he said he supported them in principle, last week he opposed them in practice. He's using this again for political exploitation, and he's flip-flopped on this one. He jumps on the bandwagon when something like this is revealed to make some cheap points.'

Tony Blair was staying above the fray. He was due in London's Docklands, to make a speech at Canada House in Canary Wharf, on investment and the economy, to an audience of business leaders. As he arrived he came upon Lord Deedes, Bill Deedes, *Daily Telegraph* journalist, former Tory Cabinet minister and immortalised in *Private Eye*'s spoof 'Dear Bill' letters supposedly written to him by Denis Thatcher. Blair said to the peer: 'What brings you here?' Lord Deedes responded simply: 'I work here.' The *Telegraph* offices are in the Canada Square tower block.

Blair was at work, too, ridiculing the Conservatives' economic policy, even as the Labour media strategists were deciding how to continue their response to Howard. The PM was in jovial mood. Perhaps it was meeting Lord Deedes. He began his address with a new joke:

It's always very strange when you begin a general election campaign. A slightly different mood seems to take not just people but the politicians who are engaged in it. You think and work in a quite different way. I was at a reception the other day and a lady, a very small lady, said to me 'I'm 80 years old, you know. I'm small aren't I' . . . *[pause for effect] And it's that vague feeling that it's my fault in some way.*

She then says to me 'You're a lot taller than you are on television' . . . *and that feeling of guilt comes upon you.*

And then finally she says, 'There's an election in a few weeks' time' – and you're thinking 'What is our policy on small old ladies? Will the Tories outbid us, y'know, we'll make you six inches taller, they'll make you a foot taller.'

Well, they laughed at the time.

The PM had some good lines on the Tories' economic policy, too, building on one of Labour's campaign themes: The Conservatives used to fight on the economy, now they hide from their record after Black Wednesday. He said:

Our attack on the Conservative programme is not simply part of the tit-for-tat of an election. It exposes a fundamentally flawed prospectus for Britain's future. It is a programme that is more alchemy than economics. It promises to cut tax, spend more, borrow less – all at once. Because of the inherent implausibility of such a programme it then promises to square it all by a 'savings' programme of £35 billion. Under scrutiny it has fallen apart. In opposition that might not matter. In government it would be dangerous.

This of course is why their manifesto is by some way the shortest produced by any major party in recent years, barely pretending to be a programme for government and with virtually nothing to say about the economy or about economic change.

It is a very odd thing for someone like me, brought up with the idea that the Conservatives were always heard first on the economy, with us trying to catch up, to see them now in the position of Basil Fawlty and the war. It is a sign of the complete transformation of British politics: that we can claim to be the party of economy, and they are the threat.

Blair argued that the manifesto Labour had published provided a stark contrast with the Conservatives' plans. 'Yesterday's manifesto is New Labour. It is the basis on which we will govern. Since 1997 we have offered the British people a new choice. We have to keep on doing so, as both myself and Gordon Brown made clear.

'I want therefore to return again today to the economy. I want to set out the case for why New Labour is the party of modern wealth creation and prosperity, and why I believe that it is New Labour, rather than the Conservatives, which understands the profound challenges facing our economy and society, and has the right policies to foster enterprise and the knowledge economy upon which future wealth creation depends.' Blair declined the opportunity to take questions after his speech and sped instead to his only other engagement of the day, a visit to a school in Enfield – linked to a pledge to boost science spending in education – where wife Cherie made her first campaign outing kitted out in a fetching pink suit. A planned televised 'doorstep' conversation there between Blair and reporters was cancelled.

The perils of the doorstep were then graphically illustrated by Labour's campaign coordinator Alan Milburn. The Labour strategy on Bourgass was now settled. The Tories were making political capital out of a terrible event. The Tories had refused to back ID cards, a measure the police and security services said was needed in the fight against terrorism. They had also caused the Terror Bill showdown. Howard had presided as Home Secretary over an asylum regime far more inefficient than the present government's. The public back ID cards and strong action on terrorism. Cue Alan Milburn to perform in the street for the cameras in Croydon. This is the version of his comments put out by Labour HQ:

The result of the ricin case trial, and the information it has revealed about terrorist activity in Britain, makes it clearer than ever that no serious party should play politics on terrorism.

The public need to be reassured that every action is being taken – by government, the police and security services – to combat terrorism. I have spoken this morning to the Prime Minister and Charles Clarke who have agreed that the Identity Cards Bill will be a major plank of Labour's first Queen's Speech if we win the election.

If Labour win, the ID Card Bill will be reintroduced before the summer. Only last week the Conservatives blocked ID cards from becoming law, after nearly three years of discussion in parliament.

A few weeks ago, they tried to obstruct the government's plans for control orders and a new Prevention of Terrorism Act. I now challenge Michael Howard to say whether the Conservatives will support or oppose the ID Cards Bill when it is reintroduced in parliament?

There is no scope for playing politics on this. This is no time for uncertainty or hesitation. Britain needs strong leadership on terrorism. Tony Blair and the Labour Party are committed to providing that strong leadership.

But that wasn't quite the whole story. Reporters with the Howard camp began hearing rumours of a Milburn apology for the death of DC Oake, seeming to accept the government's asylum policy had somehow been complicit in his death. It turned out Milburn had been asked by Angus Walker of ITV News if he apologised for the failings in the asylum system that had allowed Bourgass to remain at large.

Milburn replied: 'Of course what we apologise for is the death of that police officer, serving his country, trying to protect his country. The issue now is how we ensure that that sort of thing doesn't happen again.' Howard was quick off the mark, nailing Milburn as having accepted some responsibility for the dreadful events. He said Mr Milburn 'was right to apologise'. He went on: 'Of course that involves acceptance of the responsibility of the government for what happened.' Howard rejected suggestions that he was 'playing politics' with the issue. 'That is what Labour always say when they have no answer to the criticisms that we make. The truth is that Britain's asylum system is in chaos. That is not something I have been saying today or yesterday but something I have been saying over the course of months and years.'

Howard said that the government's claims that ID cards were the solution were 'ludicrous' when just weeks ago ministers said they would not be issued to failed asylum seekers. 'There is nothing this government will not stop at to get votes. I think the country is fed up to the back teeth. The sooner we see the back of them the better.'

Milburn had walked into Howard's elephant trap, apparently through a rhetorical slip of the brain, trying to flip round Walker's use of the word apologise, in a question most viewers, of course, never even heard. Labour HQ had to try to recover the ground given up. It rushed out a statement saying:

> There is only one person responsible for the death of Detective Constable Stephen Oake, and that is the terrorist convicted of his murder. The public will understand exactly why Alan Milburn said he was sorry a policeman serving and protecting his country was murdered, and that the issue is how we ensure it doesn't happen again.
>
> At the time of DC Stephen Oake's tragic murder, Home Secretary David Blunkett expressed the government's deepest regret. Tony Blair attended DC Oake's funeral. This is not an issue of asylum, but an issue of terrorism. As a former Home Secretary, Michael Howard should know it is completely wrong to try to exploit the murder of a police officer by a terrorist. Once again, Howard's opportunism clouds his judgement.

Former Home Secretary David Blunkett rang the PA to denounce Howard, calling on him to cease using the killing of DC Oake to score points on asylum. Labour issued another statement attacking Howard. It read:

Michael Howard tonight committed two blunders in separate TV news interviews as he tripped over himself in his attempts to gain political capital from the conviction of Kamel Bourgass.

Mr Howard got his facts wrong on asylum seeker ID cards when he told Channel Five News that asylum seekers do not get ID cards. In fact, all asylum seekers have been issued with high-tech biometric ID cards (called ARC cards) since 2002. The government's plans for biometric ID cards are for all UK citizens and foreign nationals staying in the UK longer than three months – asylum seekers are already covered.

Mr Howard also contradicted himself by saying it was 'ludicrous' to suggest that ID cards could tackle terrorism. But immediately after the September 11th attacks he wrote in the News of the World *that 'Britain is the easiest country in Western Europe in which criminals and terrorists can lose themselves. If we are serious about tackling this problem, there is one obvious remedy – identity cards.' (September 23rd 2001)*

Mr Howard also criticised the government for not knowing the number of illegal immigrants in the country – despite the fact he said he said he didn't know either when he was Home Secretary.

Labour's General Election Coordinator, Alan Milburn said 'Michael Howard is more interested in exploiting issues than telling the truth. He should know that all asylum applicants to the UK have been issued with biometric ID cards since 2002 and that the government's ID cards scheme will go even further in ensuring we know exactly who is in the country. Michael Howard is learning once more that opportunist, bandwagon politics is a

> *dangerous game to play. He should say once and for all whether he will support or oppose ID cards'.*

The rebuttal machine was in full flow. And that's how it goes with election campaign days: the surreal mixture of a terrorist outrage; a bleary-eyed new dad and a blunder; a joke and a picture caption of Cherie in a suit; a wrong word on a pavement and a political frenzy. Reality and rhetoric colliding.

3

TB–GB Shanghai'd

Friday 15 April

At 10.09 a.m. news broke that the last hope for MG Rover's Longbridge car production plant had died. It emerged that the Shanghai Automotive Industry Corporation had told the British government that it did not wish to continue talks to form a partnership with the ailing company. Blair, campaigning on what was supposed to be Labour's family-friendly, 'school gate mums' day, was caught on the hop. Even as Rover's administrators PricewaterhouseCoopers (PWC) were announcing that as a result of the collapse of the deal there would be 'significant redundancies', the PM and wife Cherie were promoting a supermarket-style New Labour magazine called *Families Matter*, complete with a foreword by former *EastEnders* star Ross Kemp at a photo-call in a community centre in Crawley, West Sussex.

Blair came out to a pre-arranged doorstep and was bombarded with questions about Rover. He may have been aware that a letter from the Chinese had arrived at the Department of Trade and Industry at 7.30 a.m., but he had few answers, telling reporters:

> *We have received a letter from the Chinese company. I think there will be announcements made about this shortly. I do not have*

anything more to say at this point in time today. But we will keep you in touch with the thing as it develops.

I think it is best that we wait and see, until we are in a position to give you the details of the letter. I have not actually seen the letter myself yet, for example, because I have been down here.

Dumping his pool reporters to travel by car to his next scheduled visit in Fulham, Blair caught the next train back to London.

Today was not supposed to be this way.

Brown, in a speech trailed overnight, was going to take campaigning centre stage with a set-piece speech at a nursery school to an audience featuring genuine mums and babies. Blair and Cherie were supposed to be the picture backdrop. Blair would go on to appear on Jeremy Vine's Radio 2 phone-in and interview show, leaving Howard and the Tories to bang on about Britishness, the unfair asylum system and travellers' sites, and Kennedy to preside over his party's attempts to highlight its green credentials. But for the second day running, events did not go to plan. Once again, events had to become the plan. And for the second week running, Blair had to scoot to the West Midlands for a Rover crisis meeting. It was exactly seven days ago that he had made the same journey on his return from Pope John Paul's funeral. But the morning had begun with no hint of what was to come. Kennedy, looking 24 hours less tired than he had yesterday, positively bounced into his 7.30 a.m. press conference. 'I'm a bit more alert today,' he told the hacks.

'The environment is at the heart of what we stand for as a party and it's something that for me personally is an issue of very considerable passion,' began Kennedy. 'On the environment the Liberal Democrats are not just the real alternative. If you want to improve the environment we are the only choice.' He warmed to his theme: 'For me, politics is not just about helping people to improve their lives now, it is also about taking responsibility for future generations.

'That is why action on the environment runs – as a green thread – through our manifesto. On the economy, education, health, transport or foreign affairs, we show how our green policies would work to protect and improve the environment.' He promised a moratorium on GM crops until proved safe for people and the environment. He also pledged not to go ahead with any major new road building schemes unless the benefits were clear, and promised 60 per cent of all household waste should be recycled by 2012; 20 per cent of electricity generated by renewable sources by 2020 and a moratorium on new incinerators and no new nuclear power stations. Kennedy said environmentally damaging behaviour cost Britain £67 billion last year – equivalent to the entire NHS budget.

On the *Today* programme he got his tuppence-worth into the Bourgass row and anticipated Howard's speech later on British values. 'What I am not wanting to do is to jump from the very specific to saying therefore you recast an entire policy on the back of this. That, I think, would be irresponsible as an approach,' he said about the clash which had drawn Milburn's apology for DC Stephen Oake's death.

'What we are not going to do is to contribute to such a climate of controversy in the country that it actually begins to run the risk of disturbing the sensitive balance of good race relations, in the main, which we have, in today's British society.'

Howard had decided to replace party co-chairman Liam Fox at his party's morning news conference on pensions, alongside spokesman David Willetts.

'I believe that people deserve to be treated with dignity and respect in their retirement,' said Howard. 'But in Britain today millions of people have seen the value of their pensions destroyed by Mr Blair's stealth taxes. Imagine putting money aside for your retirement only to find that it's not there.'

Blair was not interested in pensioners' values, only their votes, mocked the Conservative leader, standing beside a huge pile of legislation representing the red tape his party would sweep away from the pensions regime.

Willetts asked: 'How can Mr Blair campaign on the economy while saying nothing about his tax plans and nothing about pensions? A responsible government would support hard-working people who do the right thing by saving for retirement. After eight years of Labour government, we've got a society where it is easy to borrow and hard to save. The collapse of our pensions since 1997 will affect people for decades to come.'

A Tory government would reward saving by abolishing the requirement to buy an annuity at the age of 75, and would strengthen company pension schemes; the state pension's link with earnings would be restored. Howard also seized on a survey in *The Times* today which had shown up to a 500 per cent increase in postal vote applications over the last election in marginal seats, and a tripling of applications overall since rules were relaxed to allow anybody who requested one to have a postal vote. Fears over potential cheating in 5 May's poll were already running high in the wake of fraud scandals in Birmingham, where six Labour councillors were found guilty by an election commissioner, and Blackburn, where a Labour activist was sentenced to three years and seven months in jail.

Howard said the government had left the system open to abuse by failing to introduce other safeguards put forward by the independent Electoral Commission watchdog. 'I think it's a scandal and Mr Blair should be thoroughly ashamed of what he has done to our democracy.' The recommendations had only been dropped 'when it was appreciated that certain categories of voters particularly favourable to the Labour Party might be less inclined to vote,' he alleged, adding that the judge in the Birmingham case had compared the situation there to a 'banana republic'.

He went on: 'People will remember the fun we had talking about hanging chads in Florida. No one ever thought our electoral system would become suspect. What happens to our credibility when we want to complain about things that happen in places like Zimbabwe?'

Howard went on to Watford, and Brown went to a school in Camberwell, south London. Neither had an entirely happy reception. Brown met his 'school gate mums' all right, outside the Comber Primary School, and tried to impress them with details of childcare policies, balloons and autographs for the children.

He said: 'I wanted to meet parents at the school gates and the children, to say that the economy is not just abstract figures, it is about them.' But the first child he picked up for a snap in front of the waiting press was one-year-old local boy Felix Williams, who promptly burst into tears.

Parents dropping their children off at school asked Brown about inheritance tax and lowering council tax, and one mother asked for more money for special needs provisions. A passer-by shouted 'Tony Blair is a warmonger' and 'Killing Iraqi children is inappropriate'.

In his speech later, Brown got a friendlier welcome. 'In the past,' he said, 'the focus of budgets was on inflation rates and trade balances. Future budgets will focus also on childcare, family tax credits and educational investment. Children are 20 per cent of our population and they are 100 per cent of our future. So when we say for every child the best start in life, we are talking about an economic concern.

'And when we warn that failure to give all children the best start in life risks failure on many other fronts, we are talking about a social concern. If we do not find it within ourselves to pay attention to our children today, they may force us to pay attention as troubled adults tomorrow.'

Pensions, children, electoral fraud, the environment – Crikey! Thought-provoking stuff. The campaign back on track at last? Now it was Howard's turn to headline his issues of the day in his Watford speech. As he stepped off his campaign bus with wife Sandra there were smiles from the multi-racial line-up there to greet them, and there were scuffles with protestors in the background as Labour placards were dashed to the ground.

Inside the venue, Howard went straight into his assault on Blair for undermining British values by turning a 'blind eye' to cheats from bogus asylum seekers to travellers setting up camp illegally. He said: 'The people I worry about are the ordinary, decent folk who know that things are wrong but are being intimidated into silence. People who don't ask for special favours and can't believe they've been pushed to the back of the queue by a government that seems obsessed by the rights of wrongdoers.' The Tory leader added:

> *In his desire to please everyone, Mr Blair has undermined Britain's values and with it the sense of fair play that's so central to our national identity . . . people like my parents choose to come and settle here – not because of the weather, but because of Britain's tolerance, love of freedom and sense of fair play. The fact that genuine refugees look to Britain for sanctuary – that hard-working families want to settle here and make a contribution to our society – demonstrates that British values stand for something in the world. They're precious. They're worth fighting for.*
>
> *And we have to fight for them today. We have to fight for them in this election campaign: because this election is not just about policies, programmes and priorities, important though they are. It's about values; our values; British values; values which aren't recognised or respected by this government.*
>
> *It astonishes me that the people who rule us today – the government and the new Establishment – seem to have a completely different set of values to everyone else. Let me give you an example.*
>
> *Recently I spoke out against the abuse of our planning laws by the*

small minority of travellers who have no respect for the law. I didn't claim it was the most important issue facing Britain today. And I didn't tar all travellers with the same brush. All I did was point out that if you or I want to build a house, we have to get planning permission first. Yet – thanks to the Human Rights Act – a minority of travellers have been able to build what they like, where they like.

Lots of hard-working families who've seen their communities turned upside down as a result came out to support me; but not the government or its supporters. Their reaction was truly astonishing.

He had been subject to a ferocious Labour attack. 'These reactions go to the very heart of what's gone wrong in our country. Some people call it political correctness. Others call it moral relativism. I call it madness. Common sense has been stood on its head. The victims have become the aggressors and the aggressors have become the victims. It's this kind of madness that is creating a growing gulf between the people and the new Establishment.'

Howard said he could take care of himself: 'The people I worry about are the ordinary, decent folk, who know that things are wrong but are being intimidated into silence. People who see the values they grew up with and still believe in trashed. No one worries about their sensitivities. No one cares if they feel excluded. No one stands up for them. Well, I will.'

He finished with his coup de speech: 'People will face a clear choice at the election: a choice between a Conservative government which upholds the law and Mr Blair, who turns a blind eye when the rules are abused.'

This is one of the Conservative leader's favourite themes: I stand up for you, the silent majority, the forgotten majority; I say the things you say in the pub, to your mum, to your husband. All neatly wrapped up in his slogan: 'Are you thinking what we're thinking?'

We can only imagine what Howard was thinking as, during his

own phone-in on Radio 4 later, on a visit to Chatham, Kent, he came in for ferocious criticism for his remarks over the past 24 hours. Ever since Mrs Thatcher was roasted by an angry viewer on the BBC's *Nationwide* TV magazine programme over the sinking of the *Belgrano* during the Falklands War, politicians have known the pitfalls of live conversations with members of the public. They can say things humble hacks could never get away with.

'Federico from London' told listeners that, like Howard's grandfather, he was Jewish and a refugee to Britain. But Federico went on: 'Every time Mr Howard opens his mouth and talks about foreigners who are invading this country in the words that he does . . . he is making life impossible for us.'

Battling with constantly annoying feedback and intermittent reception in his headphones, an uncomfortable Howard replied:

> *I'm sorry that you've reacted in the way that you have to what I've been saying because you, and the very many people like you, play a very important part in our society and I've made that absolutely clear.*
>
> *I've said many times that we are a better, richer, stronger country because we are more diverse, because of the immigrant communities that have settled in this country.*
>
> *But I do believe that if we are to continue to have good community relations and if we are to get a grip on our security and proper management of our public services, we have to have an immigration system that is under control.*

Another caller said Howard was 'appealing to the xenophobic and racist tendency. I accuse Mr Howard of saying things which appeal to racists'.

Howard, clearly stung, replied: 'I reject that absolutely. I will not be accused of racism. My grandmother was actually killed in the

Holocaust. I care passionately, perhaps because of that, about good community relations in our country and I know very well that if you have a situation in which immigration is seen to be out of control and asylum is seen to be in chaos, it is one of the greatest enemies of good community relations.'

Blair travelled to Crawley for his community centre visit. As his battlebus – the special one in which he arrives at photo-calls; he does not necessarily travel in it between venues – arrived, Blair was greeted by a lone protester holding up a placard declaring: 'Bush, Blair, Saddam – war criminals.' The protester shouted at him: 'Tony, you are a murderer.'

Everybody seemed to getting very grumpy today all of a sudden. One can only assume that Blair got grumpier as the hours wore on.

Having endured his cornering by reporters on Rover as he left what were supposed to have been the comfortable confines of West Sussex, Blair hightailed it back to London. He had already decided to visit the West Midlands, along with Brown and Patricia Hewitt. But the Radio 2 phone-in scheduled for 12.20 p.m. was a long-standing commitment and could not be broken. Knowing he would get calls on the issue, he would use it instead to make his first meaningful comments on Rover and announce a package of help for the workers – now confirmed at 5,000 – who faced the bleakest of futures, while giving no firm details.

After wading through questions on a sea of topics, he responded to a call from an MG Rover worker:

It's been a terrible blow because the workforce is a fantastic workforce and everyone has worked so hard over the last few years to try and turn the company round.

I am going to go up to the West Midlands myself this afternoon with Gordon Brown and Patricia Hewitt and we will announce details of a package. I haven't the details myself with me now which will help, I hope, the workforce in the immediate term and in the medium term as well.

There had been reports this morning, neither confirmed nor denied as the details rapidly became irrelevant, that Blair had faced down Brown, ignored Hewitt's advice, and that of officials, to offer the £100 million government bridging loan which had featured in the doomed Chinese talks. But with a New Deal task force package to help stricken workers, Blair knew he could count on Brown's support.

Blair told the caller: 'I'm really sorry. I just want you to know we tried every single thing we possibly could to put the deal together with the Chinese company. In the end I'm afraid it has been bad news today.'

Hewitt, talking on TV, said massive investment had been needed to fund new models: 'It's that hope of new models, new investment and the continuation of Longbridge as a going concern which has now, I'm afraid, died with the Chinese saying no.'

She rang the home of Phil Hanks, who has worked in the paint shop at Longbridge for the past fifteen years and whose family had been involved in the deputation to Downing Street earlier in the week.

'She sounded genuinely upset about what has happened,' he said. 'I don't blame the government for what has happened because they have done all they can. We were still holding out some hope that the deal would go ahead so this is the worst possible news.'

Hewitt, Blair and Brown then sped to Euston to catch the train to Birmingham, for talks with 'stakeholders' – unions and local Rover suppliers chief among them – at the HQ of the local regional development agency Advantage West Midlands, in Aston, where they were to unveil the government's £150 million 'soft landing' package. After the discussions, Blair told reporters he wanted to express his 'real sorrow' for all involved. He added: 'This is a desperate time for the workers at Longbridge and their families.'

Standing alongside Blair, Brown told journalists that the support package would be made up of in excess of £60 million to help diversify industry in the area and to support the supply chain. There would be another £50 million to fund the retraining and re-skilling of workers made redundant. Another £40 million would be ploughed into statutory redundancy payments. In addition, Brown said, around £40 million of previously announced money would help with the construction of a new industrial park in the region. On top of that the government was in discussion with the European Union about additional help. He confirmed the new Pension Protection Fund set up by the government to help workers whose firms go bust could also come into play. It was not the sort of impromptu press conference either Blair or Brown had imagined when they began their day's work this morning. Blair looked wearied; perhaps he wanted to look, or simply felt, solemn. Workers were filmed removing their tools from the sprawling factory on improvised trolleys; even though they were collecting their own possessions, the TV image almost looked like looters scrambling for scraps among a deserted building, adding to the air of desolation.

Still in Chatham, where he had been meeting war veterans, Howard reacted to the announcement, saying the news was 'a dreadful blow' to workers who, in some instances, had given decades of their lives to the company. 'It is a terrible blow to them, their families and also those who work in the dealerships. This is going to have, I am afraid, very deep and far-reaching consequences. It's a tragic day for thousands of workers and their families.'

Howard confessed he was not clear on all the details, but added: 'It does seem to me that the government got involved in the nego-tiations with Shanghai Automotive pretty late in the day.'

Kennedy concurred that the government should have acted sooner. 'As it developed into such a grave situation within the last two weeks, it seems incredible that, with the level of government involvement there over such a period of time, the alarm bells didn't ring at the very top sooner than they did. It looks as if the government was moving too late,' he said.

Speaking on a campaign visit to Falmouth, Kennedy went on: 'Most people will find it amazing that it was such a 59th minute of the eleventh hour that saw Gordon Brown and Tony Blair suddenly arriving; and, of course, alas after the events, here they are back there again.' Commenting on the failure of the Treasury and the DTI to act sooner, Kennedy said, 'That is a question the government will have to answer.' Later he and Howard joined calls for an inquiry into the whole affair.

Blair, Brown and Hewitt finally headed out of Birmingham, their duty done; Howard made for home in his Folkestone constituency, to his house looking down over Romney Marsh, and Kennedy travelled back to London, to his baby boy and wife Sarah, to put his feet up for a day or so at least – although that may be an optimistic description of life with a newborn infant. They could all have watched Labour's latest party political broadcast with their cocoa.

Beginning with shots showing the Tory leader as a youthful-looking MP entering parliament in 1983, the short film ran through the introduction of the poll tax and Britain's exit from the Exchange Rate Mechanism on Black Wednesday. It also highlighted his record as Home Secretary, claiming police numbers fell by 1,132. The film then cut to the present day.

'As Tory leader, now he plans to make £35 billion cuts – and put economic stability at risk,' the commentary ran. To the strains of Gladys Knight and the Pips singing 'The Way We Were', the broadcast ended: 'We can't afford to go back to the way we were. If you want to take Britain forward not back, vote Labour on 5 May.'

You see how clever Labour had thought its campaigning day was to be: Gordon Brown's speech on 'bringing the economy home', explaining all those Budget numbers in child-friendly terms; a lovely glossy magazine for the those 'school gate mums' wooed by Gordon, Tony and Cherie – not to mention Ross Kemp thrown in for good measure. That was how it had looked at 8 a.m., in the settled imagination of Alastair Campbell. Maybe he ended the day in front of the telly, humming along: 'Could it be that it was all so simple then; or has time rewritten every line . . .'

Saturday 16 April

But if they had the chance to do it all again – tell me: would they, could they? Of course they would. A grid's a grid for all that, and sometimes it works.

Today, Patricia Hewitt sought to close down the Rover issue early on, announcing that Sir Bryan Nicholson, chairman of the Financial Reporting Council, would investigate the financial collapse of the company. So calls for an inquiry had been met, and any queries could be deflected and deferred until it reports.

Labour's grid said the rest of the day was reserved for another NHS day, and time to complain about Tory election tactics. No point in hanging around – put up the PM and 'attack dog', though he famously hates the expression, John Reid, at a 9 a.m. press conference. Especially after a story in the *Guardian* accuses the Conservatives over the MRSA superbug of using misleading figures; when you appear to have got them bang to rights, and see the possibility of Howard himself having to issue an apology. After all, Labour had been drawn into an apology over the Bourgass affair.

Tony Blair, John Reid and junior health minister Rosie Winterton hurtled into their party's press conference at Labour HQ. They were people with a mission – or, come to think of it, a double mission. The first was spelt out clear enough. The press release was headlined 'This is now the values election – Blair.' And the clearest choice on values was about the NHS. The PM duly delivered, declaring this to be, surprise, surprise, 'the values election' even as he invited voters to sign a nationwide petition to 'keep the NHS free' and presided over an announcement of 50 community hospitals to be built, refurbished, or generally done up, over the next five years. He said the public would have the choice of 'Labour values of security and opportunity for all Britain's hard-working families and pensioners – or Conservative values to govern in the interests of a privileged few at the expense of the hardworking majority'.

He went on: 'Politics is more than just the dry detail of policy. Politics is about deeply-held beliefs which drive the policy detail, the values which underpin the policy programmes. Values bring politics alive. And at this election there is a choice between two very different sets of values.' Blair said yesterday he had discussed improving childcare with parents, and, of course, been to Birmingham to discuss with local bosses, unions and the development agencies how to help MG Rover workers.

> *Both were about helping the decent hard-working families of our country – the people who play by the rules and deserve a government which believes that in a constantly changing and uncertain world its duty is to extend greater opportunity and security for all. That is what I mean when I say this is a choice between values.*
>
> *A previous generation of Labour politicians fought to create the NHS in the face of fierce Conservative opposition. This generation of Labour politicians is fighting to keep up the necessary investment to rebuild the NHS after decades of neglect, once again in the face of fierce Conservative opposition – Labour values which support the NHS – or Conservative values which oppose it.*

And so on. One feature of this campaign has been the 'cross-phrasing' of messages. Decent, hard-working families: is it a Tory phrase or Labour phrase? Discuss, as they say.

Reid praised the Labour government's record on investment in the National Health Service, reeling off statistics of new buildings and new equipment, telling reporters: 'These aren't just statistics. They are an indication of lives saved – around 50,000 from the reduction in premature deaths from cancer and heart-related disease alone. They mean a better and speedier service. So it will be in the future.'

But there was more to come. The second hit. Blair and Reid stuck the knife into the Tories, after the *Guardian* story out today that they had distributed campaign leaflets giving figures for MRSA infections which related to NHS Trusts – plural – which were described in the literature as relating to an NHS Trust – singular. The impression given to voters was that one individual hospital had the superbug infection rate attributable, in fact, to a whole region.

Blair, looking relaxed in shirtsleeves at his press conference performance after the unexpected turmoil of the last 24 hours, told reporters of the Conservative effort: 'It's a campaign that is a nasty and unscrupulous campaign, frankly, and it's descending into increasing desperation as time goes on. They do not deserve to get away with a campaign being fought in this way.' He added: 'The whole nature of the Conservative campaign on health is to forget about the improvements in the NHS and just focus on one issue, MRSA.'

For good, measure he went on: 'The major part of their campaign, talking to our candidates, is almost a one-issue campaign on immigration and asylum and associated issues.'

Reid didn't need much asking to join in. He accused the Tories of 'a systematic deception of the public over MRSA incidents in hospitals'. He said: 'Their campaign literature told people their local hospitals were affected by MRSA at an incidence which actually related to the whole region.' He said the previous Tory administration had failed to act against MRSA 'at a time when we could have killed off the superbug. The Tory government ran down the staff, ran down the hospitals, and ran down the cleaning'.

Blair posed for pictures signing a stunted-up petition in the overspill area of Labour headquarters after the press conference, before heading off to Dartford for the pre-arranged pictures at the Darent Valley Hospital, where Cherie was to join him.

Howard, meanwhile, had decided weeks ago not to be in London on Saturdays for ritual press conferences, but for the next three weeks to be in his constituency of Folkestone and Hythe. He was, after all, defending a majority there of 5,907, making him technically vulnerable to the tactical target putsch which would have been dreamed of by both Labour and the Liberal Democrats. Today, Howard was to make a speech there on 'The Britain I believe in'. The only other Tory event planned was a poster launch by party co-chairman and weekend duty bod Liam Fox, which attacked Labour on MRSA. Howard had made a feature of campaigning on the issue and had poignant reasons for doing so. His wife Sandra's mother died from a hospital-acquired infection. Conservative HQ had put out a statement on the *Guardian* story in the small hours of the morning, pointing out it was little more than a typographical error. The statement said: 'The figure [used on the leaflet] reflects accurately the number of bloodstream infection rates for the area. The letter should have read "local NHS Trusts" but unfortunately read, "Trust". MRSA has become endemic in our hospitals – deaths associated with MRSA have tripled since 1997. The issue, of critical importance to NHS staff and patients, has not been a priority for Labour. In contrast the Conservatives have set out an action plan to deliver what matters to people – clean hospitals.'

A bit of argy-bargy over an old newspaper story did not register as a cloud on Howard's horizon. He set out his stall in comfortable constituency surroundings: 'Today I want to share with you my hopes and aspirations for our country. The country we should be. The country we can be. The country we must be. My hopes for Britain are rooted in the values of the hard-working families who make our country the best in the world: rewarding enterprise; encouraging individual responsibility; and a pride – no matter what our colour, creed or religion – in being British. The Britain I believe in will reward people who do the right thing: who work hard, pay their taxes and bring up their children to respect others.'

The values of hard-working families; the Tories engaged in the 'values' debate. Not afraid of it either – you want values, they've got them.

> *Britain's hard-working families and its wealth-creating entrepreneurs need a government solidly on their side – a government that recognises and rewards their efforts.*
>
> *A government that applies a simple philosophy: reward people who do the right thing. Reward parents who raise children to respect others, reward professionals who follow their vocation, reward businessmen and -women who take risks to guarantee our future prosperity.*
>
> *Rewarding them means trusting them – with more of their own money, more control over their destiny, more freedom to believe in their dreams and to see them come true. The balance between rights and responsibilities in Britain is today out of kilter. Too many people now believe that they are no longer wholly responsible for their actions. And the rights culture rewards those who don't play by the rules.*
>
> *'I've got my rights' has become the verbal equivalent of two fingers to authority. The so-called Human Rights Act has allowed arsonists to escape expulsion from school, killers to win the right to pornography in prison, and travellers to set up illegal encampments in defiance of planning laws.*
>
> *I believe fair play matters. The same rules should apply whatever your background, whatever your religion, whatever your sex. We are all British. We are one nation. That's why I don't believe in special rules for special interest groups. And I'll carry on talking about fair play even though I'm attacked for it because I will never be stopped from saying what I know is right.*

I believe respect matters: respect for others, respect for the law, respect for property. These values are the bedrock of a successful society. The Britain I believe in would put a premium on fair play, on order and on respect.

That's why we should never tolerate abuse, whether by people-smugglers who trample over our borders, criminals who work the system for their benefit or freeloaders who demand special privileges without shouldering their responsibilities.

I believe that, given the chance, a Conservative Party which believes in recognising and rewarding Britain's forgotten majority could transform our nation.

That was the Britain Howard believed in. He went on to take some questions from the audience and soon he was asked about MRSA and the leaflets. This is the version of his answer initially released by Conservative Campaign HQ:

I'm angry about the 5,000 people who die every year from hospital-acquired infections in our country, that's what I'm angry about, Mr Blair.

Mr Blair is rattled because he doesn't have a plan to deal with hospital-acquired infections, I do have a plan, my plan is to bring back matron and put her where she belongs in charge.

And she would have the right to close infected wards, something which now when local infections teams ask to happen doesn't happen because the managers say if you close the ward we'd miss government targets. That's what we would change, that's how we'd improve things, that how we would deal with this terrible problem of hospital-acquired infections which is killing so many people in this country.

But reporters there knew what he had actually said was: 'We sent out a letter and it referred to the MRSA rates in the local hospital, the local hospital trust, when it should have referred to the local hospital trusts. And that was a mistake and I'm very sorry we made that mistake. Mr Blair may be angry about the omission of the letter 's'. I'm angry about the 5,000 people who die every year . . .'

The apology had been somehow left off the version promulgated initially by the Conservatives. It was a hit for Labour and revenge for Milburn. It fed into their claims that the Conservative campaign was 'nasty and unscrupulous'; the effect of the error – which may have been a genuine typographical slip – was to mislead voters into thinking infection rates at their local hospital were far higher than they actually were.

A Conservative spokeswoman said bashfully: 'Michael has apologised for a mistake in the leaflet, but he doesn't apologise for raising the issue.' Blair, meanwhile, was enjoying himself in Dartford. Nursing staff there surprised him by testing his heart rate and oxygen levels, using a pulse oximeter, a type of heat sensor, to take readings from the Prime Minister's finger. He recorded a heartbeat of 66 beats per minute and an oxygen level of 98 out of a possible 100. Staff said the readings indicated he was in good shape, particularly given the rigours of the election campaign. No sign of the dodgy ticker.

Blair and Cherie met staff and patients in reception, the out-patient unit and the 23-hour-a-day elective surgery 'Hotel Redwood' suite – Redwood, Redwood, that name rings a bell; surely not a ward named after the Tory frontbencher John? Among the patients was Brenda Stevens, 67, from Dartford. She told Blair that she had come to the hospital the day before for a surgical operation to address her own uneven heartbeat. When she was about to be anaesthetised, her heart went into a flutter and the operation had to be postponed, but she was full of praise for the unit: 'It is wonderful, you could not get better if I had paid private and I could not afford that. This is equal or better.' You could almost sense the

PM thinking of the TV cameras: 'Are you getting all this stuff?' In a reference to his own problems with an irregular heartbeat, Blair told Mrs Stevens: 'I was going to give you the benefit of my ignorance, but I won't.'

Another patient, 54-year-old Brian Cope, from Hextable, near Dartford, told Mr Blair that he had come to the hospital to have a fatty lump removed from his shoulder. Blair could not resist commenting on Mr Cope's impressive beard: 'That is a magnificent, spectacular beard.'

Mr Cope replied: 'Someone once told me that if I wanted to be a Labour politician I would have to shave my beard.' Blair's reply, if there was one, was sadly inaudible. Just as well for the bearded Home Secretary Charles Clarke.

Blair told reporters as he left the hospital: 'Just as the economy is at the heart of this election campaign, so should the NHS be. It is not just the fact of the new building and all the extra investment that we have got to keep going, it is the values of the health service.

'The importance of keeping the health service free at the point of use, with care based on people's need not their wealth or ability to pay, is in contrast with a Conservative plan that will actually take money out of the NHS and subsidise private health care.'

Mr Blair was asked about the Conservatives' campaigning on MRSA. He lost no time in attacking the Tories again: 'We are tackling MRSA here at this hospital. For the Conservatives to try to run down the whole of the NHS on the basis of MRSA and often misleading information about it is just an indication of what is at stake here.'

The Blairs travelled to and from Dartford by scheduled train. On their return journey to Victoria, the Labour leader encountered retired driver Raymond Bowyer, 67, from Stockwell, south London. Mr Bowyer regaled the Prime Minister and his wife with stories of how to get around London without paying the congestion charge, and details of the best routes between various points. And he proudly boasted to Blair: 'I know all the routes. I could beat your driver back to Downing Street.' The two men shook hands and posed for pictures.

Later Mr Bowyer said: 'I have seen him on TV before, but never in person. He's a very nice man. I'll vote for him.'

Reid, meanwhile, had been continuing to trade blows over the NHS with the Conservatives, while the Lib Dem President Simon Hughes had contained the party's main campaigning to a boat trip down the River Thames, highlighting his party's pledge to scrap student fees. Labour, you see, had sold students down the river – geddit?

But as well as the negative, Reid decided to accentuate the positive and promised women they would receive the results of their cervical smear tests within seven days rather than seven weeks, if the party was returned to power. They would also be able to get their test results by email, text or telephone, as well as automatically getting them in writing, as now. Saturday night brought a clutch of polls after the first full week of day-by-day campaigning and they made satisfying reading at Labour Campaign HQ. Labour's lead varied from one point to 10 per cent. Not a single survey showed the Conservatives making anywhere near enough headway to make anything other than a dent in Blair's 161-seat majority. The rosiest poll for Labour said it would barely shift at all.

The Tories began floating their plans for pensions as the first editions of the newspapers began drifting in. But Campbell could have been forgiven for singing Labour's campaign song to himself as he leafed through them: 'A Beautiful Day.'

Sunday 17 April

The tumbleweed blows down Election Street on Sunday morning, gathering empty cappuccino cups as it rolls. There are no early news conferences and the only bacon rolls are in the breakfast TV studios, where the bleary-eyed debate their message with their fresher-faced inquisitors. Especially on the first Sunday after campaigning proper began, it is time to take stock, leafing through the newspapers at more leisure than when firefighting stories from the first editions that drop into media offices on Saturday night; deciding where the strategy is going right or wrong.

The man with most to ponder today was probably Lynton Crosby, Howard's Australian media guru brought over earlier in 2005 to mastermind the Conservatives' strategy, after delivering four successive election triumphs for Howard's namesake John, leader of the Australian Liberal Party – the equivalent of the Tories Down Under. Whatever the Conservatives' private polling may be telling them about the success, or otherwise, of his techniques, targeting hit-and-run attacks on issues then moving on, the national opinion polls seemed stubbornly stuck in a rut that would lead only to a comfortable ride to Downing Street for Blair.

The crop of Sunday paper polls putting Labour's lead at anywhere between 1 and 10 per cent showed no evidence of a surge even in target seats, where a *News of the World* poll predicted Labour was holding up so well it could return with hardly a hole in its majority. Crosby, 48, has a reputation as a straight-talking and tough – even ruthless – operator, who inspires loyalty among friends and loathing among others. His arrival created a flurry of excitement in Westminster as he was hailed a 'master of the dark political arts' and 'the Australian Karl Rove', a reference to President George Bush's legendary strategist.

Along with business partner Mark Textor, Crosby's Australian winning streak started with the defeat of charismatic Labor Premier Paul Keating. However, critics focus on the highly divisive 2001 Australian election campaign which saw John Howard accused by some of racism and xenophobia. He had been lagging in the polls before turning back ships carrying Afghan and Iraqi asylum seekers and campaigning on the slogan: 'We decide who will come into this country.'

It was by no means Crosby's first brush with controversy. In 1992 the Australian Liberals were forced to pull a TV advert about the murder of a teenage girl following complaints from her family. Violent crime and immigration are what Crosby refers to as 'dog whistle' issues that, just as a dog whistle is too high for humans to hear, send coded messages to certain groups of voters. Born the son of a cereal farmer, he grew up in Kadina on South Australia's Yorke peninsula. He read economics at the University of Adelaide and worked for a petrol company and an oil exploration firm before joining the staff of a Liberal politician. Crosby was made the party's director of Queensland before setting up his own company in the early 1990s. He stood for the Australian Parliament himself only once, in 1981. He lost.

The Tories lured him to London, where he stays with wife Dawn in a rented Westminster flat, to try to counter the New Labour media machine. He has conceded that the transfer to Britain is a gamble. 'I am optimistic that the Conservative Party can do very well, and they can win. But life is not without risk,' he recently told the Australian newspaper. 'Getting up in the morning has a risk, crossing the road has a risk. We made a judgement as a company that it was something we wanted to do. And I am not contemplating there will be a [disastrous] blow-out.'

So far, Crosby had had Michael Howard out on the stump, criss-crossing the country by helicopter with a small pool of journalists. He had had him in old-style canvassing shots, putting leaflets through doors and pressing the flesh; and we had seen Big Speech Howard. We had also seen patient Press Conference Howard, refusing to make extravagant promises, facing down the press calmly and confidently and seizing on issues when they were going his way. Was there another Howard for Crosby to project?

The Conservatives' big idea for later today was the launch of its pensions prospectus, already floated in the Sunday papers. It was cautious and targeted at low- and basic-rate taxpayers, who paid into contributory pension schemes. The government would give £10 for every £100 saved, paid straight into the fund. There would be no benefit for top-rate tax earners who already received some relief on their contributions. The scheme, added to the pensioners' council tax discount of 50 per cent, up to £500, was billed as the second 'tax cut' to be sliced from the £4 billion in tax cuts the party said its plans allowed for.

Howard claimed the pensions move could increase the retire-ment pension of someone on average earnings by up to £500 a year. Announcing the scheme at a 2 p.m. press conference, he said: 'When I meet people, they often say to me "Too many politicians are inter-ested in the short term, tomorrow and next week, rather than ten years' time."

'Today, we are announcing a detailed, carefully considered and fully costed proposal to repair the long-term damage done by Mr Brown's pension tax. Only by encouraging more people to save can we ease their anxieties about their long-term security and give our economy a brighter, better future.'

Howard said the money would be paid to people whether they had personal or company schemes. He added: 'I believe in rewarding people who do the right thing and help themselves.

Though under our scheme people won't get something for nothing – they'll only get something out if they put something in.

'So to people paying basic-rate tax in their late 20s, 30s and 40s, our message is simple: if you do the right thing, we will do the right thing by you; if you save, we will boost your savings; and if you help yourself, we will help you.'

The Tories were making much of the fact that Labour had hived off its pensions review to the former head of the Confederation of British Industry Adair Turner, who was not due to report until after the election. So while the Conservatives had a policy, they claimed, Labour had none. But the Tory scheme itself was dense, modest and certainly unsparkling.

Labour retorted simply that the party's sums did not add up, and concentrated on another health pledge under their old master guru Campbell's plans. Reid went on GMTV to confirm the cervical smear test promise, saying: 'Women have said to me constantly that after a cervical smear test, having to wait up to seven weeks is just a very, very stressful period.' A quick, targeted hit. Some levers that are available to governments, even on a sleepy Sunday, are just not there for oppositions, no matter who their spin gurus are.

Also on the breakfast TV round, somewhat more controversially, was Britain's most senior policeman, Commissioner of the Metropolitan Police Sir Ian Blair. In an interview recorded earlier in the week, in the wake of the Bourgass case, but shown today, he not only backed up the government over the terrorist threat, but also came very close to throwing his full weight behind its ID Cards Bill that had been scuppered by the Tories at the end of the parliament.

The civil rights group Liberty told him to steer clear of his namesake Labour leader and stay out of the election.

Sir Ian told Sir David Frost:

There's real clarity now that Al-Qaeda affiliates are targeting Britain – that's the first thing. Secondly, I think we obviously have to mourn the death of Stephen Oake. Thirdly, the important point is to say this is one individual, not the whole Muslim community who are law-abiding and we have to work to support them. 99.9 per cent of Muslims and 99.9 per cent of Asians are law-abiding people and we've got to support them in that and understand the difference. What is it that drives a tiny number of young men and women into extreme violence?

Lastly, how does the legal system deal with cases of this sort? I think there will be a number of questions to be asked about whether the law is quite right.

The way that Al-Qaeda operates is in a sense of very loose-knit conspiracies. The way English law has developed is it doesn't like conspiracies. It likes actual offences. And where one person does something and another person does another thing but it's only when they add up that they become a conspiracy . . . I think we're going to have to just look again to see whether there is some other legislation around acts preparatory to terrorism, or something of that nature – that's what we'll have to do.

Asked if he would like to see an ID Cards Bill reintroduced after the election, Sir Ian said:

I think there has to be further consideration of that.

I wasn't particularly keen on ID cards until recently – until I began to understand the way in which identity theft is carried out, and the fact that what you and I and many of the viewers would recognise as forgery just doesn't exist any more.

There are no more printing presses in basements. The documents that are being produced are exactly identical to the real documents, they're just unauthorised. And so we have to go to a

place where we do know who people are. We now have the tech-
nology, I think through iris recognition, to go to that and I think
that would be very helpful.

One of the things about some of the [suspected terrorist]
Belmarsh detainees, and indeed Bourgass, is we do not know who
he is. At one stage or other we've got to start with a position where
we do know who people are.

Shami Chakrabarti, director of Liberty, laid into Sir Ian: 'Liberty remains clear that the case for compulsory ID cards has not been made. More importantly, however, it is time for Blair the Police Commissioner to create some distance from his political namesake. Law enforcement and other vital services must remain politically neutral – especially during an election campaign. Politicians come and go but the public needs confidence that policing goes on regardless.' Scotland Yard said later Sir Ian had been asked a question and had simply stated his opinion.

Labour swiftly confirmed it would, indeed, bring back its ID Cards Bill if re-elected, on the back of Sir Ian's comments, and repeated their challenge to the Tories to say whether or not they would support them.

And after fears of postal voting fraud, the election professionals moved today to try and damp down public concern, while conceding ID cards would certainly help shore up the system – a system, they reminded people, which had always been open to abuse but had thankfully survived relatively unscathed.

Alan Winchcombe, executive director of the Association of Electoral Administrators popped up on GMTV, saying: 'I don't think we should be at all worried about the way postal voting is taking place at this election. Our members are very keen to make sure that the integrity of the ballot is totally protected. Electoral fraud, particularly in postal voting, does takes place but the

Birmingham case which has highlighted this is a fairly small case of it.

'The AEA members are very vigilant in checking applications for postal voting and do everything they can to make sure the postal voting process is totally secure.

'But the whole of the voting process in the UK is based on trust and always has been. It hasn't significantly changed since Victorian times.

'You walk into the polling station and your identity is not checked. You are asked to confirm your name and address on the register of electors but the people on the desk do not know whether you are that person or not and the same applies to postal voting.'

There was no way of checking the signature of the voter or the witness on postal ballots, he said. 'The problem is that we don't have a database of those signatures. If we could check those signatures or other pieces of information . . . then that could go some way to checking individual voters' identities.'

ID cards would 'undoubtedly help' checking voters who turned up in person, he said. 'If you had to take an ID card into the polling station with a photograph on it, voting officials could check your identity almost without error.'

It was only to be hoped that he had not, inadvertently, given somebody somewhere some ideas.

But sometimes, among the flotsam and jetsam of a Sunday dominated by the airwaves, you can still find a little, overlooked gem. Deputy Prime Minister John Prescott went on the radio to reject claims that Blair and Brown had agreed a 'marriage of convenience' for the duration of the campaign. This is what he said:

It's about the two most effective politicians we've seen in Britain for a very long time, who have over these eight years produced the strongest economy we've seen, with sustained economic growth.

> *At the end of the day, these are two important men that made a lot of our decisions in government and have delivered for this country.*

Prescott went on:

> *He [Mr Blair] is staying a full term. That's what he's told you and you still won't believe it, will you? The matter of who gets elected leader in the party is elected by the party, as indeed I am as the deputy leader.*
>
> *In regard to the appointment of the Prime Minister, that's the Queen's appointment.*
>
> *You have got the Prime Minister making it very clear to you that he is staying for a full term. Why don't you accept it? You're getting it from the man himself saying that.*

Prescott – inadvertently? – lending currency to a rumour which had been doing the rounds at Westminster, that Blair would stay on as Prime Minister for a full term, but avoid party bloodshed and a coup by the simple device of resigning as Labour leader and calling for an orderly contest to succeed him in his party job.

The winner would sit in the Cabinet and shape the party's programme for a fourth term – the programme for the third is all but mapped out in Whitehall's five-year plans – before leading the party's next general election campaign. In the meantime the Queen would retain Blair as her First Minister.

Was that what Prescott meant? Time will tell . . .

4

Immigration, immigration, immigration

Monday 18 April

On Saturday, Tony Blair launched a petition on the NHS. On Monday, Michael Howard signed it. Now that's what you call a progressive consensus. The message was quite unremarkable: 'Keep the NHS free!' But when you have been campaigning on the same issue for the past two or three days, you have to come up with something. I think it was Margaret Beckett who introduced the sad but true notion: 'When you and I are sick of hearing it, the public are only just beginning to listen.' The public ought, by now then, to be starting to get the messages on the NHS and pensions. The Tories banged on with the pensions policies they had first floated on Saturday night. Labour and Blair pressed on with the NHS, producing pledges like so many hankies from a magician's sleeve.

Kennedy, meanwhile, went 'smart and tough' on law and order, promising more police on the streets, freed by hi-tech wizardry from all that pen-pushing paperwork. Hopefully he thinks the public will get the message quite quickly, or at least he hasn't had a long conversation with Mrs Beckett recently.

Howard signed up to Labour's petition, confusingly, at Tory HQ in Swindon, flourishing his pen beneath the slogan: 'We the undersigned are totally opposed to the introduction of charges for hospital operations.' The Tory version, it is true, added the injunction to 'Vote Conservative'. Labour's petition had been designed to draw attention to the party's claim that the Tories' scheme to offer to pay half the cost from NHS funds for patients' private operations amounted to introducing a charging regime in the health service for the first time since its inception. 'I am totally opposed to the introduction of charges for hospital operations,' said Howard as he scribbled away.

> We fully believe in keeping the NHS free and that is why we have written in 'Vote Conservative' and I am absolutely delighted to sign it. They keep telling lies about our policies. They keep saying all sorts of things about what our policies would be and I just want to demonstrate that what they say is not true, that we all agree that there should not be any charges introduced for hospital operations. We should have an honest debate about the differences between us.

Howard rejected any suggestion that his party's policy would take money out of the NHS, saying: 'It is a good deal for everyone.'

A consensual mood was not, alas, to be the theme of the day.

The Tories began it with their pensions portfolio, run out at a full-blown press conference for the second day running. Headlining the commitment was the £1.7 billion tax incentive for people to save for their retirement, unveiled yesterday. That went alongside a pledge to cut up to £500 a year from the council tax bills of pensioner households.

Howard said other measures would include a cull of red tape, raising the basic state pension in line with earnings not prices, and using unclaimed assets in banks to help workers who lost pensions when their firms went bust. Howard told his morning press conference: 'Our message is simple: whatever your age, if you do the right thing, we will do the right thing by you. If you save, we will boost your savings. And if you help yourself, we will help you. I don't pretend to be able to defuse Britain's pension time bomb overnight but our five-point action plan will begin to reverse the damage done by Mr Brown's pension tax.'

Optimism is a necessary quality in any party leader, especially during a general election campaign, but it was noteworthy today that the three leaders expressed that optimism on the following scale – Blair: v. cautious; Kennedy v. enthusiastic; Howard v. confident and optimistic.

Asked about his party's prospects on 5 May, Howard said: 'I'm very pleased with the way in which the campaign's going. We are getting our message across. Morale is high, we are getting a very positive response on the doorstep, so I'm very encouraged. I'm looking forward to the opinion poll that takes place on 5 May. I'm very optimistic and confident about the outcome.'

Kennedy's verdict: 'The key features that seem to be emerging from our point of view is that from our target seats regionally around the country, we are getting a better response from our campaign teams there in terms of what they are hearing from the electorate than frankly we have ever had at any general election. There has been no sense of squeeze – quite the opposite – on the Liberal Democrats at this stage in the campaign.'

Blair: 'I think what's happening is people are understanding, whatever their concerns and worries, that the economy is at stake and proposals for the National Health Service are at stake and we do have credible policies to deal with these things and they don't. Time will tell.'

The Lib Dems had earlier rolled out their law and order package with a perky Kennedy – daily perkiness updates now seem obligatory for the new dad – promising an extra 10,000 police and 20,000 more Community Support Officers. He also underlined the party's commitment to investing £150 million in hi-tech equipment. The party would pay for the £1 billion policy by scrapping Labour plans for compulsory ID cards and from the £5 billion they would save by switching cash from low priority government programmes such as the baby bonds.

Both Kennedy and his home affairs spokesman Mark Oaten criticised Sir Ian Blair for his comments yesterday that ID cards could be 'very helpful' in the fight against international terrorism. They warned that the Met Commissioner needed to 'tread carefully' when making public remarks about such a highly charged issue during an election campaign.

Blair and Reid showed there was nothing up their sleeves before producing the 'new' cancer waiting time pledges – although one was the cervical smear promise given at the weekend. By 2008 breast cancer patients would be seen by a consultant within two weeks of being referred by a GP, as would patients with suspected bowel cancer.

Blair told reporters the changes would 'make a difference to thousands of patients', before heading for hospitals in Milton Keynes and Redditch. He also published some glossy pages documenting his party's health policy. The Tories duly pored over them, before launching another front in the War of the Typographical Error.

A Conservative news conference was hastily convened for 3 p.m. 'Emergency Tory News Conference' it flashed up on Sky News. Well, not really an emergency, but there were David 'two brains' Willetts, pensions spokesman and treasury spokesman George Osborne with smiles on their faces. They had found the typographical error! To be honest, somebody else had probably found it, but they had had it ragged out and flashed up onto the media room backdrop.

It said Labour had decided to increase National Insurance Contributions in 1998. 1998, imagine it! The increase had not in fact been announced until after the following election. Labour had obviously lied before the 2001 election, because it had already decided to put up NICs while claiming they had no plans to do so.

Osborne said: 'We have proof that Mr Blair was not being straight with the electorate. They may have agreed these rises in 1998 but they did not tell the British people until 2003. Labour are calling this an honest mistake and they are right: they made the mistake of being honest.'

Willetts jumped in, too, having had Labour comments on pensions subjected to textual analysis. Blair was planning to means-test your pension, he warned, grimly. A new 'citizen's pension' – which Blair hadn't ruled out – would be expensive. Means-testing it – which he hadn't mentioned – would make it cheaper.

A citizen's pension, said Willetts, 'would be very expensive, provided everyone got it. Tony Blair says it would cost billions of pounds. The experts agree that Labour would need higher taxes to pay for the spending plans they already have. So they can't afford to be making more spending commitments.

'There is a way they could make it cheaper – they could means-test it.' He finished with a flourish: 'Mr Blair cannot be trusted with our pensions.' Labour was scornful. A spokesman blamed a typographical error for the date in the document ('But they got every single figure wrong in the date,' cried Osborne).

The Labour spokesman said: 'This is desperate stuff from the Tories. The decision to raise National Insurance was only made in response to the publication of the Wanless Report in March 2002.

'The Conservative Party has shown this afternoon that its faltering campaign has moved into a new phase, from cynical opportunism to total desperation.' The spokesman added: 'Of course we rule out means-testing the basic state pension. The basic state pension will remain the universal foundation of pension provision.' Ah, the state pension, yes, but what about a new citizen's pension? The games they play.

While Howard was signing petitions in Swindon, and Blair glad-handing more patients, Kennedy went to Liverpool to meet Community Support Officers. But in between visits, Kennedy and Howard were each grilled by fearsome interrogators: Kennedy by Jeremy Paxman for *Newsnight*, and Howard by Press Packer Alex Anthony, thirteen, from Warwickshire, for BBC *Newsround*, the children's news programme (memo to Howard: They Can't Vote Yet, Michael!) Kennedy was put on the spot over his fitness. Asked if – having spoken openly about the need to change his lifestyle – he faced a credibility problem with voters, he replied: 'No. I don't think so. If you look at the measures of public opinion about myself, about the party as a whole, they are positive.

'I think the biggest single question that I've always faced, that the party has always faced is: Can these people win and then, if they win, can they deliver? Now, step by step, city by city, constituency by constituency, region by region, we are demonstrating that we can win.'

He added: 'This election, this whole campaign, is about moving that onto a much higher level and I think the conditions are there and I think the party and myself are in good shape for that challenge.'

Paxman – who apologised in 2002 for questioning Kennedy too closely about his alcohol consumption – asked if his doctor was happy with his smoking and drinking habits.

Kennedy replied: 'Yes my doctor is actually rather approving. He would like to see me not smoke at all but it has drastically come down since the turn of the year and I am determined that it is going to be phased out altogether – particularly since the arrival of the new one.'

Asked if he intended to go 'on and on' as party leader, he replied: 'I hope so, that's my intention. I want to be in the next parliament, leading a much, much bigger parliamentary party for the Liberal

Democrats. I don't know how far our ambitions can go because we have got a very perverse voting system when it's three-party politics as it is in this election. 'But I think it can be substantially bigger. The opportunity in the next parliament is substantially greater and when you have devoted your working life towards that objective, heavens above, you don't want to shirk opportunity.'

Howard had a considerably tougher time. Cover your eyes if you are easily frightened. Young children should read this with a parent or responsible carer. In this transcript 'PP' stand for Press Packer Alex and 'MH' for the brave Conservative leader.

PP: Will you improve what we can do with our free time?

MH: Will I improve what you can do with your free time?

PP: Yes, the options?

MH: Well, what sort of options would you like that you don't have at the moment?

PP: Things like more youth clubs

MH: Yes, we've actually said we would provide money for increasing the number of youth clubs so that is something I can say we would do.

PP: Next question, do you support the campaign for better school dinners?

MH: Jamie's Oliver's campaign? We do. But I'm now going to say something very controversial which you may not like because there's a difference between us and the government on this. The government says that you should have a choice at school and one of the choices should be healthy dinners. I'm afraid we are much tougher and we say you shouldn't have a choice – junk food should be banned. You and your friends may not like that very much but we think that it's very, very important that you have healthy school dinners. It's very important for your health, it's very important for your behaviour.

PP: How long would it take you to pull troops out of Iraq?

MH: I would keep troops in Iraq as long as both the Iraqi government wanted them to stay and I thought they were doing some good.

PP: Now, in this bag are fifteen mystery questions. You have to pick three of them – good luck.

MH: I'll need it, won't I? Thank you very much. So I pick them out do I, give them to you to read out or do I read them out myself?

PP: I read them.

MH: You read them – OK. Is that one or two?

PP: Wait, I need to ask you it.

MH: Oh, you do them one at a time do you?

PP: What's Posh and Beck's new baby called?

MH: Cruz.

PP: Yes.

PP: What time is Newsround *on each day on BBC One?*

MH: Pass. I know I should have known that but I don't. So I'll have to pass on that.

PP: Last question.

MH: Last one. See before my kids left home I knew the answer to all these questions but they've grown up and left home so I don't know the answer to them now.

PP: What's been your favourite pop tune in the last year?

MH: My favourite pop tune in the last year . . . [thinks] well, I guess I'll go for the easy one which is 'Amarillo' which is number one at the moment, will that do you?

PP: OK. Thank you.

MH: Thank you very much, Alex.

No, thank you very much. You were warned he couldn't even vote. What if you'd got Cruz wrong?

Back on the fringes of the election, Reg Keys, the father of a Redcap soldier killed in Iraq, who was standing against Blair on an anti-war ticket, announced an election coup.

Sedgefield Labour Party Executive Committee member Derek Cattell ended a 30-year association with the Labour leader's local party at a news conference in support of Keys. The 52-year-old Independent candidate was accusing Blair of misleading parliament over the reasons for going to war. His son, Lance Corporal Tom Keys, 20, was one of six military policemen killed by an Iraqi mob in Al Majar Al Kabir in June 2003.

Cattell, a retired GMB union official, of Windlestone, County Durham, was at the modest Keys campaign headquarters in an office unit in Newton Aycliffe to explain his decision to leave Labour. He said: 'My conscience would not allow me to continue my membership. The war in Iraq has raised issues over the Prime Minister's integrity and honesty. I was not prepared to vote or campaign for the Prime Minister in this constituency.

'I was not prepared to vote Labour through gritted teeth. I think there is a sea-change happening which has been reflected within the local Labour Party which has lost in Sedgefield a third of its members since 1997. I believe there were at one time 1,000 members and a third of them have been lost. I am not the first person to resign my membership of the Sedgefield Labour Party over the Iraq war.'

Cattell said he had campaigned for Blair in the past, despite the fact the Labour leader was more 'conservative thinking' than him, and denied being on the extreme left of the party. He said he wanted Labour to win the general election but with a new leader.

'I am proud to give my support to Reg Keys, an Independent candidate whose circumstances, with his son's tragic death in Iraq, have brought him to Sedgefield. Reg has a mountain to climb but I believe he is the person who can do it,' he said.

Keys added: 'What better endorsement can I have than from a staunch Labour member for over 30 years? With Derek we obviously have a man of integrity who felt he can no longer function within a Labour Party whose leader has the faith of his flock. Mr Cattell has done the honourable thing here and I think Tony Blair should follow his example. Such a catastrophic political blunder has taken the country into an illegal war.'

Martin Bell, the former reporter, turned one-time Independent MP for Tatton and now backing Keys, said Cattell was 'a man of great honour and principle' as he attended his press conference.

John Burton, Blair's long-time agent, agreed membership in Sedgefield had fallen since 1997 following a successful major recruitment drive in the run-up to that election – a phenomenon repeated nationwide. But he added: 'It remained steady all through the Iraq issue and has been for the last two years or so.' He said the party had modernised to make itself electable but claimed Cattell had remained to the left of the party.

'We have changed the party to get in power but we could not change Derek Cattell,' Burton added. 'As a strong union man, Derek needs to remember what the Labour Party has done for the working people.'

But Blair was not the only Cabinet minister to face a single-issue candidate in his own backyard.

A grandfather-of-five today announced he would stand against Defence Secretary Geoff Hoon to win support for a medal to be awarded to those who served in the Second World War Atlantic convoys, the doughty campaigner not satisfied with a special badge Blair agreed should be struck instead. Eddie Grenfell, 85, said he thought he could be the oldest parliamentary candidate as he announced he would be standing as an Independent against Hoon in his Ashfield constituency.

The retired Royal Navy commander said he would be travelling from his home in Portsmouth to compete for the Nottinghamshire seat. He would, he said, represent the 3,000-strong Arctic Medal Campaign, lobbying on behalf of thousands of British seamen and sailors who served in the convoys. They were a vital supply line for the Russian forces between 1941 and 1945, transporting by sea provisions and weapons to help the fight against the Nazis. The journeys were among the most dangerous made by British forces during the war, with the ships becoming regular targets for U-boats and dive bombers. There can scarcely be an MP in the Commons who over the past four or five years has not equally been bombarded by letters from some of the most determined campaigners, dedicated to gaining recognition for their comrades – alive and dead.

The government has yet to recognise the medal campaign, said Mr Grenfell, who was among only a few to survive the sinking of the *Empire Lawrence*, a catapult aircraft merchant ship.

He went on: 'We think that it was such a terrible thing that every other campaign received a medal even if they were not in action. You could spend a few days in the Mediterranean without action and get a medal, but spend five and a half months in the Arctic and be in a ship that sunk and get nothing.'

Mr Grenfell said he failed in a recent attempt to persuade the government to decorate the convoy veterans.

'I spoke to Mr Hoon and I put in front of him documents saying it would be easy to go to the Prime Minister to say we have got a good case,' he said. 'He refused. We fought against Nazi injustice for five years and here we are, still fighting against injustice, but this time it's Geoff Hoon.' Mr Grenfell said he would fight on behalf of all veterans if elected next month. Hoon's majority at the last election was 13,268. Mr Grenfell will need all his fighting spirit.

The former BBC director general Greg Dyke came out fighting, too, today. Still fuming over his clash with the government over the famous Andrew Gilligan 'sexed-up' Iraq dossier claims which cost him his job, the one-time New Labour supporter announced he would be voting Liberal Democrat – although, confusingly, he called them the Liberal Party. He meant the Lib Dems.

Before his appointment as director general Dyke had made donations totalling at least £50,000 to the party and once stood unsuccessfully as the Labour candidate for the Greater London Council constituency of Putney. The ex-BBC boss made his announcement on the *Live with Alastair Stewart* show on the ITV News Channel. 'I have decided to vote Liberal and decided to support the Liberal Party for a number of reasons, some of which are that I find some of their policies much closer to what I believe than I find the Labour Party to be,' he said.

'I actually happen to believe that people like me who earn more than £100,000 a year should pay more tax.'

Dyke added: 'If it had been a Gordon Brown Labour Party, yes, I might have voted for him because I have much more trust in him. I could not vote for a Labour Party with Tony Blair as its leader. We know that Tony Blair has on two occasions promised to step down in favour of Gordon Brown and has not done it.'

The Lib Dems welcomed him with open arms. President Simon Hughes said: 'I welcome Greg Dyke's support, and that of the many thousands of former Labour supporters who are now turning to the Liberal Democrats to offer a real alternative to Tony Blair's government.'

Blair was at his rampant, defiant best at a rally later in Birmingham, storming through the crowd of activists shaking hand after outstretched hand, telling them there was 'an awful lot at stake for the future of this country' on 5 May.

A shirt-sleeved Blair, complete with red tie, denounced Conservative health policy as 'typically Tory . . . utterly unfair . . . completely contrary to every founding principle the NHS has ever held dear'. Blair on the 'core vote' stump.

Howard made a late-evening TV appearance on Jonathan Dimbleby's ITV show, too late for the newspapers' first editions.

Dimbleby asked if he feared a repeat of the race riots seen in some northern towns: 'Are you fearful that if there are more newcomers than is desirable there will be more Burnleys, more Oldhams?'

Howard replied:

> *Yes. I think people have to have confidence in the system. They have to understand there is a proper system of controls and that gives people reassurance.*
>
> *And I think that when people believe that there is no proper system, that immigration is out of control, I think that these anxieties . . . makes it more difficult to have good community relations.*

Asked again if he was warning of a repeat of violence, Howard said he would not put it in those terms but added, 'We have to be vigilant if we are to make sure we continue to have good community relations'.

Defectors, protestors, campaigners, petitions, promises and pensions. Immigration. Tonight Ladbroke's changed their odds on a Tony Blair third term for the first time since the campaign began.

They shortened Labour's victory odds from 1/16-on to 1/20-on. The bookies thought there was a different sea-change.

Tuesday 19 April

The bookmakers were not alone. The newspapers may have gone to bed before Howard's Dimbleby programme appearance, but they had a story of their own to tell. After seven days of intensive campaigning, and months of softening up the voters, the Conservatives were still swimming against the tide.

An NOP poll for the *Independent* put Labour on 37 per cent, down one point since the previous week, with the Conservatives and Liberal Democrats unchanged on 32 per cent and 21 per cent respectively. A Populus poll for *The Times* put Labour on 40 per cent, up three points since the last poll two weeks ago, the Conservatives on 31 per cent, four points down, and the Liberal Democrats on 21 per cent, two points up. And a Mori poll for the *Financial Times* put Labour on 41 per cent, the Conservatives on 31 per cent and the Liberal Democrats on 21 per cent.

Politicians will rail against opinion polls; but all they really mean is that they don't want to believe the ones they don't like, and they dare not believe the ones they do. They spend a small fortune on their own. Howard faced his morning news conference on law and order knowing that by now reporters would have caught up with his comments on immigration last night. It had been a feisty encounter, but not shown until gone 11 p.m. After Howard's response to Dimbleby's 'race riot' question, in an angry exchange, Asian gap year student Dean Velani, eighteen, accused the Tory leader of 'shambolic opportunism to pander to Middle England'. He said: 'You don't realise what it is like for me', adding: 'You are pandering to xenophobia and hatred in our country.'

Howard hit back, saying: 'I profoundly disagree and what I say frankly to people who hold the view you hold is if you disagree then tell us what you would do to deal with the problem.'

However, Mr Velani was not alone in taking issue with the Tory leader. Gilbert Barthley said that ever since he had come to Britain in 1954 he had heard campaigns based around immigration. 'When you talk in the street and you make these remarks you hear bits and pieces that "they are coming here for this, they are coming here for that"' Roger Chandra described himself as a disillusioned Tory voter and attacked what he said was the detail-free rhetoric of the Conservatives on immigration. 'You talk about immigration, asylum seekers and terrorism. You mix those up, are you playing on the fear of people?' he said.

There was a 'primeval fear' within voters on the issue, said Mr Chandra. 'I can't vote for a party that plays on those basic instincts,' he added. Anthony Dunn accused Mr Howard of suggesting immigrants were 'bringing dirty diseases'.

Had the show gone out at a different time of day, its impact would have been immediate. Instead, it had a slower-burn effect. It would not be until much later today, in a very unexpected forum, that it would really explode. Immigration was first raised with Kennedy, speaking on health at his party's breakfast news conference. He lambasted Howard for implying other parties wanted uncontrolled immigration: 'I'm not aware of any mainstream political party in British politics that hasn't argued for a system of controlled immigration. To try and use that phrase as if everybody else would just let the borders of our country go to pigs and whistles and only the Conservatives care about controlled immigration is a complete misrepresentation of the case. I think that is not because the Conservatives want a perfectly responsible and sensible discussion about immigration policy, I think it's because they are trying to appeal to a core vote at this stage of the campaign . . . at the exclusion of a sensible discussion.'

Howard, launching one of those 'five-point plans' so beloved of politicians to deal with binge drinking and the 'yob culture', decided first to tear up his pre-prepared script on the issue and attack Labour 'lies', specifically Blair lies, about the Conservative campaign. But he knew what he would be questioned on. He said:

Mr Blair started this campaign by lying about our spending plans. When it became clear that he could not sustain these claims, he dropped them. Now he denies he ever made them and now he's resorting to false claims about our plans for hospitals. He has put false claims on his posters, on his campaign literature and on his leaflets.

But last night he was forced to admit that his claims about our hospital policy are false too. So this morning I challenged Mr Blair to withdraw every poster, every leaflet and every piece of campaign literature which has that second Labour lie on it.

How can anyone trust Mr Blair when his campaign is based on these lies? It's time Mr Blair started telling the truth and had an honest debate about the real challenges facing our country.

Last night, in a separate ITV interview, Blair had changed tack to accuse the Tories of leeching money from the NHS through their private part-payment plan and skirted round the claim of imposing NHS charges for the first time. Having got his dig at Labour off his chest, Howard was back on track with his largely familiar attack on the government's record on crime, standing side by side with shadow Home Secretary David Davis.

The questioning, though, as he expected, was largely about immigration. The first reporter, Andrew Neil, asked if the Conservative leader had had his 'Enoch Powell moment'. Howard said:

I have always said that we benefit from immigration, that we are a stronger and richer country as a result. I also believe immigration has to be brought under control so that we have good community relations in our country, so that we get a grip on the security problems we face and so that we effectively manage our public services.

That's the case I have been making in this campaign. That's the case I will continue to make.

Another reporter asked: Was it true that some frontbenchers had contacted him, urging him to tone down his rhetoric on the issue? 'No. We have had no such calls, neither to me nor to my office.'

How could community relations worsen, as he feared?

We clearly believe that there should be a limit on immigration, that's our view. I have always believed, I'm sure it's true, that good community relations and firm but fair immigration controls go hand in hand together. We have seen immigration triple under Mr Blair. No one's ever been asked their views about that.

You can't specify what might happen but I believe, as I've made clear very many times, that if we are to continue to have good community relations in this country you have to be vigilant. And if people lose confidence in the system and believe it's out of control, I believe that breeds a sense of insecurity and that's damaging to good community relations.

With that, he left the room and headed for Battersea heliport to catch his helicopter to Peterborough, where he was scheduled to visit a local police station on what was, after all, a Law and Order Day. His helicopter had developed a technical fault. It could not take off. The lunchtime TV news showed Howard desperately running up the platform at King's Cross Station looking for all the world like a man about to miss a train.

He missed the train. He boarded another, more elegantly, half an hour later. Tory co-chairman Liam Fox, meanwhile, had taken to the airwaves to deny talk of a rift within the upper echelons of the party over the play the immigration issue was getting. 'I have been talking to a lot of my senior colleagues and, in fact, it is quite the reverse message. Individuals may have their views but I am telling you what the view is of the vast majority of my colleagues because we are talking about the issues that really matter. One or two malcontents talk to Labour-leaning papers like the *Guardian* or *The Times*.'

He said it was 'nonsense' to suggest that the Conservatives were campaigning just on immigration. 'This is far from a single-issue election and I think it is preposterous to portray it as such.'

Blair had stayed in Birmingham overnight after his rally the previous evening, and hosted his morning press conference from there, campaigning on health issues for the fourth day running. Today it was to be children's health. And he refused to bow to Conservative demands to withdraw his campaign posters.

Said Blair: 'In this election, the NHS and its future is at stake. The Tory patients' passport plan would effectively end the principle of treatment only according to need and replace it with treatment according to wealth.' The Conservative proposals would take at least £1.2 billion out of the NHS to fund part of the cost of patients who chose to go private. He added:

> That NHS money would be given in vouchers for private treatment. To cash in the vouchers, you would need to be able to afford the charge for the rest of the cost of the hospital operation. That is the reality of the Conservative policy.
>
> So under their proposals, there will be two classes of NHS patients. The first class of NHS patients will be offered fast-track private treatment as long as they are willing to pay an additional

charge on top of the value of their voucher. And a second class of NHS patients – those who cannot afford thousands of pounds to pay for private treatment – who would have to wait longer for a service that will remain free.

So there would be one slower route without an additional charge and one faster route where you would be expected to pay half the cost of the operation. A policy in which the many subsidise the few.

Blair added: 'Mr Howard has asked us to withdraw the allegation. We will not. It is his policy, not ours, and if he is embarrassed by it, it is up to him to withdraw the policy.'

Flanked by Culture, Media and Sport Secretary Tessa Jowell and Children's Minister Margaret Hodge, he highlighted Labour plans to improve child health by giving all schoolchildren access to a school nurse, cutting fatty and salty foods from school meals, introducing clearer food labelling, restricting advertising of unhealthy food to children and expanding sports at school.

When the local case of an asylum seeker who had caused death by dangerous driving was raised, Blair spoke of the government's record on removals of asylum seekers. Asked about Howard's comments he would say only: 'Immigration and asylum are issues that need to be handled with care.' Asked if he believed that any politicians were failing to handle the issues with care, Blair moved on to the next questioner without responding. He had consistently refused to be drawn into attacking the Conservatives on immigration ever since it became clear it would feature as one of the opposition's five main themes.

He explained to friends earlier in the campaign that if he, in effect, repeatedly accused the Conservatives of playing the 'race card' that would be exactly what they would like him to do. Then they could protest that they were in touch with the public's real concerns while Labour was obsessed with political correctness. He would address the issue on his own ground, at a time of his own choosing. A 'typically Tony' calibrated response.

While Blair was hosting his press conference, repeating a promise to deliver healthier 'Jamie Oliver-style' school dinners, Cherie was on a 'private' solo visit to the Worlds End Infant and Nursery School in Birmingham. She was sporting a black and white jacket with a long cream pashmina and white trousers as she toured the class-rooms chatting to parents – and providing the London *Evening Standard* with a front-page splash.

With youngest son Leo, five next month, now at big-boy school, she fell, naturally enough, into conversation about his school dinners: 'They are not terrific, to be honest,' said Cherie. 'I am seriously thinking about sending him in with a packed lunch.'

A frosty Westminster Education Authority declined to comment. But a trip for the Blairs, accompanied by Blair Minimus, to see the beak is probably unlikely.

It was a wives' day out. Sandra Howard was appearing on an ITV afternoon programme with the risqué title *Loose Women*. She reduced its audience to titters when asked how many more years she thought her husband could remain in public life. The former model said: 'I won't say he can go on for ten – but he can certainly do five.' Host Kaye Adams was unable to resist the temptation to add: 'I don't think we want to know how long Michael can go on for.' Others were left to ponder: Why do they go on these shows?

Now arrived safely, if a trifle late, in Peterborough, Michael Howard met officers at Thorpe Wood police station before holding private talks with commanders. If he had wanted to avoid further comment on immigration he was to be predictably disappointed as he was confronted by reporters as he left. 'I have said many times I believe we benefit from immigration. We are a stronger and richer country,' he repeated. 'But I believe it's important that it's controlled immigration.'

Asked about the polls, he replied: 'We're doing very well. I'm delighted to be here with a very good candidate.'

He may not have been so delighted to arrive in Nottingham to address a crime forum, where he was supposed to hear first-hand tales from the victims of crime. Instead, at the carefully stage-managed event in front of an invited audience, on Law and Order Day, Howard was rounded on in dramatic fashion – by police officers themselves – over his immigration remarks.

Rob Lawrence, coordinator for the Nottingham Black Police Association, asked him how he expected to engage voters 'when you have taken the stance towards immigration' and raised the spectre of 'race riots'.

'You are pandering towards the fears of many people in the community on the issue of immigration,' he said.

Howard said his belief that the pace of change was too great was shared by the government's own Community Cohesion Panel, set up to investigate the Bradford riots. His answer slowly dripped flammable fluid onto the burning issue.

'Let me quote to you one statistic and you can draw what conclusions from it you like. I will leave that to you. In 1997 there were no BNP councillors in this country. Today there are fourteen. Draw your own conclusions.'

That brought a furious response from Glen Williams, the Deputy Chair of the Nottingham Black Police Association.

The statement you have come up with, the discussions of fears around immigration, these are all issues that pander to the fears of people who have not been allowed, a public who have not been allowed, sensible dialogue and discussion going on about these issues.

When you talk about political correctness you are talking about people like me, a black police officer who is basically being told to shut up and deal with racism.

*When you use words like that they are emotive and they are
pandering to basic instincts. Why don't you stop using that sort of
language and deal with the issues in a sensible way that does not
produce fear?*

Howard stood by his claim that the 'Stop forms' being introduced
for use when police talk to people on the street, recommended by
the inquiry into Stephen Lawrence's death, and which he is
committed to scrap, were an example of unacceptable political
correctness, attracting more flak.

Afterwards Williams, a prominent campaigner, dismissed the
event as a stunt.

He said: 'My greatest concern is that what I saw here today, and I
did come as an observer, was another example of pandering to the
fears that people have. This was not a debate. This was not a discussion. It was a situation where people were invited in and Mr
Howard was allowed just to give a party political broadcast.'

On a visit to Guildford, Kennedy kept up the pressure on the
Conservative leader, saying:

*When you are in a prominent public political position you have
access to the airwaves – as the party leaders enjoy every hour of the
day at the moment. When you are addressing an issue like race
relations and immigration you have got to tread with responsibility and sensitivity.*

*We are a multicultural, multiracial society and I think un-
ambiguously we are far better as a society because of that.*

*That does not mean you cannot have a responsible discussion
about the best way to have a controlled immigration policy. What
you must not do is play upon people's apprehensions or misappre-
hensions about race relations in this country.*

He added for good measure: 'The interesting story of the election so far in terms of the standing of the three parties is that the Conservatives have not been able to get to a point higher than that at which they lost the last general election with their worst results for 150 years, and indeed today the trends are that they are going down.'

Back in London, the Muslim Council of Britain (MCB), a moderate umbrella body which represents mosques, schools and charities across the country, was holding a press conference to publicise a list of ten questions for the UK's one million Muslim voters to ask prospective MPs. Issues included whether the candidates supported the immediate publication of a timetable for the withdrawal of British troops from Iraq and legislation to outlaw religious hatred.

Before the press conference could even begin, there were chaotic scenes as a group of more than a dozen men, two of them masked, broke down the door of the library in the Central London Mosque in Regents Park. The men who burst in said they represented the Saviour Sect, believed to contain former members of the disbanded Al-Muhajiroun group and be headed by firebrand cleric Sheikh Omar Bakri Mohammed.

As the group streamed into the meeting, one of the masked men shouted: 'Kaffirs. MCB are dirty kaffirs.'

Another man yelled: 'The MCB are a mouthpiece of the British government of Tony Blair and George Bush. They don't represent Islam. They don't represent British Muslims.' One protester threw a punch at MCB secretary general Iqbal Sacranie but only succeeded in knocking off his glasses. For fifteen to 20 minutes, the militants remained in the centre of the meeting room, surrounded by photographers and cameramen as they chanted militant slogans. They handed out a leaflet reading: 'Vote today . . . become Kaffir tomorrow!' It bore photographs of Blair, Howard, Kennedy and

George Galloway of Respect, branding them crooks, criminals and devils. Eventually, the uninvited guests left. Mr Sacranie said the disturbance was 'part of democracy in action'.

He added: 'In every community you have these fringe elements. It does not reflect the Muslim community.'

Meanwhile, fears, however far-fetched, that the election may not even go ahead were raised when it was announced a judge would on Thursday hear an initial application from Birmingham City Council deputy leader John Hemming for a judicial review of the 5 May poll, in the wake of the postal vote fraud cases. Hemming, the leader of the Liberal Democrat group on the council, is to ask the judge – expected to be Mr Justice Collins – to rule that he has an arguable case which should go to a full hearing as a matter of urgency.

His application followed that elections court hearing in Birmingham which removed six Labour councillors from office over widespread and systematic abuse of the postal voting system and led the election commissioner Richard Mawrey QC to warn that the postal voting system was wide open to fraud. Hemming was also arguing that the lack of a secure system for postal voting breaches the Human Rights Act because it compromises the secret ballot. He wants postal votes in this election to be counted separately from non-postal votes and for the political parties to be given permission to check postal voting applications.

A legal deadlock resulting from the ruling could even postpone polling day, he predicted.

It was also announced that representatives of the Association of Chief Police Officers (Acpo) were due to attend talks in Whitehall on Thursday in an attempt to identify potential problems with postal voting in the run up to polling day. The meeting, to be chaired by the Permanent Secretary at the Department for Constitutional Affairs, Alex Allan, was called to bring together senior representatives from the Electoral Commission, the Royal

Mail and returning officers. Officials from the Office of the Deputy Prime Minister were also summoned.

A spokesman for the DCA denied that it was a crisis meeting, saying that it was normal for the bodies involved in running an election to get together before polling to ensure the proper arrangements were in place. However he confirmed that the issue of postal voting fraud would be on the agenda.

'Inevitably they must discuss it because it has been such a big issue. It is definitely going to be talked about,' the spokesman said.

A spokeswoman for Acpo – which has drawn up new guidelines with the Electoral Commission for police forces on how to deal with complaints of ballot-rigging – confirmed they were expecting to see a rise in postal voting at this election. 'I think it is safe to say that postal voting has become greater and that is why we are dealing with that and taking it seriously,' she said. 'This is an opportunity for us to be able to say what is happening on the ground.'

David Monks, the chief executive of Huntingdonshire District Council, deputed to represent returning officers, said they were struggling to cope with an 'explosion' of postal vote applications. 'The real problem is resources. The ultimate killer is time because people can apply for postal votes up to six days before the date of polls and it is our duty to turn these postal vote applications around as quickly as possible.'

Whatever the outcome of the Hemming case, and however unlikely the postponement of the election itself, the prospect of legal challenges to close election results loomed ever larger in the minds of party managers. The 'hanging chad election' was coming ever closer to home, even as nominations for 5 May officially closed at 4 p.m. today.

Far away, in Vatican City, the bells of St Peter's tolled to announce the result of a different election, of a new Pope, the German Cardinal Joseph Ratzinger.

His Holiness will never know that, in one of those bizarre twists of political life, it was the first puffs of smoke from the Sistine Chapel chimney announcing his elevation to become Pope Benedict XVI which meant the 24-hour news channels pulled away from Michael Howard's stage set in Nottingham, before his awkward confrontation could appear live; sparing his blushes for a few hours at least.

Nobody could fix that.

Wednesday 20 April

Tony and Gordon settled down together on the sofa. Blair may have promised to reform his sofa style of government, but has yet to give up the sofa style of interviewing. He would, you suspect, be loath to do so. Nestled next to Brown on the GMTV settee this morning, Blair embarked on his latest round of 'Heineken campaigning', named after the beer advert which promised a lager that would refresh the parts other beers can't reach. Breakfast TV, *Richard and Judy*, *Ant and Dec*, in New Labour land these are all niche TV shows which refresh your message with electors in ways other campaigning can't reach.

Brown, whose last top-of-the-bill day had been eclipsed by the MG Rover crisis, was joining Blair in the battle for 'school gate mums' again, and three of those mums were perched on stools in the studio ready with their questions. But first, Blair wanted to make something clear: why GMTV had got GB as well as TB.

'I think the economy is a big issue in the campaign obviously, but also all the stuff we are trying to do for families is something very much Gordon has been pioneering over the past few years and I think it's important to come together.

'I think it's good to show people that there's a unified leadership at the top of the party that's trying to do what I hope are the right things for the country. In particular when there's been people speculating about it, sometimes it's good to come out and show we have been working together for 20-odd years and we are going to go on doing it.'

Blair added: 'I hope it is good when people see a strong team working together. I'm not saying we are not doing more together, that's exactly why we are doing it.'

Brown, asked if he wanted Blair's job, said wryly: 'It's not the job that's important, it's doing good things, it's doing the right things. We have been working together for 22 years. We shared an office in the Commons for five years that had no windows!'

It is a well-known fact that if you sit in an office without windows with someone for a few years it removes from your psyche any desire to covet your neighbour's job. And when you have worked with them for 22 – not '20-odd', Tony – the very fact precludes you from brooding over your relative fortunes. At least neither of them muttered 'whatever love is' when asked about their relationship.

Heineken segwayed seamlessly into masochism as the 'mums' were invited to put their questions. Michelle was angry with the Child Support Agency.

'I can tell you what's going to happen, but I should start with an apology for what has happened,' said Blair. 'The CSA has been a problem ever since it was set up in 1993. In 1993 it was set up, and that system was a complete nightmare. We are trying to make sure mums get the payments they need from their partners who don't want to pay. We have got a new management team, we have brought in a computer system we are trying to sort out, the payment system is going to be simpler, but there's a long way to go.

'The previous system was a nightmare, this system is a nightmare, we are doing our best to sort it out.'

More masochism as the PM was asked how people could survive in 'rip-off Britain' with soaring house prices. Blair replied: 'I can't stop modern life being a struggle for people because it is, it's hard. What we can promise people is this: we will keep the economy strong, we will keep interest rates low, we will keep a large number of jobs in the economy and we will do our level best with work–life balance.'

The two colleagues went off to Robinsfield Infant School in St John's Wood, a community school in a highly multicultural part of north London where pupils speak a total of 30 different languages.

Blair met, in fact, a 'school gate dad', Hailu Gourmu-Sorsu, who said: 'I told him he was doing a good job with respect to child poverty but he really should do more to increase school budgets.'

The other parties were having their Council Tax Day. Kennedy confirmed the Lib Dems would scrap it, and replace it with a local income tax. Today, unlike manifesto launch, just-back-from-baby-being-born, day, he had his figures more or less off pat. The policy would have its gainers and losers, with 50 per cent of households paying less, 25 per cent broadly unaffected, and 25 per cent paying more. The average household would be £450-a-year better off.

Blair and Kennedy also pre-butted the Tories' announcement, trailed in the morning newspapers, that Howard's party would scrap the revaluation of seven million homes in England planned for later in the year. The houses were last valued in 1991 and that valuation determined which tax band they were in for council tax purposes. There were obvious fears that the revaluation, though promised to be overall 'revenue neutral', would land some with big increases given rocketing property prices in the last fourteen years. Howard's party had seemed, until today, to accept the revaluation would take place – or at least had never made scrapping it an issue until now.

Before Howard had even formally shown his hand, Blair said: 'From the Conservatives this really is the most desperate opportunism because a week ago they said they were going to proceed with the revaluation. The only reason we have got the council tax is because of the poll tax Michael Howard introduced.'

Kennedy said the Tory plan was 'naked opportunism' and accused the Conservatives of dodging the issue of their support for an unfair tax. Howard was adamant as he hosted his morning news conference:

We voted consistently against this revaluation every time there was a vote in parliament. We are not ruling out a revaluation for all time. We are ruling out a revaluation in the course of the next parliament.

You only need a revaluation where there are disparities that have emerged in property prices. The most important disparities are regional disparities. We have been looking very carefully at the information which has become available.

The latest information has only become available in the last seven days from the Halifax, which shows that regional dispari-ties are becoming much less acute. Given that, there is absolutely no justification to spend £100 million on the cost of a revalua-tion unless you have a big black hole in your accounts and you plan to use that revaluation as a stealthy means of partially filling it.

The Tories, of course, maintain Brown has that black hole and they would not.

Howard later remained upbeat about his party's chances on 5 May, saying on a campaign visit to a pub in Lancashire that 'all the signs are that they [the voters] are coming our way'. Something else in the shape of a voter was coming Blair's way as he left Brown behind for a classic 'meet the people' mission in a shopping centre in Leeds. Half an hour before the PM's arrival, Labour staff fanned out asking people if they would like the chance to interrogate a 'senior minister' about issues such as childcare or education. Those, you see, were the themes of the day. Labour wanted to inject some spontaneity into campaigning; some masochism even, for the two words are synony-mous in New Labour vocabulary.

Jessica Haigh, 20, a creative writing student at the city's university, was out shopping with a friend when the Labour team descended. She was no stranger to politics. Her father Mick, who lives in Scarborough, had been a Labour councillor before, disillusioned, in 2001 he had turned to the Liberal Democrats, ending, Ms Haigh said later, 'generations' of family support for the party Blair now led.

The Labour officials did not quite have enough time to get all that detail down.

Blair's arrival into the Atrium of Light centre down an escalator prompted a hum of surprise and excitement among passers-by and diners at the Nando's and Brown's restaurants in the food hall. He briefly diverted from his route to pop into a Starbuck's coffee bar and shake hands with surprised customers.

He told one woman who complained of the length of waiting lists for NHS dentists in the area that the government was training up new dentists, but acknowledged it would be some time before there were enough to meet demand. Another woman told him that young offenders were 'laughing at the law' because of lenient sentences handed down by courts and urged him to ensure that in future they received 'a short sharp shock'.

Blair told her: 'It is a bit of a lottery, depending on which courts you go to. Some local magistrates are very, very tough, some aren't. We are introducing sentencing guidelines so courts get some guidance.' He acknowledged it was 'dispiriting' if members of a community came forward to give evidence and then saw offenders given 'a slap on the wrist'. Emma Cooper, 21, from Leeds, urged Mr Blair to make the environment his top priority, warning: 'Obviously, our planet's going downhill rapidly.' The Prime Minister told her that he had made the environment one of the two issues at the top of the agenda of the G8 group of industrialised nations during Britain's presidency this year.

And he added: 'I would like to make it an issue in the election, because I think long-term it is the biggest problem we face.'

Blair, to the surprise of the gathering crowd pulled in by the mesmeric power of TV paraphernalia, then sat down in the food court and shook hands to the chosen few hunched over a coffee table in front of the cameras. Ms Haigh just, well, let rip:

In 1997, I was eleven and we were so happy when you got in and now all our family's trust in your party has gone.

It is heartbreaking when you work so long to get a Labour government in power and then they turn into a Conservative one.

I come from a very Labour family and my dad was a Labour county councillor, but he lost faith in the party and I am going to vote Liberal Democrat. What are you going to do to persuade us you are the party of the people? What are you going to do to regain people's confidence?

Blair, in true masochism mode, asked her what her concerns about Labour policies were. Then he asked her whether she appreciated elements of the government's record, such as the stable economy and the introduction of the minimum wage and tax credits for low-income families.

She responded: 'It's not just Iraq, it's everything together. You are promoting globalisation and linking with a foreign government in a foreign war. You are pushing these good things you are doing, which is wonderful, but at the same time you are still being seen as Conservative.

'It's the image, it's the spin, it's trying to get the UK to be what the world wants it to be rather than what it can be.'

Blair replied: 'What you are saying is exactly where the debate is in the country for a significant number of people, and I've got to find a way of persuading you, because otherwise you may vote Liberal Democrat and you're going to end up with the Tories.'

Ms Haigh responded: 'I know, that's the scary thing.'

Mr Blair moved on, but Jessica suddenly found herself much in demand. As reporters crowded round she told them what had happened:

I told him, 'You have taken a good socialist party and turned it into a Conservative one. What are you going to do to get disillusioned voters back?'

He looked a bit taken aback. He seemed a bit nervous and he was really thinking about how to answer the question. He came up with quite a good response and told me about the working tax credit, but I said he was pandering to globalisation.

He said 'Yes, but we're living in the real world', but he seemed to just be making excuses to me. He never answered my question.

I don't know what my fellow students will think. It's all been a bit confusing. I didn't really think I had said anything particularly controversial. I hope they will be pleased with what I said. I don't regret it and I think I'll look back on today with pride.

What would her dad think?

I haven't had the chance to talk to him yet, but I hope he's going to be proud of me. We've been feeling this way for a while. I think this was my chance to get it all off my chest and tell him exactly what I think of him.

I think they asked me and my friend if we wanted to ask a question because we looked like students. We couldn't believe it when we saw it was Tony Blair. They were expecting us to ask something about being a student or Iraq but I just thought, no, I'm going to tell him exactly what I think.

Such is the fickle nature of politics, that the identity of Jessica's friend, and what question she asked, if any, are not recorded in history. It is to be hoped they do not go into politics and end up sharing a windowless room together.

But Blair was not the only one having interesting encounters today. John Prescott had been touring the country in his People's

Express bus, famous in the last election campaign for depositing him on Wednesday 16 May 2001, in Rhyl, north Wales, where he thumped Craig Evans, a 29-year-old farm worker from Denbigh, who had thrown an egg at him.

Last week, another egg had been hurled at him by a veterinary student protesting about the government's hunting ban. But it had hit only his bus, not him.

So what is it about Wales?

Prescott's bus took him to the principality again today, Cwmbran to be precise, where local *South Wales Argus* reporter Mark Choueke asked the Deputy Prime Minister about the case of Peter Law, a long-serving Labour politician in Wales and Welsh Assembly member, who had announced he was leaving the party and standing as an Independent in the Blaenau Gwent constituency.

Mr Prescott 'blew his top', according to Choueke, when the reporter asked how he and his Cabinet colleagues had reacted to Mr Law's decision. The reporter said that Prescott told him: 'It didn't even register with us.' When Choueke pressed him further, Prescott, he said, retorted: 'Why are you asking me about this? I don't care. It's a Welsh situation. I'm a national politician.'

Choueke again pressed him and Prescott replied: 'Where do they get these amateurs from? You're an amateur, mate. Go get on your bus, go home.' Choueke asked: 'Are you too big for the regional press now, John?' Prescott replied: 'Bugger off. Get on your bus, you amateur.'

The Deputy Prime Minister's spokeswoman later explained he had already answered questions about Mr Law earlier.

She said: 'In this particular situation the approach was quite unreasonable and quite unprofessional. There was just one question and the reporter kept going back and back on it.'

Brown, by contrast, was having a whale of a time. Abandoned by Blair to the outer reaches of Hatfield, Herts – one of a string of seats that used to be called the aerospace marginals because of the industry there – he was free to make a classic set-piece speech on his family and child-friendly theme of the day.

The Chancellor thundered that the Tories' 'Right to Choose' policy, subsidising parents' private school fees, would 'cut from investment in the many in order to pay the fees for the few'. And on his 'vision thing' he spoke of his ambition for the welfare state to open up a 'new frontier' through the completion of a comprehensive system for nurturing young children.

Brown in full cry can be a formidable, though for reporters uncomfortably rapid, speaker:

In the next parliament we will complete the creation of a new frontier for the welfare state, a comprehensive service for the under-fives, extending nursery education and creating a SureStart Children's Centre in every community.

Today there are 500 SureStart Children's Centres. By 2010 there will be 3,500 – a Children's Centre in every community. In time the Children's Centres will be as vital a focus of community life as the local hospital and local school.

And having created more than a million more childcare places since 1997, we will, in the next parliament, create the next million.

He seemed to be enjoying himself:

At every election the choice people face is which government can best meet the needs and concerns of hard-working families. In this election I believe that parents' and children's concerns are so important that this election is now rightly called the school gate election campaign.

And today after visiting school gates and talking to parents, my colleagues and I are making a direct appeal to mothers and fathers.

Election 2005

The personal touch:

> *Being a parent has changed the way I think of the needs of children and families. All parents want the best for their child. And what every parent wants for their children, I also want for all children. Every child is precious, every child unique, every child special, and all our children count. And every parent knows, as I do, that they can do better for their children if the appropriate help and support is there for them. That is what parents tell us they want.*

Howard, meanwhile, had gone out on the stump in Bolton, haranguing Labour over the council tax and reinforcing his 'yobs' message for good measure.

> *I have got a message. If there are any yobs watching, or burglars or criminals, I would not advise you to vote Conservative at this election.*
>
> *Because you may think you are tough but a Conservative government would be tougher.*

His wife Sandra, however, revealed she had more immediate concerns. Her own personal website disclosed that earlier in the campaign she had faced a crisis.

> *Back to Campaign Headquarters where Susie in Michael's office tells me my hair looked a mess on television. We agree it's time for action.*
>
> *I have heard on the grapevine that a certain other leader's wife has booked arguably the best and certainly the priciest hairdresser in town for the entire campaigning month ahead. I reckon that gives me some good leverage in getting across that my hair deserves a look-in, too.*

Sadly my own hairdresser doesn't go a bundle on the idea of home visits at dawn and tells me I'd faint away at his out-of-hours charges.

Susie offers her services. She does an instant, on the spot blow-dry; it's marvellous, she's a genius and we make plans for regular early-morning hair-salvation sessions – one panic off my long list.

Blair's hair was OK when he faced his ritual grilling by Jeremy Paxman tonight. Asked if he had told Brown when he would stand down, Blair said: 'No, I've said to Gordon the same as I've said to everyone. If you elect the Prime Minister, you serve the term.'

Asked if he had done a deal with Brown, he replied: 'You don't do deals about jobs like this. Gordon and I have been working extremely closely together. It has been a great partnership. I hope it has also been a good partnership for the country.

'He has been a magnificent Chancellor. He has produced tremendous economic strength in this country. We can be proud, I hope, of what we have achieved for the country.'

Blair denied wanting to be 'shot' of the job, saying, 'I still think we have got things to do'. He added:

The irony of this job is that you are less popular as you go on but, in some ways, you are better equipped to do the job.

I feel we are just really poised on the health service, education reform, a lot of the stuff we are doing on law and order.

There's masses for me to do and that's what gets me up in the morning. I've set a limit for my time . . . and then it's for somebody else to take on the baton and run with it. But I still feel there's things we've got to do and I think we can accelerate the change, drive it faster in a third term.

Blair paused for thought only once during the grilling when Paxman, having routinely badgered the PM on immigration, picked on one of the most sensitive issues of Blair's eight years in power.

He was asked if he accepted any responsibility for the death of weapons expert Dr David Kelly, the Ministry of Defence scientist at the heart of the Iraq dossier row.

Blair thought for a while before saying:

It was a terrible, terrible thing to have happened.

I don't believe we had any option, however, but to disclose his name. Had we failed to do so, that would have been seen as attempting to conceal something from the committee that was looking into this at the time.

I feel desperately sorry for his family and the ordeal they were put through.

5

Tough on votes ...

Thursday 21 April

Twelve years ago a youthful Labour home affairs spokesman had a soundbite slogan so successful it must have irritated his opposite number across the Despatch Box no end. In 1993 the 40-year-old Tony Blair was taunting Home Secretary Michael Howard with his mantra: 'Tough on crime, tough on the causes of crime.' Neither could have imagined the sequence of events, beginning with the sudden death of Blair's party leader John Smith the following year, which would lead them to fight a general election as leaders of their respective parties in 2005.

Today Blair sought another winning formula on crime, as he piggy-backed his party's campaign on the publication of new police figures on recorded offences, and – the statistics favoured by Blair – the latest British Crime Survey, which asks people about their experiences of crime.

Violent crime recorded by police rose 9 per cent in the final three months of 2004 to a total of 295,400 offences, announced the Home Office at 10 a.m. But the total number of crimes recorded by police in England and Wales fell 5 per cent in the quarter to 1,381,400, compared with the same period the previous year. The British Crime Survey (BCS), showed an 11 per cent fall in overall crime year-on-year in 2004. It also indicated a 10 per cent fall in the offences it records as violent crime. OK, now we've all got the facts and figures.

Blair opened his morning news conference looking back to Howard's days as Home Secretary:

When I was elected an MP in 1983, the public did not associate the Labour Party with credible law and order policies. By the time I was elected leader of the Labour Party in 1994, the Tories had squandered their credentials on crime as comprehensively as they had on the economy; crime had soared and police numbers were being cut.

A guiding principle of the establishment of New Labour was standing up for the interests of the many, not the few.

With New Labour, the public have had a government on their side in tackling crime and its causes. We have record police numbers, tough powers that are taking on anti-social behaviour and a reformed criminal justice system which is being rebalanced in favour of the victim and witness, not the criminal.

As a result, crime has gone down by 30 per cent since 1997 and concern about loutish behaviour has begun to fall. But it was never going to be an overnight job. Today, there will be two sets of crime figures. The British Crime Survey will measure crime as experienced by members of the public. The recorded statistics will count the number of crimes reported to the police.

For years, when Michael Howard was Home Secretary, police recorded crime did not count many scuffles and minor assaults which should have been classed as violent crime. The Association of Chief Police Officers wanted to change that and we agreed. It was the right thing to do. Every crime should be counted, even if it gives the wrong impression that violent crime has gone up.

He conceded: 'On any basis, crime has fallen since we came to office, yet we know that for many people in local communities it doesn't feel like that.' Blair promised a massive increase in uniformed Community Support Officers, from 4,000 to 24,000. Even though they have no more powers of arrest than the ordinary citizen, the PM believes their presence on streets reassures the public.

Over to Home Secretary Charles Clarke to make the big pitch, a Labour promise to cut crime by 15 per cent in a third term in office. 'The fight against crime, and particularly violent crime and anti-social behaviour, is a number-one priority for Labour.

'It is under a Labour government that overall crime has fallen by 30 per cent and violent crime by 26 per cent but of course we want this to fall further. That is why we commit to reducing all crime by a further 15 per cent and within that to ensure that violent crime continues to fall.'

Blair was asked whether increases in violent crime meant that something had 'gone wrong' with society. He replied:

First of all we should get the facts straight. It is not just that crime overall has fallen. If you measure crime on the British Crime Survey violent crime has fallen too.

The recording of violent crime has risen, that is because, for example, we are asking people to come forward in domestic violence cases or rape cases. There are common assaults that are now included in violent crime figures that were not included before.

Having said that, the fact that even violent crime has fallen is no consolation to anyone who has been a victim of a mugging, a gun crime or a knife crime.

Blair, not surprisingly, described the British Crime Survey as 'the most authoritative' measure of crime, but said statistics made no difference to anyone who had been a victim.

'There is a level of ugly disorder in some local communities which makes life hell for people.'

At one point he appeared to reminisce fondly of the days of the Krays: 'Some of these drug gangs – when you watch the films back in the 1950s about this type of criminal there were certainly rules or a code that even some of those people seemed to have – it was not of the same nature as some of the really appalling ugly violent crime that you get today linked with drugs.' Challenged, he said bashfully: 'Perhaps I'd better put out a correction on that.' Later he said: 'I'm not being nostalgic for the days of the Krays.'

The Conservatives and Michael Howard were kept waiting in Tory Campaign HQ by Labour's press conference. The Labour policy of not scheduling a regular slot was paying dividends, at least in the trivial – but psychologically telling – War of Victoria Street. Howard's news conference had been scheduled for 9 a.m., so Blair slipped his in at 8.30, forcing a delay on the Conservatives. They could read the latest email from their Campaign Director Lynton Crosby while they were waiting. Leaked to this morning's *Guardian*, it said the campaign was at a delicate stage:

> *The media get bored and start to look for stories of division and disunity. Our opponents throw everything at us to distract our attention and focus from the issues that matter.*
>
> *National opinion polls are published nearly every day – some go up, some go down, some stay the same. None of them accurately reflect the reality on the ground. All this amounts to a difficult period of the campaign. Understandably people are tired and it's easy to lose focus.*

The public appeared to be being particularly awkward: 'They are angry about being lied to by Mr Blair for so long but aren't yet convinced anyone can make the difference,' wrote Crosby; presumably after his Sunday morning pondering.

Eventually the reporters drifted away from Labour HQ and walked the few yards to where Howard was waiting to unveil the final instalment of his £4 billion tax cuts package. It was a characteristically measured, yet populist move. You can see how it would look to Crosby: believable, deliverable. But unspectacular.

'I'm announcing today that we will abolish stamp duty for the average home in Britain,' said Howard.

'This will help young people on to the property ladder and it will make it easier for young people starting a family to buy a bigger house.'

He added: 'Life is a struggle for too many families in Britain today. Last year average incomes fell for the first time in a decade thanks to Mr Brown's punishing taxes. It's time for practical help.'

His announcement trumped both the doubling of the stamp duty threshold Brown had announced in his Budget – from £60,000 to £120,000 – and the Liberal Democrats who had promised to raise it to £150,000. Under the Tory proposals the 1 per cent tax on house transactions would not be payable on deals below £250,0000. Shadow Chancellor Letwin said 80 per cent of house sales would now attract no stamp duty.

Letwin insisted: 'This policy is not aimed at the housing market; it's aimed at hard-working families who have a problem raising the money for a deposit because of the stamp duty. It will put money into the pockets of people who are home-buyers and hard-working families.

'We are absolutely confident that it is the right thing to do. It will help people to help themselves.'

The Liberal Democrats notionally had today down as the day to reinforce their commitment to scrap student fees. Kennedy hosted the news conference. He said: 'The Liberal Democrats don't just oppose top-up and student tuition fees because we disagree with the policy. I personally oppose them because I think there is no more nauseating sight than politicians pulling up the ladder of opportunity behind them.'

In fact the party had something else on its mind: it's so-called 'decapitation strategy'. It was pouring resources and people into carefully targeted seats aimed at ousting the Tory high command. Shadow Home Secretary David Davis, defending a majority of 1,903 over the Lib Dems in Haltemprice and Howden, Letwin defending 1,414 in West Dorset, ex-Party Chairman Theresa May, defending 3,284 in Maidenhead and even Howard himself defending a 5,907 cushion in Folkestone and Hythe were in their sights.

Today Kennedy would lead the charge, visiting Howden and West Dorset. And Lib Dem President Simon Hughes issued a naked appeal to Labour voters to help the project:

> *This electoral system is not of our making and we've tried to change it for many years, and it is not a fair system.*
>
> *As a result, I always say to people in seats like Oliver Letwin's in Dorset, who would naturally be Labour voters, that given that all the evidence is that your candidate will never win, and your second objective is to remove a Conservative MP and prevent the Tories from making progress, then we ask you to lend us your vote to help us do that.*

As the leaders began to fan out from their press conferences for their day's work, all was not going smoothly for Blair's crime launch. The party knew the official figures would show a rise in violent crime, but the issue was brought into sharp focus when news broke shortly after its announcements of a headline-grabbing vicious attack in Surrey.

A 26-year-old mother was stabbed in the neck as she pushed a buggy along a lane in what was immediately dubbed 'one of the safest areas of England'. The woman, who had a two-year-old son in the buggy, had been found by a member of the public in the lane off Burnhams Road, a private residential street in Little Bookham, Surrey, shortly after 4 p.m. on Wednesday. The little boy was unharmed.

And it also emerged today that a 38-year-old businessmen had been shot in the chest as burglars raided his home in Bradfield, north of Sheffield. Politically, worse was to come as Blair braced himself for yet another radio phone-in, this time on BBC Five Live.

A police officer, who identified himself only as Carl, from Boston, Lincolnshire, called in to ask Blair:

> *Why is it that you continually make my job harder by telling the general public that there are more police officers than there have ever been, when for every police officer you have put in the rank and file on the street, you have probably put another four in offices?*
>
> *My job is increasingly harder. I have heard this morning that you are going to be tough on crime, and you have set new figures. How do you propose to achieve those figures when you don't have the police officers to actually go out and do the policing?*

Blair responded: 'I speak to a lot of police officers, Carl, who don't actually share that perspective and who actually believe that they are getting on top of the crime situation, difficult though it is.'

But the officer told the PM: 'I don't know one. I couldn't give you one colleague who would share that view, not one, not one who works on the streets, who would share that view.'

Blair replied: 'Well, I'm sorry that you can't give me one, but I can assure you that I have spoken to police officers who believe that the new measures on anti-social behaviour, and the introduction of community support officers and the new measures that we are now introducing in respect of drugs and crime are actually of assistance to the police.'

The policeman was not done yet:

> *My point is not about legislation, it is not about what powers you give to police officers. I haven't got a problem with the powers you give police officers. There are some good measures, anti-social behaviour orders.*
>
> *But you can put as many different powers towards us as you like. If we don't have the police officers to support them . . .*
>
> *Yes, we have got community support officers . . . I was sat in the police station the other day and we were running three or four patrol cars, and I was the only police officer there.*
>
> *We had five community support officers, but none of them can arrest people. None of them can go out and tackle crime the way I can.*
>
> *What I'm saying to you is, yes, you have given us these powers, but how the hell am I supposed to use them if I'm the only officer there? There are two problems. One is that we need to get back to getting police officers on the street. The second problem is we need to employ more police officers to get them out there.*

The thing about masochism is that sometimes it hurts too much.

Howard had left London in search of swing voters in the Treetops Housing Development in the marginal constituency of Redditch, held by Labour's Jacqui Smith, a junior industry minister with a 2,484 majority.

The Tory leader was meeting young families in a show home, like those he hoped to be helping up the housing ladder with his stamp duty cut. Labour protesters dressed as workmen had other cuts in mind as they demonstrated on the edge of the site with placards claiming a Tory victory would damage public services.

Safely inside the show house, Howard faced disturbances of another kind as 22-month-old Josh Kelso performed for the cameras.

The youngster repeatedly climbed on the table as Mr Howard attempted to explain his policies to parents Penny and Brandon in front of a TV camera. Young people were on Howard's mind later with a speech to a youth rally in Leeds, where he highlighted education and had a neat rhetorical shimmy into Blair's crime territory. All politicians repeat sections of speeches, and jokes in particular. But Mr Howard has a particular fondness for certain passages. Stop me if you have heard this passage from his speech tonight before (it won't take long): 'If the teenage Michael Howard were applying to Cambridge today, Gordon Brown would love me. My socio-economic background ticks every one of his politically correct boxes: the child of immigrants; from a small town in Wales; a family with modest means; educated in a state school. And of course, Gordon Brown would despise Tony Blair . . .'

That's right, you read it a few pages ago. It's not against the law, but . . . Howard smartly found his way onto crime:

> Now it's a fact that young men are more likely to be the victims of crime than an older person like me.
>
> It's quite wrong that in many towns and cities today young people have to put their own safety at risk to have a good night out. Tony Blair has quite simply lost the plot when it comes to crime. Just look at what he's been up to today – he's been patting himself on the back for the latest crime figures; trying to explain the problem away; even claiming that violent crime has fallen. Mr Blair – welcome to the real world.
>
> Violent crime has almost doubled and there are now a million violent crimes committed every year. I know: my wife Sandra and my daughter Larissa have both been mugged.
>
> And now after eight years in power, and just two weeks before an

> election, Mr Blair's promising a new target to cut crime by 15 per
> cent if he gets in again. What planet is he on? Crime's gone up by
> over 15 per cent since 1998. And behind those statistics are people –
> real people who've been robbed, assaulted, mugged.
>
> What's Mr Blair's message to them? 'Give me one more chance.'

The expression was perhaps not one carelessly chosen. For this
morning, the decision they had all been waiting for was revealed to
the world. In a stunt set up with typical élan the *Sun* had yesterday
erected a chimney pipe on top of its Wapping printing plant and
invited film crews to watch as the smoke first billowed white to
signal an editorial decision had been made . . . and then turned red
to signify: 'The *Sun*'s Backing Blair!'

The paper's front-page headline this morning read: 'One Last
Chance.'

Howard, Crosby and Conservative communications boss Guy
Black could never by now seriously have expected the Currant Bun
to switch sides; but all politicians and their henchmen live in hope.

Howard was quizzed on the newspaper's backing for Blair as he
took to the GMTV sofa this morning. He said simply: 'They are
entitled to their opinion as everybody else is. But, they say one last
chance – I wonder whether the people who feel that they have so
many promises broken, that they are paying so much more in tax, they
are so worried about violent crime increasing out of control, I wonder
whether all those people do want to give them one more chance?'

Had he tried to 'work Mr Murdoch over' or talked to him,
Howard was asked. Howard replied:

> I talk to all sorts of people and they are entitled to their opinion.
> The question is, do people really want to give Mr Blair one more
> chance? I think last time they were giving him one more chance.
> I think a lot of people were disappointed last election and they

said, 'Maybe he has only had four years, let's give him one more chance'. But now the choice is, do you reward him for eight years of broken promises and vote for five more years of talk? Or do you vote Conservative for a party that has taken a stand on the things that really matter to the country?

Last year, Howard had been invited to deliver on 18 March a 'wide-ranging speech' to senior executives of Mr Murdoch's international publishing empire at the Mexican beach resort of Cancun. He was the first Conservative leader to be courted in any way, publicly acknowledged even, by the media baron since Margaret Thatcher. Conservative media chief Black, a former Director of the Press Complaints Commission had been hired not least for his high-level personal contacts in Fleet Street, and he is known to be friendly with *Sun* editor Rebekah Wade.

There must have been a time when they dared to dream. Newspapers don't, of course, win elections. But they can help knock the stuffing out of your opponents and the psychological boost of the *Sun* deserting Blair would have been considerable, as would the reverse effect have been on Labour. But Howard's pitch in Cancun had obviously not quite cut the mustard. In 1995, Tony Blair, leader of the Labour Party for just a year, had been invited to address Murdoch executives at a similar private gathering on the Hayman Islands, off the Australian coast.

At the 1997 election the *Sun* backed the fresh-faced leader of the opposition as he toppled John Major's government. Including its Home Secretary Michael Howard.

Friday 22 April

Blair chose his ground for his intervention in the immigration debate with care. Dover, a town of 33,000, had borne the brunt of asylum-seeking from France at its height – with the Conservative county council leader Sandy Bruce-Lockhart warning six years ago that the numbers flooding in were creating a 'tinder box' atmosphere there. But times have changed. With the closure of the notorious Sangatte camp across the Channel, just outside Calais, and British immigration officials stationed in France, the number of those seeking refugee status has dwindled dramatically. A perfect demonstration for Blair of the 'reality' not the 'rhetoric'. And, incidentally, adjacent to Howard's Folkestone constituency.

Labour's Gwyn Prosser is defending Dover with a 5,199 majority. And even his opponents concurred that immigration was no longer the number-one issue for the town.

Conservative candidate Paul Watkins said:

> *Immigration is not the main issue, but it is still an issue. I would say it is third or fourth rather than the top issue on this occasion.*
>
> *The subjects I hear most about from local people are crime, transport and health. There is a second-class road infrastructure into Dover and a third-class rail system.*
>
> *The former acute hospital, Buckland Hospital, has been downgraded over the last eight years and acute and emergency services have been removed and sent to Ashford and Margate. Local people now have to travel 20 or 30 miles to receive acute or emergency care.*

Liberal Democrat candidate Antony Hook agreed that immigration and asylum had slipped down the agenda locally. 'People recognise that there is an important debate about the asylum system but people's lives are going to be far more radically affected by whether we can succeed in reforming council tax and abolishing tuition fees,' he said. Blair could almost have scripted their remarks himself.

According to latest Home Office figures, at the end of 2004 there were 2,155 asylum seekers being supported in the whole of the south east, excluding London, compared with 10,030 in Yorkshire and the Humber, 7,330 in the North West and 7,505 in the West Midlands. There were just under 16,000 in London.

Blair's blue helicopter swooped over the White Cliffs of Dover to land near the harbour's cruise liner terminal and he launched into a lengthy exposition of his position, and an uncompromising criticism of the Conservatives.

> I said at the manifesto launch that I would deal with the issue of asylum and immigration during this campaign. I do so today, and have chosen to do so in a detailed speech, so that this issue can be examined in detail and in perspective.
>
> Concern over asylum and immigration is not about racism. It is about fairness.
>
> People want to know that the rules and systems we have in place are fair; fair to hard-working taxpayers who deserve to know that others are playing by the rules; fair to those who genuinely need asylum and who use the correct channels; fair to those legitimate migrants who make such a major contribution to our economy.
>
> People also want to know that those they elect to government get it. That we are listening. We do get it. We are listening.
>
> It is precisely because we have been working hard at it, that over the past few years asylum claims have fallen in Britain faster than anywhere else in Europe. But we know we have to tighten the

asylum system further. I also understand concern over immigration controls. We will put in place strict controls that work. They will be part of our first legislative programme if we are re-elected on 5 May. These controls will include the type of points system used in Australia, for example, to help ensure our economy gets the skills we need.

But I never want this to be an issue that divides our country, that sets communities against each other. We are a tolerant, decent nation. That tolerance should not be abused. But neither should it be turned on its head.

It is the duty of government to deal with the issues of both asylum and immigration. But they should not be exploited by a politics that in desperation seeks refuge in them.

Blair was scathing about Howard's position.

Their campaign is based on the statement that it isn't racist to talk about immigration. I know of no senior politician who has ever said it was. So why do they put it like that? Why do they say we 'pussy-foot' around on this issue when they know perfectly well we have been legislating on it, from 1998 onwards, tightening the system, often in the face of their opposition.

It is an attempt deliberately to exploit people's fears, to suggest that for reasons of political correctness, those in power don't dare deal with the issue, so that the public is left with the impression that they are being silenced in their concerns, that we are blindly ignoring them or telling them that to raise the issue is racist, when actually the opposite is true.

The Tory party have gone from being a One Nation party to being a one-issue party. Afraid to talk about the economy, embarrassed by the sheer ineptitude of their economic plan, unable to defend their unfair and elitist NHS and schools policies, unable to explain how they would finance the extra police they are promising, they are left with this one-issue campaign, on asylum and immigration.

Worse, since it is the issue they are pushing so hard at local constituency level, street by street, you might at least expect them to have a coherent policy on it. Instead, their policy on asylum is a joke, an incoherent babble.

Blair went on to confirm plans for 600 extra immigration officers to police Britain's borders; increased use of detention and electronic tagging for failed asylum seekers, to stop them disappearing or going 'clandestine', like the police killer Kamel Bourgass and for UK visa applicants overseas to be finger-printed before coming to the UK.

'Not ignoring the issue and not exploiting the issue, but dealing with the issue – that is our duty, that is our pledge,' said Blair.

As he was making his speech, it was Howard's turn in the Jeremy Paxman hotseat, recording at London's Canary Wharf an interview to be aired this evening. He thus could not respond directly to Blair, but was pressed on the immigration issue. The history of Paxman–Howard interviews is unfortunate and dominated by the confrontation between the two during the 1997 Conservative leadership contest in which Howard was a (very) unsuccessful candidate. Paxman asked him fourteen times about an incident when he had been Home Secretary, asking him if he intervened to overrule the director of the prison service Derek Lewis and suspend the Governor of Parkhurst Prison. 'Did you threaten to overrule him?' the journalist kept repeating. Paxman was later reputed to have said, jokingly or not, that he was just trying to fill time.

Today's encounter was robust but less bruising. Howard even appeared to be rather enjoying himself at one point, producing from his pocket a piece of paper bearing a quote from the late Roy Jenkins, whom Howard described as 'the patron saint of liberalism'.

The quote read: 'There is a clear limit to the amount of immigration this country can absorb. And it is in the interests of the minorities themselves to maintain a strict control.'

Howard went on, triumphantly: 'That is what I think. It is not what Mr Blair thinks. That is the difference in principle between us.'

Whatever the difference in principle, the difference in practice was that Blair was PM and he was not.

Asked where the Conservatives would find a home for their overseas asylum processing centre for those wanting to enter the UK – dubbed 'fantasy island' by Labour – Howard could only reply: 'I'm in opposition. I can't negotiate with other governments.'

After Blair's speech it was left to Tory co-chairman Liam Fox and Davis, the party's home affairs spokesman, to perform the rebuttal.

Fox said there had to be an end to 'uncontrolled immigration' and repeated the charge that 'no one has any idea' how many illegal immigrants lived in the UK.

'The Prime Minister should have addressed these issues over the past eight years. How typical of him with two weeks to go until an election that he now says he will do something about it next time.'

Davis chipped in: 'A rattled Mr Blair hopes that one speech, thirteen days before a general election, on an issue he's ignored for eight years, will make people suddenly trust him. We've heard it all before. He's spent years pussy-footing around this issue, during which time our asylum and immigration system has become chaotic and out of control.'

He had earlier turned on Labour over crime, at the Tories' set-piece morning press conference, where he fleshed out plans for 20,000 extra prison places to keep offenders off the streets and aid their rehabilitation by trying to end the merry-go-round of prisoners constantly being shuffled around the country, from prison to prison, meaning they were never settled long enough to complete a rehab programme.

Davis said: 'Mr Blair's complacent response to the rise in violent crime is to say crime is falling and his Home Secretary even believes violent crime is falling.

'That attitude is absolutely typical of Mr Blair's behaviour over the last eight years. Try and manage the issue off the front pages with a blizzard of misleading denials.'

The shadow Home Secretary said the reality was: 'The violence and lawlessness of some of Britain's inner cities is already spreading to suburbs and market towns across the country.

'Let me tell Mr Blair straight – life in Britain today is very different outside your security bubble.'

The Liberal Democrats refused to be dragged into the row over immigration, insisting they would not let the other parties set their agenda. They stuck determinedly to their focus on discrimination against women.

Party strategists said the Conservative campaign had been damaged by focusing on immigration. They insisted they were happy to sit back and let Labour and the Tories do battle over it.

Kennedy also insisted he had plenty still to say on the major issues and indicated he would play his trump card soon – his opposition to the war in Iraq.

He said he had not pushed Iraq to the forefront of the Lib Dem campaign yet because he did not want the party to be seen as a one-trick pony.

In terms of ploughing our own furrow, we have said from the outset that, particularly in the early stages of the campaign, we wanted to set out very clearly for people the key principles and priorities and policies that the Liberal Democrats are promoting in this election.

That is what we are doing. It does not mean to say we have not got something to contribute on the issues of the day. Of course we have. Currently other parties – one in particular in opposition –

have been banging on about what they believe are the agenda-setting items. And a fat lot of good it seems to be doing them.

Kennedy continued: 'You can rest assured I will have plenty to say about Iraq in a few days' time. But we have been quite clear about this. Had we simply started the election as a party by saying we believe this is all about Iraq and we are all about Iraq, we would immediately have been pigeon-holed as that is the only thing the Liberal Democrats have got to talk about.'

The Lib Dems instead talked of closing the gender pay gap and providing a proper 'citizen's pension' for women, based on residency not National Insurance contributions. The worst joke-makers said the party was not talking about its Manifesto but its Mummyfesto.

Blair's immigration speech was his one hit of the day. He did not take to the campaign trail again.

Howard moved on to Milton Keynes where, almost as if to disprove Blair's 'one issue' campaign jibe, he did not mention asylum or immigration but focused instead on the government's house-building programme. The Conservative leader, in cheerful mode, again adopted his 'stump' persona, talking to a crowd through a hand-held microphone.

'Labour has imposed massive house building programmes on greenbelt and green fields that will destroy the character of many quiet rural areas forever,' he said.

He gave short shrift to a heckler who demanded to know if he would reform the honours system. 'If that's the best you can come up with that is a pretty poor show,' said Howard.

He had also begun to look uncomfortably like John Major, with his famous soap box.

For light relief, the Johnsons – father and son – were also out on the stump today. *Spectator* editor Boris, defending his Henley seat, went to the aid of father Stanley, 64, fighting Teignbridge for the Conservatives.

Boris trumpeted: 'Vote Johnson, vote often – there is a ready supply of Johnsons waiting to step into whatever breaches are left in whatever constituencies.'

Stanley disclosed: 'My campaign has been to go from pub to pub.' Kennedy continued on the 'decapitation' strategy trail, visiting Theresa May's Maidenhead constituency.

Decapitation was not a word he used personally, he assured reporters. And no doubt to their complete relief he said the tactic was 'nothing personal' against the Tory frontbenchers involved.

'The fact these seats are precariously held by prominent Conservatives is by the by,' he said. 'But for us they're target seats and we are going to win them.'

Speaking at an old people's day centre in the town, Kennedy claimed the Tory campaign was in real trouble. 'There is a residual centre-right vote in our country but I don't think it's much more than that and it is certainly not the makings of a winning vote.'

In the unique way that only election campaigns, and Lib Dem ones in particular, can zig-zag the country, Kennedy later visited St Monica's Church-in-Wales Primary School in Cardiff. There, in his best throaty, Scottish burr he read pupils 'Gerry's Story' about a giraffe. Just practising for Donald.

There was now the almost palpable air of exhaustion that infects every general election campaign halfway through. It was what Lynton Crosby had been referring to in his leaked email. Even though you would suspect Australian general elections have a travelling rhythm somewhat different to British contests, Crosby had identified the symptoms.

There were more jokes at the press conferences; more snide remarks, too. There were fewer constituency visits. Blair simply didn't make one today. The first weeks have taken their toll, but there is not yet the excitement of the final burst to polling day. Nor was there yet anything to suggest that the sprint to the finish would be a close-run thing, which at least would pump some adrenalin into tired party workers, struggling to remember what day of the week it was, whose families had gone unacknowledged day after day, whose wedding anniversaries and children's birthdays had come and gone uncelebrated ever since their call to the cause had come.

And for the Conservatives, not only was the hope of victory fading bar a political miracle, there were the first rumblings of the old Tory syndrome known to political scientists as 'fighting like ferrets in a sack'. As always, those now out of the frontline were leading the charge. Michael Portillo had already cautioned against a perceived stress on immigration. Now it was former minister and failed London mayoral candidate Steve Norris's turn to attack the strategy.

'I can't say I am all together delighted by it,' he said in extracts from a GMTV interview to be broadcast this weekend but released tonight. 'The dog whistle approach to politics is about as cynical as you get and I am not entirely sure that I would subscribe to it,' he said.

> *More to the point, from a purely tactical perspective, it is pretty clear that that sort of message appeals to Tory core voters.*
>
> *Whilst it is always important to shore up the core vote, the Conservative Party isn't going to win unless it attracts about two million more people who didn't vote Conservative in 2001.*
>
> *My strong advice to the Tory leader would be that shoring up your core vote is not enough, it simply isn't enough to get the people who will always vote for you come hell and high water.*

Another rumbling in the election undergrowth came from the fuel protestors who had proved so powerful in the past. They threatened to disrupt the general election with direct action, including refinery blockades and go-slows on major routes.

Farmer and haulier Andrew Spence, a spokesman for the Fuel Lobby, said their campaign was set to begin on 3 May, two days before polling day, if the government did not bring down tax on fuel. The lobby said it was prepared to recreate the week-long protests of September 2000 which caused shortages and buying panic at the pumps.

Mr Spence, from Consett, County Durham, said: 'Don't rule anything out. The election would be stopped if we had our way. Tony Blair will not be able have enough fuel in his car to get to the polling station.'

He said a large meeting of hauliers had been fixed for tonight in Stirling, Scotland. 'Those boys up there want to do something now,' said Mr Spence. 'The hardest part will be stopping them from protesting until 3 May.'

The Road Haulage Association also warned members could be stirred into – strictly legal – action. It claimed anger was mounting around the country about fuel prices. Its chief executive Roger King said meetings had been held in Scotland and North Wales and attitudes among those present were 'increasingly militant'. He added:

We recognise that the price of oil is a world problem. But the fact remains that we are paying the highest levels of fuel duty in the world.

We equally recognise that government has frozen fuel duty for some while now but this has done little to stem the huge increase in costs hauliers must pay before they receive any return from the customer – even if that customer is paying something towards the extra cost.

We desperately need some kind of fuel stabilisation formula which would result in tax levels on fuel being reduced as world oil prices increase.

But he added: 'Whatever we do as an industry, it must be lawful but to the point.

Another, theoretical, threat to an election already plagued by 'noises off' receded after John Hemming, deputy leader of Birmingham City Council, lost his court bid for a review of polling in the wake of the postal ballot fraud cases yesterday. The government said it would launch a new drive to tell people how to use their postal votes securely.

The threat to Howard's peace of mind this weekend, though, was more prosaic and more immediate. He had another batch of opinion polls to look forward to and the battle to retain his own seat to fight. All senior Tories are haunted by the spectre of their Party Chairman Chris Patten, who engineered a surprise general election victory for John Major in 1992, but at the expense of neglecting his own Bath constituency, which turfed him out of parliament.

And Howard also had to find a way of revitalising those exhausted Tory campaign staff, and local canvassers whose feet were already aching.

Saturday 23 April

Howard decided to leave his dog whistle in his pocket, and shout 'Here, Rover!' instead.

He went to Hastings to deliver his blunt message to the Conservative faithful. No jacket, pale blue shirt, pink tie. Podium, audience of activists. Opening words of speech:

Today I want to cut to the chase. There'll be none of the usual pleasantries, I'm afraid. Eighteen days ago, Mr Blair announced that he had decided to call an election because he wanted five more years in power.

Since then, a much loved Pope has died, there's been a royal wedding, and a new Pope has been elected. All of them are big, important events. So is this election.

In twelve days time, Britain will go to the polls. The election is different from those events, historic as they are. The citizens of this country were observers of those events. In this election, they decide.

At this election you are the decision makers. It is your decision. Your vote is your voice.

But there's one person who's crossing his fingers in the hope you'll keep silent – praying that our country will sleepwalk its way to another five years of Labour. And that person is Mr Blair. If you stay silent, you will send him a clear message: 'Carry on, you're doing just fine.'

So now, with just twelve days to go, it's time to focus on what really matters. How you use your vote – because if you stay silent you'll have to live with the consequences for the next five years.

To cast a vote is to take a stand, to have your say about what's going on in our country, to send people to Westminster who will stand up for the values you believe in, and get on with the things you want done.

If you're unhappy about high taxes, uncontrolled immigration, rising crime and dirty hospitals, then why reward Mr Blair's Labour Party with your vote? Why don't you take a stand? Isn't it your duty to take a stand? Your duty to yourselves and your duty to our country.

So think carefully about the message you want to send. In twelve days' time, you have the chance to take a stand – in fact it'll be your last chance to take a stand on Mr Blair.

Now, if it would not have looked odd on television you suspect the Conservative leader would have rolled up his shirtsleeves. He rattled off denunciation after denunciation of Blair's Labour administration before issuing this cry from the heart:

Look back at the last eight years and think about the things Mr Blair has said to get elected, and you realise that character IS an issue at this election.

And that's why I've got to say it as I see it.

Quite frankly, Tony Blair's lost the plot. He's talked a lot and failed to deliver. He's told lies to win elections.

And he's only taken a stand on one thing in the last eight years – taking Britain to war. And he couldn't even tell the truth about that.

Well, I don't believe in saying one thing but doing another. With me, what you see is what you get.

I don't care what the armies of do-gooders have to say about it: I think we've been too soft on crime for too long. We've been too lax about immigration for too long. We've turned a blind eye to the lack of discipline at school for too long.

I want the chance to act on these issues.

My message to Britain is simple: you don't have to settle for this. Britain is the fourth richest country in the world – we should be doing so much better than we are today.

By supporting your local Conservative candidate, you can vote for a party that has taken a stand on the things that matter – cleaner hospitals, school discipline, more police, controlled immigration and lower taxes.

To cast a vote is to take a stand. It's your duty to take a stand. How else do you think Mr Blair and his wishy-washy, pussyfooting government are going to get the message? We've all had enough, and now we want action.

Be true to yourself. Be true to our country. On May the 5th take a stand on the things that matter. On May the 5th take a stand for change. On May the 5th take a stand and vote Conservative.

Howard took the applause and walked off stage. He had used the phrase 'take a stand' or said he had 'taken a stand' seventeen times in a brief six-page speech. After a spell canvassing in Hastings he went home.

The Conservatives opened up another full-frontal assault on Blair's trustworthiness over the David Kelly affair, following on from the PM's Paxman interview where he used the words: 'I don't believe we had any option, however, but to disclose his name.'

Blair had always maintained the government had not named Dr Kelly to the media, but had instead simply taken a decision to confirm his identity – as the civil servant who had come forward to his bosses to admit he could be the source of reports about the controversial Iraq dossier – if a name was put to the Ministry of Defence press office by reporters.

Shadow Foreign Secretary Michael Ancram seized on Blair's use of the word 'disclose'. He wrote to the PM asking him now to 'come clean', reopening a tortuous – though important – argument about the 'naming strategy' that preceded Dr Kelly's suicide in July 2003.

Ancram wrote:

> *Following your admission to Jeremy Paxman that you did disclose Dr David Kelly's name to the media, you must now give a clear account of why you have failed to admit this before and why you disclosed the name of a distinguished civil servant to the press, although he had been told that it would not be necessary to reveal his name.*
>
> *In your interview you said that 'I don't believe we had any option, however, but to disclose his name.'*
>
> *This directly contradicts what you told journalists on 22 July 2003. You were asked: 'Why did you authorise the naming of David Kelly?' You replied: 'That is completely untrue.'*
>
> *Again you were asked 'Did you authorise anyone in Downing Street or in the MoD to release David Kelly's name?' You answered: 'Emphatically not.'*
>
> *But now you have admitted that you 'disclosed' the name.*
>
> *In light of the admission you have finally made, it would be right for you to come clean and explain in full your role in deciding how Dr Kelly's name was disclosed.*
>
> *Will you now admit that you took the decision that inevitably led to Dr Kelly's name being made public?*

A Labour Party spokesman said: 'The Prime Minister was simply restating the already well-known fact, covered for example in the Hutton report, that the Ministry of Defence confirmed to the *Financial Times* that they were correct when they rang their press office and put David Kelly's name to them.'

Turning the screw later, Ancram said: 'David Kelly was a highly respected scientist. He was effectively driven to his death by what happened.'

Blair was not interested in the points Ancram had made, when he hosted his party's news conference. He dismissed it as 'personal stuff' which was bound to be raised, and marched back onto his chosen ground.

One side effect of the expected surge in postal voting was that so many more ballot papers would start to be completed before 5 May. Blair wanted his message out early and out often.

He went to Billingsgate Market in the City of London to unveil posters bearing Labour's 'second phase' campaign slogan: 'If you value it – vote for it'.

Then at party HQ he hosted the press conference, joined by Brown on a video-link from Edinburgh. In his own way, his message was as uncompromising as Howard's, as he sought to wring every last 'X' from every last voter whether in person, or by post.

> Over these coming days people have got to make up their minds as to which government to elect for our country and I know the British people will give very serious thought to the choice that is before them.
>
> We have had the programmes and manifestos from the parties. I think I can say to you without any doubt, certainly in my mind, there is only one serious programme for government that has been set out.

He said the Tory manifesto was 'threadbare and contradictory' and the Liberal Democrat blueprint 'simply doesn't add up'.

Blair went on: 'People are going to have to think very, very carefully about this over the coming days. In the end, it's a big choice, it's a fundamental choice for our country. There will either be a Conservative government or a Labour government that people wake up to on 6 May, so that choice has now got to be made.

'The real point about the election is that at a local level this election is going to be decided often by a few hundred votes either way in marginal constituencies.

'If people value a strong economy they have to vote for it. If they value the low interest rates, the record number of jobs, they have got to vote for it'

Brown warned: 'The danger of wasting your vote on the Liberal Democrats is real – it is not the easy way out, it is a backdoor way to a Tory government.'

Blair stressed the need to slug it out in every corner of Britain: 'This election is tough and tight. It will be decided in marginal constituencies.'

He said a few hundred votes in those key marginals could decide its outcome. The message was plain enough, both to voters and activists: Don't be fooled by the polls. Don't be complacent. Like a soccer team three-nil up at half time, Labour were determined not to sit back and allow their opponents to retrieve some hope. They would rather win six-nil.

So John Prescott went to Edinburgh; specifically Tesco's supermarket in the suburb of Colinton. There had been numerous reports recently about ex-BBC boss John Birt's role in and around No. 10 as a 'blue skies' thinker, or 'unpaid advisor' in proper Whitehall-speak. He was going to run this unit, that unit. Prescott was having none of that.

'First of all, let's dismiss John bloody Birt,' he said.

> He might walk in and out of No. 10, he might whisper in ears. There are thousands of advisers like that. He obviously thinks he is a bit more important.
>
> That is what advisers do – but they don't make decisions.

That's cleared that up, then. And don't forget to attack the Liberal Democrats, Mr Prescott.

'You have a Liberal Democrat council here,' Mr Prescott told innocent bystanders, much to their bemusement, since they had a Labour-controlled council.

> *When you see Charles Kennedy saying he's tired after a day looking after the baby: Blimey! What does he think women are doing all day?*
> *It seems to me like the Liberals are on the run. They are tired and they can't get their policies over.*

Charles Kennedy, meanwhile, was serene in his Ross, Skye and Lochaber constituency, where generations of his family have been crofters, apart from a brief foray into employment into the whisky industry. The *Daily Telegraph* unearthed, with scholarly diligence today, that Donald Kennedy (the elder, born in 1850) had moved away from the land to take up a post as a 'mashman' in the Nevis Distillery in the parish of Kilmallie, Inverness, the ancestral home of the Lib Dem leader's family. The current Kennedy, new father of the youngest Donald of that ilk, was in confident mood as he spoke against the background of green fields and blue sky.

He said of the next phase of his party's campaign: 'Iraq, the United Nations, and our relationship with Europe and all manner and means of other issues including the environmental agenda – those come into play very strongly indeed.'

Kennedy went on: 'I'm not one of those in the pessimistic game about voter participation.

'I will risk a prediction. I think the participation rate will go up in this general election overall. And it will be up because people do see there are big issues, big values at stake.'

People did not want 'Tony Blair being returned with a three-figure majority so he can do what he likes, whether it's war and peace or the domestic agenda'.

He said voters knew the Conservatives could not win power: 'The key issue for the remainder of the campaign now is who can provide the real alternative based on a positive and fundamentally optimistic agenda.'

Cheerful Charlie. And well he might be. Nobody was predicting that his party would lose seats, and he was still wrapped in the euphoria of a new baby son.

Blair had to believe a fight to the end was on, or risk ending up with an ever smaller majority – and the smaller Labour's majority, the more peril to his carefully-laid plan to transfer power by the next election; whatever it is. Howard knew a fight to the end was on.

If he was not to walk into No. 10, he had to slash Blair's winning margin somehow, in his own way, to avoid the calamitous infighting that had become such a feature of his party in recent years. And which would rob him, too, of the chance to bow out at a time of his choosing. With or without Tony Blair back in Downing Street, he did not want to be drafting a resignation statement in the early hours of 6 May.

Margaret Dixon, whose shoulder operation was cancelled seven times by Warrington Hospital. Her case was highlighted by Michael Howard as proof of the failure of the government's health spending.

The launch of the Labour manifesto. Tony Blair said, 'There are no weak links here.'

Michael Howard launches the Conservative manifesto.

John Prescott's battlebus (above) on the campaign trail. Charles Kennedy (right) arrives at East Midlands airport for a visit to Leicestershire. Michael Howard (below) crosses the country by helicopter.

(Above) Charles Kennedy celebrates the arrival of new son Donald with wife Sarah. (Left) Speaking at the launch of the party's manifesto 48 hours after the birth.

Families of workers facing redundancies from the MG Rover
plant take their protests to No. 10 Downing Street. Liz Hanks (left)
and Gemma Cartwright with Daniel Hanks, fouteen,
Tia Cartwright, seven, Pearce Cartwright, six.

(Left) British pro-fox hunting protester Otis Ferry is removed by police officers after shouting at Tony Blair.
(Below) A protester is led away by police during a confrontation between fierce election rivals Oona King and George Galloway at Queen Mary, University of London.

Conservative leader Michael Howard addresses a rally on the subject of immigration. Howard's repeated focus on the issue drew criticism from some senior Tory figures.

Greenpeace activists invade Deputy Prime Minister John Prescott's home in Hull. A spokesman for Greenpeace said the group were attempting to install a solar panel on the roof of Prescott's constituency home in a bid to highlight the government's record on energy.

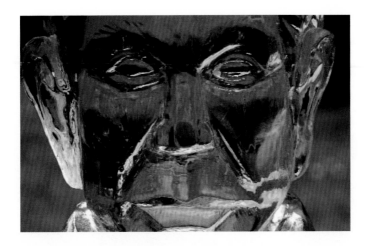

Ice sculpture depicting Tony Blair, unveiled by the Green Party in central London to illustrate their claim that Blair's credibility was melting away day by day.

Mark McGowan kisses a laminated portrait of Tony Blair opposite 10 Downing Street. The artist was attempting to kiss the picture 100,000 times as a token of his support for the Labour leader.

Militants disrupting a Muslim Council of Britain press conference which was unveiling a list of ten questions for Muslim voters to ask parliamentary candidates.

Former Downing Street communications chief Alastair Campbell sitting in on a press conference given by Tony Blair and Education Secretary Ruth Kelly.

Tony Blair meets pupils at Lilian Baylis Technology School. The booing sounds which greeted the Prime Minister were later described by some pupils as a 'Boom!' of approval.

Gordon Brown and Tony Blair during a joint press conference as the two continued to campaign for re-election with a display of unity.

TV impressionist Rory Bremner, dressed as the Tory leader, stands with Conservative candidate Peter Bone and Michael Howard during a visit to Rushden.

Tony Blair buys ice creams for himself and Gordon Brown during a visit to Gillingham.

Robert Kilroy-Silk, leader of Veritas, canvasses voters in Ilkeston, Derbyshire.

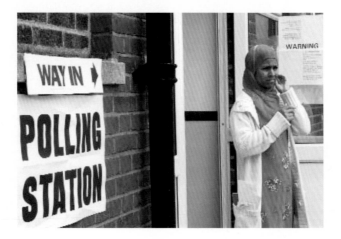

A voter leaves a Luton polling station after casting her ballot.

(Left) Robert Kilroy-Silk after his heavy defeat in Erewash. (Below) George Galloway, former Labour MP and new Respect MP for Bethnal Green and Bow, greets supporters in London's Brick Lane.

Friday 6 May: Tony Blair, his wife Cherie and youngest son Leo outside 10 Downing Street.

6

A question of trust

Sunday 24 April

The *Mail on Sunday* landed with a thud on Alastair Campbell's desk. 'THE PROOF: Blair <u>was</u> told war could be ruled illegal,' its front page screamed. The newspaper said it could 'now reveal for the first time exactly what counsel Mr Blair received' over the legality of the Iraq war.

Blair had always maintained that Attorney General Lord Goldsmith's final advice that the war would be legal without a second United Nations resolution had been delivered orally to Cabinet, on 17 March 2003. The Attorney then released some details in a parliamentary written answer. But there had been constant calls for Lord Goldsmith's 'full advice' on the potential conflict to be published, amid claims that he had earlier warned it could be illegal in international law without such a UN mandate, exposing British troops to the risk of legal action.

The *Mail on Sunday* claimed to have been given details of the worries expressed by the Attorney General in a paper drawn up on 7 March 2003. The concerns were said to include the fact that Security Council Resolution 1441, warning Saddam Hussein of 'serious consequences' if he continued to cock a snook at the UN, singularly failed to use the normal language reserved for the threat of United Nations-authorised military action: 'all necessary means'; and a warning that reviving earlier resolutions passed over the first Gulf War ejecting Saddam from Kuwait might not be sufficient to cover future action.

Lord Goldsmith's spokesman said simply: 'The Attorney General presented his view to Cabinet on 17 March 2003 that military action in Iraq would be lawful. It was his own genuinely held independent view.

'Legal advice is confidential, protected by legal professional privilege and we don't comment on the process of giving legal advice. The parliamentary statement of 17 March 2003 never purported to be a summary of the Attorney General's advice.'

Howard was appearing on BBC1's *Breakfast with Frost* this morning, and having first questioned Blair's integrity in his speech yesterday, decided to go for the jugular, accusing Blair directly of lying over the war – which he had stepped back from doing in Hastings. It may seem an arcane distinction, but in politics to accuse someone of not telling the truth is not quite the same as accusing them of lying.

Howard decided to go the extra mile on TV: 'This is the last chance the British people will have to send a message to Mr Blair, to say to him we are fed up with your broken promises, we are fed up with the way you lied to win elections, as over tax, and we are fed up with the way you lied to us over the war.

'This is an opportunity for the British people to take a stand, to make a judgement on Mr Blair's character. It is the last chance they'll have to do that.'

Alastair Campbell had been expecting the Liberal Democrats to launch their long-promised assault on the PM over Iraq next week. He had not necessarily been expecting Howard to jump in so enthusiastically.

The Conservative leader explained his view:

If you look at what happened over the war, the intelligence he had, as we know from the Butler Report, was limited, sporadic and patchy.

When Mr Blair came to report back to the country he said he had intelligence which was extensive, detailed and authoritative.

Maybe you can reconcile those two different sets of words. I can't. I think that portraying the intelligence in that way was not true.

And to think today had been pencilled in as Armistice Day in the campaign. Hostilities were to be suspended while each party leader made a speech to mark World Poverty Day, more or less presenting a united front. Just as well nobody suggested a friendly soccer match.

Even as Howard arrived at the Tabernacle Christian Centre in west London to deliver his pre-planned address, he had another go at Blair:

I think today's revelations confirm what I said yesterday. Character is an issue at this election.

There is one thing about which Mr Blair has taken a stand in the last eight years and that was taking the country to war. Even on that issue he did not tell the truth. It is time he did.

Then he remembered the truce:

I'm particularly pleased that the cause of making poverty history is something that has united the parties in this country.

There is not much in this election campaign on which we agree but we do agree we should substantially increase our international aid by £800 million over the next three years, that we should work towards meeting the United Nations target of 0.7 per cent of national income by 2013 and that we should work towards cancelling the debt of the poorest countries in the world.

> *If we can work together to achieve that, we will all be performing a service to the rest of the people who share this planet with us.*

A few miles away in Barnes, Kennedy echoed Howard's sentiments:

> *Britain is a wealthy country, a prosperous country. It is the duty of countries such as ours, with the means to help, to take action to make poverty history.*
>
> *It is not only the right thing to do, it is in our national interest too.*
>
> *In an increasingly interconnected world, problems – and responsibilities – have become internationalised. Only strong and concerted action by states in partnership will achieve sustainable development. We have an historic opportunity to make the world fairer.*

But he did not want the Tories stealing his thunder over Iraq, as his party prepared to launch its own attack to woo those anti-war voters.

In an interview for lunchtime BBC radio he dismissed Conservative attempts to exploit the issue as 'laughable', saying they had been the 'principal cheerleaders' for the invasion of Iraq.

He added: 'The longer it goes on, the more corrosive it becomes for Tony Blair as Prime Minister, for the government, and for people's sense of trust in the whole political establishment.

'The longer he remains unwilling to publish in full the Attorney General's advice, the more people are going to view this election as an issue of trust and as a referendum on the trust which they felt was so badly lacking over the decision to go to war.'

With Labour's high command refusing to be deflected from their scheduled rally on world poverty at London's Old Vic theatre, it was left to the Leader of the Lords, Baroness Amos, to defend the government on the airwaves. 'To continue to undermine the integrity of the Attorney General in this way is, I think, appalling,' she told Sky News's *Sunday with Adam Boulton* programme.

'Our view was that the war was legal then, it remains legal now. There is no issue about that for this government.'

Blair had been looking forward to his rally. Africa was a favourite cause – and he had a surprise for everybody up his sleeve.

Blair describes African poverty as 'a scar on the conscience of the world' and means it. He and Cherie have for years privately supported an orphanage in Cape Town, South Africa, called Nazareth House, which cares for children with HIV/Aids and who are often abandoned and cast out from their families and villages. As the children are now starting to live longer with access to better drugs, some are successfully placed back with their relatives. It is still, however, a heartbreaking place in the shadow of beautiful Table Mountain. Blair was deeply moved as he played with youngsters there on a visit in 1998.

Blair has travelled widely on the continent: Mozambique, Nigeria, Sierra Leone, Senegal, Sudan, Ethiopia, Egypt, Libya, as well as South Africa. He has seen some of the most wretched people on the planet, visited some of its most opulent mansions and residences, and met some of its more idiosyncratic leaders.

Earlier this year his Commission for Africa, comprising leading politicians and campaigners, including Bob Geldof, published its weighty blueprint for action, designed to stimulate discussion later in 2005 when Blair hopes to use the UK presidency of the G8 to focus attention on the issue.

The Chancellor has become a convert too, travelling to Africa himself earlier this year and drawing on the experience in speeches ever since in his unsuccessful campaign to persuade the United States to support his debt relief initiatives.

So Blair and Brown had been looking forward to their set-piece event; complete with surprise cameo appearance by an old friend and the Frank Sinatra of the campaign trail: Bill Clinton.

In an emotional, 25-minute, apparently unscripted speech Blair told the 1,000 Labour supporters at the rally: 'We have to make 2005 the year of the new beginning for Africa.' Blair said the scandal of Africa wasn't just that thousands died needlessly every day.

The scandal is that they die when, with the right political will and effort, we can prevent their deaths.

In eighteen years of Conservative government, aid each year to the world's poorest as a proportion of our national wealth had halved.

In the last eight years, aid every year as a proportion of national wealth has risen. Overall aid has doubled. Aid to Africa has trebled.'

He asked: 'What cause could be more noble than millions of people dying preventatively? If the wealthy nations wanted to stop it, they could do so.

'If we are given the chance and are re-elected, I can make you this commitment. We will work night and day to end the scandal of poverty in Africa.'

Clinton appeared live via video-link from New York, and slipped neatly into Blair's new 'If you value it, vote for it' slogan.

He warned: 'Our people get a little easily disillusioned. They don't like this policy or that policy. They sometimes fall into the trap of thinking it doesn't matter and there are no consequences.

'But if you believe that, look at the difference in the US between now and four years ago.'

Describing himself as a 'semi-retired' politician he told the Labour faithful: 'If you do value the progress you are making in

Britain, if you value the idea you can end world poverty – you have to vote for values.' He ended with a characteristic flourish: 'I'm just here to say thank you, amen and go get 'em.'

Amen.

In a memo from Campbell to Labour's strategy team, published on the party's website today, he made clear just why the party wanted supporters to 'go get 'em'.

The *Sunday Times* had published part of the document, under the headline 'Home and Dry', quoting Campbell as saying Labour's election plan was working, and on track for victory. But his real underlying message was the need for activists to drive the campaign forward in key constituencies. Labour decided to publish the full text to make his message clear. At first sight, it provides a fascinating glimpse into the inner working of Labour's campaign. The politicians' initials are self-explanatory; p/c stands for press conference, PG stands for party polling guru Phillip Gould:

Date: 23.04.05
To: Strategy Team
From: AC

TB has asked me to set out a campaign overview as we enter the final full week of the campaign. Here it is.

Private polling reflects published polling. Lead is stable. TB rating up. MH down. CK failing to make headway. TB–GB joint campaigning has seen our lead on leadership in the economy rise even further, leads on health and education have also risen. When asked 'who do you trust to run the country/economy?' we have a growing lead.

So the strategy – root everything in the economy, focus on values/dividing lines in public services – is on track and working.

The overnight tracking polls show we can be confident on asylum and immigration. TB's speech had huge awareness and he seems to have got the balance right, between action on the one hand, tolerance on the other. In the focus groups, there are now signs of a negative halo effect for Howard i.e. when the Tories focus on asylum and immigration it has the effect of skewing the perception of the party to the Right and turns off centrist voters.

People are beginning to ask if MH ever talks about anything else. Men in particular have begun to notice MH never speaks on the economy. People are beginning to compare him negatively with Mrs Thatcher (and even with John Major!). His nastiness and a sense that he is extreme are now being raised without any prompting.

Asked where to place the Tories on a Right to Left scale of −100 to +100, where 0 is the centre, people placed the Tories at an average of +36 at the start of the campaign, in the last few days that has risen as high as +57, indicating that they have been seen to move sharply to the Right. Labour has moved from −3 to −6, on the same scale. We are now very close to the centre. This appears to be very good news for us. It means the Tories are increasingly being seen as extreme. It is also clear as per Crosby's memo in the Guardian, that they are sticking to their 'send a message' strategy, rather than going to win, and they are not even putting forward a programme for government.

However, TB is concerned that we understand fully the kind of campaign they are running. Of course we have to say they have vacated the field on the economy, and that they do not have a serious or coherent programme for government. But in terms of their strategy, that misses the point. They are fighting a different sort of campaign, focusing ruthlessly on the marginals, targeting specific voters with specific messages designed to arouse fear and grievance. It is, as TB has said, nasty and unscrupulous, but it still has the capacity to be effective in some parts of the country.

So the big national poll leads do not matter. What matters is that we understand the nature of their campaign, expose it, and fight it very hard on the ground, by making sure our messages and policies are heard, and theirs rebutted. We have gathered a good deal of their local material which will allow us to continue to expose what they are up to through the week. It is a deliberately sneaky strategy which once fully exposed will damage them. Allied to this, we need to build on the argument that just as voters used to punish us in the 80s because we failed to listen, and because of the nature of our campaigns, so the public should see this election as an opportunity not just to support us, but to punish them, send them a message that they deserve to lose and need to go away, rethink, start compromising with an electorate that has moved on from the Thatcher years.

TURNOUT:
TB is anxious that we understand fully the implication of the analysis PG presented on turnout yesterday. The reality is, as we succeed in our attacks on the Tories, and as Howard becomes more and more visible, we rise in the polls, which then has a direct and immediate impact on the prospects for turnout.

Among certain groups, there has been a sharp decline in certainty to vote in the last week. Certainty to vote for Labour has dropped by around 7% and among the people who are most strongly aligned with us on issues such as health and education, the drop has been bigger. This has little or nothing to do with apathy or disillusion. It is more that if the poll lead widens, they feel sure we are going to win and less compelled to vote. This again plays into Crosby's Queensland strategy.

In summary, we are very well positioned in the debate but there is a strong risk low turnout could hit us very hard, indeed. So far we have been engaged in making and winning arguments. This job is largely done. Next week, we will be back on the economy,

TB–GB, dividing lines in public services. The arguments keep going but we will be shifting to a greater emphasis on the importance of voting. We have new posters planned for today, on schools and hospitals, with the slogan, 'If you value it, vote for it.'

We have an economic version planned for Monday's TB–JP–GB cities event. We then get up the choice on public services, tax credits, before launching the business manifesto to get another day on the economy. It's pretty simple: when we are on the economy, we win the arguments. But we now need to inject a greater sense of this being about values every bit as much as competence – with a real focus on the importance of voting, moving eventually to the line that if people stay at home, or go with the Lib Dems, they will wake up with Howard.

The rest of the campaign should be relentlessly about why voting matters, and we should be focusing on issues which are more likely to convince our supporters to vote. That means the economy, health, education, family tax credits, minimum wage, which every poll has shown to be our singly most popular policy.

Finally, on the Lib Dems, GB is setting out at this morning's p/c the argument that serious people cannot take the LDs seriously. We know CK is going big on Iraq next week. It is to him what immigration is to Howard. Our answer is twofold: defend the points on Iraq, on the grounds that if CK's view had prevailed, Saddam would still be in power. But also point out CK focused on this because his policies on the economy and crime/legalising drugs in particular, are a joke.

Intriguing stuff. But did Alastair Campbell really put his master plan for his party's final week's full campaigning on an open website for all to read? Hmmm . . . are you thinking what I'm thinking?

Monday 25 April

In London early this morning it rained, and it rained and it rained. On the Underground, the Victoria Line was shut. The Northern Line was flooded. Rush-hour commuters limped drenched and late into work. And it rained, too, on Charles Kennedy's parade. Rhetorical wars, just like real ones, do not always go strictly according to plan. Kennedy set out to launch his all-out attack on Blair over Iraq, the moment that had been in the Lib Dem grid for so long. If he was hoping for an easy ride at his news conference, he was to be disappointed; and Howard had already pilfered his headlines with his 'liar' attack yesterday.

Today, there were sharp exchanges between Kennedy and reporters, as he wheeled out his condemnation of Blair over Iraq, and stretched his denunciation to a warning about a possible strike against Iran in the next eighteen months – which he said that the PM, unlike Foreign Secretary Straw, had refused to rule out.

Kennedy told his morning news conference: 'Iraq deserves to be a central issue in this election, not only because of what has happened, but because of what may yet come to pass.'

He said some analysts were predicting a strike against Iran within eighteen months. It's clear that military option is under active consideration in Washington,' he added. Straw had been 'commendably unequivocal in his insistence that such action would be inconceivable'.

Kennedy went on:

Tony Blair as Prime Minister, by contrast, has only gone so far as to say there are no plans for an attack on Iran.

The problem the Prime Minister has is that we don't have sufficient reason to trust his word when it comes to this issue.

Britain's international reputation has been damaged by the way Tony Blair took us to war.

It has undermined the United Nations. It has undermined international law. It has undermined Tony Blair's own standing as Prime Minister. It has undermined trust in government and politics generally.

The Lib Dem leader called, finally, for a full public inquiry into the war against Iraq. But reporters wanted to know what Kennedy himself would have done about Saddam Hussein.

'Had the United Nations weapons inspectors been given the additional time that they sought from the international community they would presumably have concluded there were no weapons of mass destruction so history would have been different,' he said. 'There is quite a body of evidence to suggest that Saddam's regime was internally becoming untenable.'

But asked to produce or name any of that 'body of evidence' he could not. He waffled. And he refused to put the boot in to Blair.

Asked if he thought the Prime Minister was a 'liar', Kennedy said:

The answer is we cannot know, and we cannot know in the absence of the full disclosure of what was the definitive legal advice that the Attorney General proffered to the government.

If I was in the Prime Minister's shoes right now, I would publish, if I was confident, and let people make their minds up.

I genuinely cannot understand, despite all the institutional hostility towards making public an Attorney General's set of recommendations, I cannot understand, given the political context, why he just does not put it in front of people.

Kennedy went off to Bournemouth to be questioned in the friendlier surroundings of a school hall by a group of youngsters. He had used the whole of his morning media time on Iraq, with so far not much to show for it. Some TV bulletins simply picked up on his hesitations when pressed, rather than his attack on Blair, and he had had nothing new to offer. Not yet, anyway.

Alastair Campbell's focus groups might call it a 'negative halo' effect; others might simply call it the 'banging on' effect. Minds, even Kennedy would surely admit, had already been made up on the issue.

At his morning news conference, Howard decided to make another council tax announcement, knowing he would be bound to get his chance to attack Blair on Iraq again under questioning. He said the Tories, as well as cancelling the planned council tax revaluation, would also scrap plans to bring in a new, wider range of tax bands.

He also announced, though with little fanfare, his party's business manifesto, promising, among a sprinkling of un-glitzy pledges, to reduce the burden of red tape on small firms.

Hammering home his lower tax message, he told reporters:

If I came up to you in the street, took money out of your pocket and threw it down the drain, that would be a crime.

Well, that's what Mr Blair's government does every day of the week. But you don't have to settle for this.

It's time to take a stand against government waste. People work hard for their money. They deserve a government that takes a stand, stops the waste and gives them lower taxes and value for money.

The Tory press conference podiums now carried a new logo, replacing that gift to satirists and state-of-the-art dog-whistle, 'Are you thinking what we're thinking?' It now read: 'Taking a stand on the issues that matter'.

Why?

'We are taking a stand because we think people are thinking what we are thinking, and given that, we are inviting them to make a stand and we are confident they will,' said Howard. Hopefully the memo explaining that will never be leaked.

Why had he called Blair a liar?

'I'm afraid I tell it as it is and I tell it as I find it, because I think this election is about trust. This election is about whether people in our country can continue to trust Mr Blair.'

Blair's news conference was low-key, too. The heavyweight clash of the day was supposed to be Brown, followed by Howard, making consecutive, but dry, speeches to the British Chambers of Commerce at London's QEII conference centre.

But at the morning follies, both Brown and Industry Secretary Hewitt, trying a new tack and building on Campbell's comments in his strategy memo, compared Howard unfavourably with Margaret Thatcher. Brown said Lady Thatcher would have been 'appalled' by the Conservatives' plans to 'spend more, tax less and borrow less'. They were reckless proposals that Thatcher 'would never have countenanced'.

Hewitt said that though she disagreed fundamentally with much of what Thatcher had stood for, 'nobody could ever say that she had failed to grasp the centrality of the economy to any serious general election campaign'. She went on: 'Lady Thatcher's Tory Party used to run the economy. Mr Howard's Tory Party runs away from it.' A sign of the times for Thatcher to feature at a Labour election press conference in terms any other than scathing condemnation.

Lady Thatcher, long ago ordered by doctors not to undertake any further public speaking engagements, had not figured in Howard's campaign at all, for understandable reasons. Would the Labour jibes and her absence tap into the secret heart of Conservatives worried that their man was not up to the job? Or would it provoke one last hurrah on the campaign trail from the Iron Lady? Win, win, Labour strategists probably reckoned, remembering fondly their 2001 election poster depicting the then Conservative leader William Hague wearing a Thatcher wig with the slogan: 'Get out and vote or they get in'.

The PM decided on a new line of defence, too, when, with increasing exasperation, punctuated by forced smiles, he faced repeated questioning on Iraq from reporters. He appealed:

Let's stop having this argument about whether it's my character or my integrity that's at issue here and understand the decision had to be taken.

I have no disrespect for people who disagreed with me over Iraq.

I simply ask them to conduct the debate on the terms of whether the judgement was right or not, rather than attacks on my conduct and integrity.

Blair went on, talking straight from Campbell's script:

You have got to ask yourselves why this is happening. Why is it that the Liberal Democrats and the Conservatives have got back to this issue?

I would suggest to you this is because they have got nothing serious to say about the issues facing our country for the future.

I know there's a disagreement over Iraq. That disagreement we will never resolve, but I also know it's right to look to the future now.

Up hill and down dale the questioning went, but Blair was never rattled. He has faced every possible sort of interrogation on the subject, even a quasi-judicial probing by Lord Hutton sitting in the witness box at the Royal Courts of Justice.

Blair said the Conservatives were mounting 'a full scale assault on my character' because they had nothing else to offer. 'They can call me what they like,' he said dismissively.

Of the decision to go to war: 'I can't say I am sorry about it. I am not sorry about it. I think I did the right thing.'

He went on to brave Bristol, where once students had pelted him with tomatoes. Today the welcome was generally kinder as he highlighted government plans for inner-city regeneration. But, with the Prime Minister reaching into a line of well-wishers to shake hands, one woman snubbed his advance.

She rejected Blair's outstretched arm and shouted: 'I will not shake the hand of a killer.' On the campaign trail, an unremarkable event, and something Blair has lived with for years as Britain's forces have seen action across the world. But in the small hours, does it still sting? Not a baying press pack or organised demonstration – just a woman refusing to shake your hand.

The PM got on with his job and stuck to his theme for the week, saying: 'Never mind what the opinion polls say, the thing that counts is going to be in constituencies, often marginal constituencies, where a few hundred votes or a few thousand either way can decide the course of this election.

'The only way of getting a Labour government on 6 May is to vote for it on 5 May.'

The weather brightened up a bit at lunchtime.

Howard, having breezed past only the occasional umbrella in a market in the London suburb of Croydon, and not being caught pocketing any tomatoes to pelt at Blair, and avoiding any disastrous heckles, had another bash at being grilled by 'ordinary voters' on an ITV show, *Ballot Boxy Jury*, to be screened later tonight.

The Conservative leader, though proud of his education at the rugby-loving Llanelli Grammar School, as those who have heard his speeches can testify, also once horrified its headmaster by asking if he and fellow sixth-formers might play soccer instead. In the most heroic version of the story, Howard goes on to start a soccer team. So, under questioning from the television audience about his party's fortunes, he groped for an analogy from the Beautiful Game.

'I am a football fan. You often find if you are a football fan there is a team that might be two goals down at half-time, [pause] they win the game,' he said. 'I went to the Carling Cup final a few weeks back to watch my team Liverpool play Chelsea. We were ahead until the last ten minutes and then we were screwed.

'So the election is not over until 5 May and I am confident we can win that.'

Gaffe, or strategy? Blair had been insisting that the Tories were deliberately playing the underdog card, as part of their 'Australian tactics'; the idea being that people don't need to vote Labour, because the party is home and dry, and as the Conservatives cannot win, it is safe to vote for them since they will not form a government. The Tories then sneakily target the swing seats that will shift the balance of power at Westminster, thereby creeping up on the rails, and, Hey Presto! A Conservative government on 6 May. In a three-party, first-past-the-post system with unpredictable turnout, it is doubtful the tactic could work as well as it did with an Australian electorate where, for a start, voting is compulsory. But Labour's strategy team needed something to invade their sleep.

Election coordinator Milburn confirmed their fears:

> Michael Howard's 'two-nil down' comments are part of the Crosby backdoor strategy. They are designed to show the Tories are losing and are unlikely to win.

In reality, as the Prime Minister has said, this election is close in the marginals. Michael Howard's private polling shows just what ours does: there is a real contest which will be settled by a small number of votes in the battleground seats.

His tactic is clear: on the one hand he wants to talk down the Labour vote, to make voters think this is an opportunity to protest rather than a big choice about who governs Britain for the next four or five years.

At the same time the imported dog-whistle tactics of his Australian campaign team are designed to maximise the Tory vote.

Our message to every Labour supporter is simple and direct. If you vote Tory you get Michael Howard. If you vote Liberal Democrat you are in danger of getting Michael Howard. And if you don't vote at all you are in danger of getting Michael Howard.

For the record, Howard might have mentioned another football match this season, when his beloved Reds – he is, by the way, a genuine fan – were two-nil down against Fulham at half time, but went on to win four-two. The Carling Cup defeat was obviously fresher in his memory.

Back with the *Ballot Box Jury*, Howard yet again came under fire for his comments on immigration. Eemaan Elmougy, who converted to Islam when she married her Egyptian husband more than two decades ago, said: 'You sound as though you are trying to frighten people and turn things back to 40 years ago and Enoch Powell's days. 'I really feel you are just pandering to the racists of the country.' Howard replied: 'That is an easy thing to say. I think it is a very unfair thing to say.'

His arguments did not persuade nurse Sue Owner, a former Conservative voter, to back his party on 5 May. Asked if she would once again vote Tory she said: 'No. Because I feel it is not just about immigration, which seems to be the main issue.' The Conservatives should be talking about issues like education and Europe as well, she said.

A forlorn Howard complained: 'I wish you had been asking questions about education and Europe this evening, but you were asking questions about immigration.'

The once-feared fuel protestors, who five years ago had caused Blair to turn on his heels in Sheffield, cancel a regional visit and speed back to London, were not having much luck so far either. They had trouble with their turnout.

Farmers For Action (FFA) tried to blockade the Shell oil refinery at Stanlow, Cheshire – the seat of those nationwide protests of September 2000. The county constabulary reported 20 men in around fifteen tractors had arrived at the plant, near Ellesmere Port at 5 a.m. Protest organisers claimed there were 30 vehicles.

They were greeted by a unit of 30 police officers, after the force had been alerted to the protest by media inquiries on Sunday night. The police refused to let the protest vehicles park on the road and instead the farmers spent nearly three hours circling a roundabout more than two miles from the refinery gate.

The protest caused mild congestion and some tanker drivers apparently chose to leave via a different route, but there was no disruption of fuel supplies.

By 8 a.m. the farmers agreed to park their vehicles on the round-about while their leaders met Shell management, in the hope of using the firm to influence the government. The meeting proved fruitless.

The leaders then met a representative from the Transport and General Workers Union to ask the Shell tanker drivers to refuse to cross the unofficial picket line. However, the union representative declined to play any part in the action, as it was not an official dispute.

David Handley, of FFA, who had originally described the action as a 'blockade', promised that numbers would increase throughout the day. The dairy farmer, from Monmouth, Wales, explained that many farmers found it difficult to leave work before lunchtime.

But by 3 p.m. numbers had dwindled to less than fifteen men, with around seven tractors and a number of private cars, including three Range Rovers and a Land Rover Discovery with the private registration 'H8 FFA'. A single Volvo lorry had also joined the protest, and a few hauliers arrived in cars.

Staffordshire-based sheep and arable farmer Roger Hopley said the fine weather might have influenced the low turnout. 'Last week it was raining and we had nothing to do, so the turnout would have been excellent,' he said. 'This is the first fine day for a while, and the lads have a week's work to catch up on, so it's been quieter.'

Derbyshire farmer Harry Holland said: 'We were quite pleased with the way it was going this morning but it has gone a bit flat.'

No need for petrol panic-buying just yet.

Howard moved from one TV studio to another, to be interrogated now by Sky's Adam Boulton, who winkled another admission from him. Despite his 'liar' attacks on Blair, the Conservative leader said he thought the Iraq war was 'probably' legal.

'I have not seen the Attorney General's opinion. From where I see it I think it probably was. I think it was. But I have not seen the Attorney General's opinion,' he told Boulton.

'But let me tell you what I would have done differently. If I had had the Attorney General's opinion I would have taken it in full to the Cabinet. I would have had a full Cabinet discussion on it.

'They never saw the written opinion. The written opinion was never put before the Cabinet. If there was a written opinion that should have been placed before the Cabinet.'

Howard said he would have made sure that he knew that the infamous claim that Saddam Hussein's weapons could be deployed in 45 minutes related only to battlefield weapons. A Conservative government would then have corrected any misleading headlines, he insisted.

'There is nothing more serious than taking our country to war. And if you are going to do that most serious thing as Prime Minister, the one thing above all you have to be is straight with the British people.' Howard continued: 'My case is not that the intelligence was flawed. My case is that Mr Blair deliberately distorted the intelligence he was given.

'There is a huge difference between an honest belief that turns out to be wrong and misrepresenting what you were told to the British people.'

Iraq was about to claim another headline, too.

At 10.50 p.m., the contents of the front page of tomorrow's *Independent* newspaper became widely known.

Brian Sedgemore, 68, fully paid-up, if not founder, member of Labour's awkward squad, dogged opponent of the war – and of much else Blairite besides – who had decided not to contest his Hackney South and Shoreditch constituency after 27 years at Westminster, was quitting the party he had belonged to for 37 years . . . to join the Liberal Democrats. Kennedy said tonight in a statement:

> *Brian Sedgemore's message for other people who are considering voting Labour but who are unhappy with the party's policies on Iraq, tuition fees and civil liberties is clear.*
>
> *At this election, the only party which has taken principled stands on these issues is the Liberal Democrats. They should follow their beliefs and vote Liberal Democrat – certain in the knowledge that however they vote, Michael Howard's Conservatives cannot win this election.*

Which begs the question: If a dog hears two whistles, which way does he run?

Tuesday 26 April

Sedgemore was guest of honour at the Liberal Democrat press conference. With his teacher's jacket, check shirt and red tie, he still looked the very model of a veteran Labour backbencher. It would have been a brave, or foolhardy, 'spin nurse' who suggested some nice amber neckwear instead. The ex-MP pushed his large-framed square glasses up onto his nose and delivered his bitter valediction to the Labour Party. 'Only one thing can be said with certainty about the results of this general election,' he said.

> *The number of abstentions will be colossal, and who could blame the electorate. The public are surely right to hold politics and politicians in ill repute. What about the policies, ideas and values which will determine the result of this election?*
>
> *If being British does not entail a longing for liberty, then having such an identity is worthless. If a political party does not yearn for freedom based on the rule of law, habeas corpus and due protest, there is no point being a member of it or voting for it.*
>
> *It is against this background that I finally decided I could no longer support the Labour government and will join the Liberal Democrats.*
>
> *The idea and practice of Britain as a liberal country has always been under threat but it has taken a Labour prime minister to secure its demise. For Tony Blair, his scorn for liberal Britain is surprising for one who has an expensive liberal education and he entered politics as an aspirant liberal lawyer, an ardent member of CND and a standard-bearer for the left.*

Sedgemore insisted he was joining the Lib Dems to 'work for a nobler vision of Britain'.

He continued: 'All the deeply illiberal measures passed by the government were ferociously and heroically opposed by a number of backbench MPs, myself included, as well as by the Liberal Democrats collectively. I urge everyone from the centre and left in British politics to give Blair a bloody nose at the election and to vote for the Liberal Democrats in recognition of the fact that the tawdry New Labour project is dead.'

He added: 'The Tories have no chance of winning the election so the bogeyman Howard argument is very much an Aunt Sally, easily put up and even more easily knocked down.'

And he hinted that others might follow his lead, albeit not until after the election, saying there was a group of those similarly disaffected with Blair. 'I can be absolutely sure what I am saying is right because I was one of them.'

Cheekily asked if he was expecting a peerage in return for his defection, Sedgemore replied: 'No, I've got a wonderful place in the Gwaun Valley – five acres of land and an acre's lake, cormorants, herons, ducks, fish – and I think I'm going to have a lovely time down there in north Pembrokeshire – and I'm learning to speak Welsh.' Sounds a long way from Hackney, though.

Kennedy was clearly revelling in his coup: 'Brian Sedgemore's message for other people who are considering voting Labour but who are unhappy with the Party's policies on Iraq, tuition fees and civil liberties is clear, he said.

'At this election, the only party which has taken principled stands on these issues is the Liberal Democrats. We are a Liberal Democrat party and by definition that means we are not part of the control freak tendency of British politics.

'People are sick and tired of being spun and spun and spun again in British politics and that is not our approach.

'I think we are quintessentially, characteristically, instinctively a Liberal Democrat society in this country.'

Although even he tempered his enthusiasm by remarking that the big 'challenge and opportunity' for the party was to get hold of 'this innate sense of Liberal Democrat values' and convert it into votes for his party. Sedgemore's jumping-ship, long planned, was aimed at giving reassurance to Old Labour diehards and others in his old party with a grievance that it was 'safe' to vote Lib Dem and to counter Blair's argument that to do so risked letting the Tories in 'through the back door'. Although the ex-Labour MP may not be a household name, he is well known and (perhaps until today) respected in old left circles.

Blair, meanwhile, simply shrugged off Sedgemore's decision to swap sides. 'If he wants to choose to vote Liberal Democrat, and there's not going to be a Liberal Democrat government, that's up to him.

'What he does is up to him. He is not even a candidate at the election.'

He was speaking at the Lilian Baylis Technology School in Kennington, south London, an odd venue for a press conference and even odder given Blair's history of schools and election campaigns. He announced polling day in May 2001 not from Downing Street as he did this year, but standing in front of an impressive stained glass window in the main hall of the selective, church girls school St Saviour's and St Olave's just off the Old Kent Road. It was the very school that Harriet Harman had declined to send her daughter to three years previously, provoking unpleasant memories for some in the party. And it had a headmistress, Irene Bishop, who was not best pleased at her school being used for an election stunt. She also later publicly attacked the government's education budget and its plans for performance-related pay.

But Blair was on safer turf today – or so he thought. The Lilian Baylis Technology School had hit the headlines two years ago, when the then shadow home secretary Oliver Letwin, who lives nearby, said he would rather 'go out on the streets and beg' than send his children there. Letwin, now shadow Chancellor, later apologised for his remarks, made at a Tory Party annual conference fringe meeting in October 2003. But at the time they were attacked by headmaster Gary Phillips, who said they were upsetting for parents and children at the school.

Mr Phillips was still in charge, and he had nothing of the Mrs Bishops about him. He was unashamedly for Tony. Introducing the Prime Minister, ostensibly there to unveil a plaque commemorating the refurbishment of the school once he had finished hosting his news conference, reporters expected a few cursory remarks. But Mr Phillips waded in: 'I believe much of what we have done at Lilian Baylis has been made possible by the policy of this government. I believe the commitment of the Prime Minister and the government to schools like ours has been outstanding.

'Just as we have more to do at Lilian Baylis, so this government has more to do, and I personally hope they are elected to do it.'

He acknowledged that he was not supposed to be 'overtly political' on such occasions but insisted he had a 'unique insight' into the differences between the two main political parties and the politicians who led them. Insisting that he was not a member of any mainstream political party, Mr Phillips – sporting a collar whose top button badly needed doing up and a tie that needed straightening – said:

> When Oliver Letwin said he would rather beg on the streets than send his children here, it had a huge impact on the morale of our students. It took staff and families a long time to rebuild that morale.
>
> Our transformation into a good school was made possible by the resources and support the government has made available.
>
> I believe this government has made a difference – a difference to the life chances of our students.

It would be interesting to hear Mr Phillips being 'covertly' political. Thus effusively welcomed, Blair, alongside Education Secretary Kelly, went on to trumpet Labour's ambitions to refurbish the nation's schools and swat away questions about Sedgemore.

Alastair Campbell was spotted at the back of the schoolroom, lounging in characteristic pose: arms folded, against a wall, his eyes flicking across the assembled reporters like a buzzard surveying so many rabbits in a field. It is a truism in political presentation that the more stage-managed, micro-managed, spun and set up an event is, the more it is likely to go wrong. This is because anything that happens which is not in your plan is automatically something that has Gone Wrong. Something was about to go wrong. As Blair and Kelly moved from the schoolroom to the plaque-unveiling ceremony, several hundred pupils were lined up dutifully to welcome them. What happened next will be one of the enduring, and unsolvable, mysteries of this election campaign.

Most of the children clapped. Some, to the horror of staff and Labour's fixers, booed. Or did they?

Within minutes of the 'booing', Labour officials guided reporters to some of the youngsters, who they claimed had been making the relevant noise. They were invited to explain to the reporters what they had been doing.

The youngsters insisted that they had, in fact, been giving their VIP guests the warmest of welcomes to the school, which has sizeable numbers of students from various ethnic minorities.

The pupils insisted that they had been chanting the word 'boom' – a slang expression, said to be in south London argot roughly equivalent to 'hurray!' Mr Phillips backed up that interpretation, telling reporters: 'Different cultures celebrate in different ways.'

But other students told journalists that they had indeed been booing. Expert analysis was needed.

Within minutes, slang expert Tony Thorne, head of King's College Language Centre in London, who has compiled the Bloomsbury *Dictionary of Contemporary Slang*, confirmed 'boom' was a exclamation signifying 'approval or delight'. The term could have come from the US through hip-hop or from America, the Caribbean or 'home grown London black', he said.

He explained boom originally meant party or big celebration in black Caribbean language, adding: 'It has been around in black British for some time.'

But he was sceptical about whether the pupils' explanation was correct:

> *I think they are probably trying it on. They were probably booing and it is a good get-out because nobody really is expert in slang. You can tell people anything: kids often try it on.*
>
> *I can't believe they would see Ruth Kelly and shout 'boom, boom' in an exclamation of delight or praise, but it is certainly authentic.*

A full-scale crisis was now threatening to overwhelm the Labour presentational team. Sky News were running a super-text caption saying 'Pupils boo Blair at school' with viewers having to wait several seconds for a subsequent caption to say 'Some kids say they were shouting boom'. Blair left the school to catch his daily helicopter. From Battersea Heliport a Downing Street aide, seconded to the campaign team by virtue of their hybrid special adviser status, made an urgent phone call: 'The kids were saying Boh! It's a greeting. DJs have used it when Tony has had a private meeting with them. It's Boh!'

Doh!

These issues need to be closed down, you see. Eight hours later, Mr Phillips issued a statement.

> *Contrary to reports in some sections of the media, the Prime Minister was not 'booed' in a negative manner by students at Lilian Baylis Technology School this morning.*
>
> *The sounds the journalist misinterpreted for booing were simply the pupils welcoming Tony Blair in their own way.*
>
> *The 'boo', 'boom', or 'booyakka' is a familiar term that means 'excellent', as the pupils themselves explained to journalists at the venue at the time.*
>
> *They were in fact very happy to see Tony Blair and we were all grateful for his visit this morning.*

Yeah, as Blair might say. But what about Boh!?

John Prescott was not having a good day, either. He has been running a largely invisible campaign touring the country by coach in his egg-attracting Prescott Express. But at home in the Humberside village of Sutton, near Hull, all was not well for wife Pauline. In the early hours of the morning, Greenpeace protesters struck. Eight scaled onto the roof and erected a solar panel. Hanging below the ramparts, they displayed two large fluorescent banners saying 'Oi, 2 jags! Hit targets not voters' above the Greenpeace logo.

Prescott was not amused. A spokeswoman refused to reveal his whereabouts as she released his statement to the PA. It said: 'I do not intend to add to what is now clearly a publicity stunt.

'However, in the early hours of this morning these people terrorised my wife which I find utterly deplorable.'

TV pictures showed the mysterious Mr Prescott arriving a few minutes later in Gloucester. He moved on to Stourbridge and had recovered his humour. As he finished his unscripted address at the Swan pub, on Hagley Road, he quipped: 'I've just got to go and have a cup of tea with Greenpeace.' Prescott later spoke to reporters and repeated his condemnation of the protesters.

'I just think it's a deplorable publicity stunt, particularly as I was one of the negotiators at Kyoto,' he said.

'It was a terrifying incident for my wife in the early hours of the morning to see people scrambling up ladders on to the house. That's just unacceptable.' He added: 'I feel very strongly about my wife being terrorised by people at 5 a.m. and 6 a.m. in the morning. Wives shouldn't be there for terrorising.'

Before going their separate ways across the country, the three party leaders came together in a rare – but entirely genuine – display of unity when they joined the Queen at the unveiling of a memorial in the Mall to all police officers killed in the line of duty.

But the occasion also served to highlight the advantages of campaigning from government. Only Blair got to speak.

Tearing up a prepared Downing Street script, he said:

> *The purpose of this memorial is very, very simple. It is to say thank you to those police officers that have been killed in the service of their local community and in the service of their country.*
>
> *Thank you for your courage, thank you for your dedication, thank you for your commitment. Through them and through this memorial we thank all the police officers in our country today. We thank them for the work that they do. We thank them for being there when we need them.*
>
> *We thank them for their service and their dedication. Sometimes they pay for this dedication with their lives but every day and in every way they help people, help them even in the most difficult circumstances, help them when they know themselves they are in grave and serious danger.*
>
> *It takes a remarkable type of person to give such service.*

He ended: 'And through the memories of these officers who have been slain, people can remember every day the work they do and give thanks for it.' No spin doctor required.

Howard, meanwhile, was supposed to be having an MRSA Day again. He was also having another opposition leader day when the toast just lands butter side down.

At his morning news conference, Howard highlighted his party's £10 million campaign to combat the bug, putting matron back in charge. Shadow Health Secretary Andrew Lansley – unfortunately as it turned out – reminded reporters: 'Hand washing is important.'

Howard could afford to be dismissive of Sedgemore when asked about the overnight development. He joked that the former Labour MP was not 'very high on our list of target converts'.

He added: 'I am very realistic about the things we can and can't hope for in this election. I do not think that Brian Sedgemore was ever very high on our list of target converts. The fact that he has chosen to go to the Liberal Democrats is something we can accept with a fair degree of equanimity.'

And with that the Conservative leader went off to provide a 'visual context' for his theme of the day at London's National Hospital for Neurology and Neuro Surgery. He dutifully scrubbed up and washed his hands with alcohol gel before meeting patients. But . . .

But he failed to repeat the process between shaking hands with patients Sallie Hillman and Sophie Merrington. An aide reminded him, too late, to use the bedside dispensers before he went on to talk to other patients on the Lady Ann Allerton ward.

Catherine Cook, the hospital's infection control nurse, said the gel should be applied 'before you touch a patient and after you touch a patient to disinfect your hands'.

Conservative HQ rushed out a statement:

Michael Howard washed his hands with alcohol gel before he entered the ward and at least a further three times when he was on the ward.

If he inadvertently failed to do so between these two patients, he regrets this very much. This issue – for very personal reasons – is one he takes extremely seriously.

Howard's mother-in-law, as he had reminded voters, died from a hospital-acquired infection.

Jean Lawrence, chair of the Infection Control Nurses' Association, said all members of the public, not only politicians, should be aware of their actions in a hospital situation.

'I think it is a message to all of us, that we should all be considering it and it's every member of the public and not just politicians,' she said. Ms Lawrence said that doctors, physiotherapists and other health workers all had contact with patients and needed to be aware of hygiene issues. 'It's not only about putting alcohol gels in place, but about seeing that it [hand-cleaning] is done,' she added.

Kennedy was also at a hospital – but having an altogether jollier time. Speaking on a visit to the University Hospital of North Durham he said: 'Brian Sedgemore – 27 years a Labour MP – leaving the Labour Party and joining the Lib Dems and urging former Labour voters to do the same. I think that is indicative of what is a massive shift of grassroots Labour opinion away from the government, not just on Iraq but on other issues as well.' Mr Kennedy toured a children's ward in the hospital, assiduously washing his hands before meeting each patient, thereby avoiding the pitfall Howard had fallen into earlier. He said: 'At least one party leader can say, "My hands are clean".'

Oh, do play nicely.

He zipped on to a tub-thumping rally in Cambridge. Dozens of supporters were shut outside as the hall was filled to overflowing. Kennedy described the atmosphere as 'revivalist'.

Blair was rallying the faithful, too, in full 'Campaign Tony' mode. He addressed nine hundred Labour supporters amid the civic splendour of Liverpool's St George's Hall, arguing his case that the Conservative strategy was to demoralise voters about the state of Britain and thereby persuade them to stay away from the polls.

Speaking without notes and pacing up and down the stage, Blair – accompanied to the event by his wife Cherie – urged Labour voters to see through the plan and ensure a high turnout on 5 May.

Blair, buoyed by an inevitable standing ovation as he entered the hall, told supporters:

> *I simply say to the people of this country, understand this Tory strategy: it is devious, it is underhand, it is back-door.*
>
> *But let us make sure it is not effective. Let us make sure it does not work. Because I do not believe that the people of this country want to go back to that Tory government, but we have got to make sure that that does not happen.*
>
> *We have got to get every single person out to vote.*

The Tories back in London were taking the wraps of their latest weapon. It was a poster ramming home their attack on Blair's character. It portrayed his face against a red backdrop with the words: 'If he's prepared to lie to take us to war, he's prepared to lie to win an election.' In a take-off of Blair's own slogan it added: 'If you value the truth, vote for it'.

Conservative co-chairman Liam Fox said: 'Trust is now at the centre of this election campaign. We've had eight years of broken promises by Tony Blair. We think it's time to replace a Prime Minister who has a callous disregard for truth and untruth.'

Dr Fox – he is a real medical doctor – defended the personalised attack on Blair's honesty, insisting the election was now being fought over questions of 'truth, trust and honesty'.

But will we ever find out the truth about boo, boom and booyakka?

Wednesday 27 April

Scotland is not just another country, as far as Westminster politicians are concerned. It is an entirely different country. One Blair aide on a visit there during another general election campaign was heard to mutter: 'The sooner we're out of this [expletive deleted] place, the better.' Politics are tribal in Scotland, the public debate and journalism livelier, and events even more unpredictable. But all party leaders have to venture there. Today it was Howard's turn, and the surest touch-stone for all opposition politicians who want to play safe is to promise to keep the Scottish infantry regiments the government wants to amalgamate as part of its army reorganisation. The Conservatives are the lost tartan tribe, with only one MP north of the border after the last election, and they have to try and be seen to be trying.

'It's wonderful to be here in Edinburgh today,' said Howard as he addressed reporters in a hotel. 'For the last few weeks, Conservative candidates have been setting out our action plan for Scotland. Two issues stand out. First there is the question of tax. And second, Scotland's historic infantry regiments. They've both been tests of Mr Blair's character.'

Nod to Scotland. Then back on the attack. Howard basically, as the media would say, kept his standard anti-Blair script and 'put a kilt on it'. He was going to play truth or dare with Blair again – a tricky game for politicians to indulge in. But one with which Blair was more than familiar.

In November 1997, a few months after taking power, a row blew up over Labour's relationship with Formula One boss Bernie Ecclestone who had donated £1 million to the party. There was the question of a ban on tobacco sponsorship in sport which would affect Formula One. Blair argued for an exemption for Grand Prix racing. The obvious link was made. Blair's integrity was impugned. He went on TV to set the record straight.

'I hope that people know me well enough and realise the type of person I am, to realise that I would never do anything either to harm the country or anything improper. I never have. I think most people who have dealt with me think I'm a pretty straight sort of guy and I am,' he told John Humphrys on the BBC's *On The Record* magazine programme.

'I couldn't understand that anyone would impugn my motives in taking the decisions that I did. You know I guess I should have, you know we should learn the lesson of that and when something like this happens again, you deal with it quicker and in a better way and we should have done that.' Fast-forward eight years. Howard had certainly impugned the PM, and was determined to carry on doing it.

In Edinburgh the Conservative leader pressed on: 'The message I think people should send to Mr Blair is: "We have had enough of your broken promises, we have had enough of your talk, we have had enough of you".

'Mr Blair doesn't like being held accountable, but I think it's very important he should be held accountable. I think that's what general elections should be about.'

He told voters: '5 May is your chance to tell Mr Blair where to get off.' Howard stressed he still supported the war to oust Saddam Hussein but added: 'You could have gone to war and told the truth. That's what Mr Blair didn't do.' Asked by a reporter if he had ever told a lie, the Conservative leader responded: 'I'm not aware of any occasion when I have deliberately or knowingly misled people and that's the charge I make against Mr Blair.' The feud between the two appeared to be becoming ever more personal, at least on the Tories' part, as the hours went by.

Blair was in Bolton for a speech on education – a familiar tactic by now: while the Tories want to talk about 'personal stuff', the Prime Minister spells out his vision for the country. But he began by saying the Tories had an 'inept' economic plan and had campaigned on immigration 'in a profoundly unpleasant way'. He went on: 'Finally, when that fails, they turn to personal attacks on me.

'My response? I will carry on talking about the issues that matter to the hard-working families of this country: the economy, the NHS, our schools, law and order.

'I don't care in the least about the Tory attacks on my character. I do care about the future of this country. I will continue to expose the choice this nation faces on 5 May. I will talk about policy. I will talk about values.'

Labour held no news conference this morning, but at the Liberal Democrats' dawn chorus Kennedy found even his education proposals – already published – drowned out by questions about the Howard–Blair drama unfolding. Kennedy said the Tories had 'concluded they are losing this election', causing them to mount 'the most negative form of personalised campaign'. He added: 'It won't do them any good. I think they are the losing team in this election while we are looking increasingly the team which is winning.'

He again refused to follow the Conservatives and brand Blair a liar. 'I've not used that particular four-letter word. I'm not persuaded it's guaranteed to be true.'

Kennedy said that he still believed Mr Blair 'was sincere in his views at the time' on Iraq. He continued: 'And I feel he was wrong in his views and political judgement.

'That's how we've approached it from start to finish, I'm not about to change that fundamental judgement.'

Blair, shirt-sleeved in Bolton, was sticking to his message: 'Let the Tories keep up their personal attacks on me. I will keep setting out the policy choices that matter to the British people.

'Let them go negative, negative, negative. I will stay focused on education, education, education – yesterday, today, and tomorrow.'

But the folk memory of the Ecclestone affair was still there for at least two members of Blair's campaign team: his head of communications David Hill – who had been running Labour's media operation at the time, before leaving to join an outside firm – and the man he had ultimately come back to replace at No. 10, Alastair Campbell. Something would have to be done, sooner rather than later, to take the issue head-on. The ideal solution, in classic Campbell style, would be to 1: Knock the 'liar' jibe on the head; 2: provide a substitute story to fill the vacuum and knock it off the headlines.

Less profound thoughts than the integrity of the Prime Minister were troubling Kennedy as he carried on campaigning on education. He visited Weston Park Primary School in Hornsey, north London, where he was questioned again by pupils. He told the children that too little attention was being paid to the environment during the election campaign. 'We are saying a lot in this election about green issues. It is the biggest single issue facing all of us long-term. I don't think there's been nearly enough talk about the environment.'

He also gave his backing to a ban on smoking in public places: 'I am a sinner myself but even so I think the rights of those who choose not to smoke should prevail because it is bad for us.'

Kennedy told the children that Blair had done a number of good things since coming to power. But he said he had also done an awful lot of things which he disagreed with.

'I think we could do better as a country if we had people like us arguing for the sort of things we are talking about.'

Asked what his favourite food was, he opted for steak pie made by his local butcher and also revealed he was 'a bit of an ice-cream addict'.

Howard's plans for a campaign visit to Staffordshire had to be abandoned when his helicopter developed a technical fault for the second time on his leader's tour. He caught a scheduled flight back to London instead, which bumped through thunder-laden clouds as lightning flashed across the sky. Blair had a stormy flight back, too, with one report claiming his plane had actually been hit by lightning. It wasn't, but it was not the most comfortable journey preparing for a pre-arranged interview with Adam Boulton of Sky News at their Millbank studios over the road from a deserted parliament. Hill and Campbell, increasingly seen out and about with The Boss, thought through the lines to take for the programme which would go out at 7 p.m., after a pre-record at 3.45 p.m.

Boulton is a robust interviewer, unflappable and with a work schedule that would bear fine comparison to Blair's own, if not exceed it. He likes to get stories. And he got two. Maybe three.

1: Nail the jibe.

Blair told Boulton:

> *I have never told a lie. No. I don't intend to go telling lies to people. I did not lie over Iraq.*
>
> *I don't want to get into a debate with people who want to trade insults. What I would like to do is debate the policy and the future of the country.*
>
> *In the end you can play the ball or play the man and if they play the man that's probably because they don't dare play the ball.*
>
> *You have got a Conservative Party whose economic plan has collapsed, whose health service plan they do not want to debate, neither their education policy.*
>
> *We're the only party in this campaign actually making speeches on policy.*

2: Fill the vacuum
What about the euro?

AB: It doesn't look very likely at the moment that your economics are going to change dramatically.

TB: At the moment it doesn't look very likely, does it, because the economics aren't in the right place.

If the economics aren't right, if it won't help your country economically, you don't do it. Now, at the moment there is no part of business and industry clamouring to say we need this for our economy, so it doesn't look very likely.

Those in the know said that Blair had even pointed out the newsworthy nature of his remarks, following as they did a speech by Brown earlier this week in which he had hardly enthused about the single currency.

And the referendum on the EU Constitution? After all, Blair had always said, and in parliament to boot, that there would be a poll in the UK no matter what other countries did. But France was due to vote on 29 May and opinion pollsters there said Jacques Chirac's chances of a 'yes' vote were looking shaky.

'If there is still a constitution, there has got to be a referendum on it,' shimmied Blair. 'If what was to happen was France was to say "no" and then the rest of Europe were to tear up the constitution and say we're forgetting about it – you wouldn't have a [referendum] on nothing.'

Reporters and TV producers began ringing each other as soon as word of Blair's assorted comments began to filter round Westminster. Just suppose there had been a strategy – well, it looked like it would have worked.

3: And don't forget Gordon . . .

Brown gave an interview to the BBC *Ten O'Clock News*, which was played out earlier on radio outlets.

Asked whether he personally trusted Blair, he responded: 'Yes, I do. He is not only respected internationally and nationally, we are part of a team that is working for a common purpose.'

Challenged on whether Blair was a liar, Brown said:

I don't think that's correct at all.

Anybody who has worked with Tony Blair over the Iraq war knows that those were difficult decisions to make, but that the central issue in the Iraq war was 'Should we allow Saddam Hussein to continue to ignore, for year after year, the decisions of the international community?'

The war was right because Saddam Hussein should not be allowed to continue to ignore the decisions of the international community. If we had left Saddam Hussein in a position where he could continue to ignore the decisions of the international community, then the world would not be as safe as it is now and we would not have a democratic Iraq.

Asked whether Blair had told 'the whole truth' over Iraq, Brown responded: 'Yes, Mr Blair did tell the truth.'

Asked if he would personally have taken the same decision to go to war Brown said simply: 'This was a collective decision. It was a team decision. We have collective responsibility in our country. Governments make decisions, not individuals, and this was a team decision that was made.' OK, but don't forget also that Gordon will be Gordon.

Howard, safely back in the capital, went to Barnes in west London and ploughed right on, unaware of Blair and Brown's comments which had yet to be broadcast.

The Conservative leader had already today come in for criticism from party heavyweight Ken Clarke, and a bishop, for his hardline attacks on Blair. Clarke said he was 'not sure' he would have sanctioned the 'liar' poster unveiled last night.

The Bishop of Oxford, the Right Reverend Richard Harries suggested the Tories 'could have made the same point more honestly'. He said it was 'quite wrong' to suggest Mr Blair was 'somehow fundamentally dishonest'. Howard rejected the criticism, saying: 'I'm not going to be stopped from telling the truth. When something needs to be said I will say it. I will carry on saying it.'

He added for good measure: 'We are going to put the do-gooders back in their box and the criminals behind bars.'

The Liverpool fan then reserved the evening to watch his Reds take on Chelsea at Stamford Bridge in the Champions League semi-final first leg. Some other bits on the TV news might have caught his eye as the evening wore on. Or if he was really channel-hopping there was another Labour Party election broadcast scheduled, spelling out the choice between 'investment in education or Tory cuts' or 'an NHS that's free or Tory charges'.

But out and about in the country, away from the TV studios, there was that other election going on – the one the leaders keep talking about, the by-election-style fights deciding who goes to parliament.

A Labour parliamentary candidate today apologised to a family of mourners who were approached by canvassers as they waited for a funeral. Carol Hughes, her partner and daughter were sat in a black funeral limousine before her father's funeral when the activist knocked on the window and asked which way she would be voting.

A Labour Party spokeswoman said the canvasser, in Stroud, Gloucestershire, had made a genuine mistake and thought it was a limousine hired for a wedding.

The candidate, David Drew, who has been the MP for Stroud since 1997, has written to Ms Hughes.

His spokeswoman Hilary Fowles said:

David has written a complete, whole-hearted apology for the incident. It is very unfortunate.

The poor woman who was canvassing is mortified because she made a stupid mistake.

She saw the black limo and she thought it was a wedding car, she went up and told them to have a nice day.

A colleague then said to her 'For God's sake, it's a funeral', and she thought she would make it worse if she went back.

She saw people in smart hats and she just had a complete mental aberration.

The woman is now delivering leaflets rather than canvassing. There is no way she would have done this deliberately, she is devastated.

Describing the incident, which happened about ten days ago, Ms Hughes told the *Stroud News and Journal*:

I was in the funeral car outside my house because the car was early.

We were sitting there waiting to depart – myself, my partner and my daughter.

Two women came by and started to talk to us. My daughter leaned over and said, 'Not now, please,' but they just carried on.

I opened the car door and they said, 'Just wanted to ask you if you're voting Labour this time'.

I told them I would, just to get rid of them, at which one of them replied 'Oh good – have a nice day.'

I don't think they even took it in. They just didn't seem to bother. It was quite unnecessary. They were more interested in whether I was going to vote Labour than that I was in a funeral car.

I find it quite upsetting and insensitive and I couldn't believe they would bother anyone at that time. There's a time and a place for everything and that wasn't it.

I might well have voted Labour, but if that is how they treat their voters I don't think so now.

A vote lost, an unhappy memory for Ms Hughes.

And still some uncomfortable viewing for Blair, Campbell and Hill. You think you're in control of events – but you can't control everything.

Channel Four News revived the *Mail on Sunday*'s Iraq story about the Attorney General Lord Goldsmith's claimed equivocation about the legality of the conflict. But unlike the newspaper it broadcast what it said were pictures of the actual document itself.

And its account of the 7 March advice was more detailed than the newspaper's, although that may simply have been for space reasons when the paper was splashing its coverage. It was on 17 March that Lord Goldsmith had declared the war legal to the Cabinet.

Channel Four also broadcast what it said were extracts from letters exchanged about the legal advice.

The Lib Dems' deputy leader Sir Menzies Campbell told the programme: 'What we now have are ten lost days between the 7th of March and the 17th of March, in the course of which the Attorney General who had previously been of the view that war was of doubtful legality somehow coming to the conclusion that it was legal. That's why we must now have a full account of his reasoning.'

The *Guardian* tonight released a poll to be published in its first edition tomorrow. Blair's personal rating had shot up six points to 44 over the last week in the 'who would make the best PM' stakes, despite some of the public perceiving him as 'slippery and a liar'.

Overall, Labour increased its lead by one point to a seven-point gap over the Tories – 40 per cent to 33 per cent was how the parties stood.

Thursday 28 April

Nine hundred miles from the westernmost tip of Europe, and four hours' flying time from London, lies Lajes Field airbase on Terceira Island in the Azores, a Portuguese dependency. Its red-roofed, whitewashed houses are home to 55,000 people living among its rolling hills.

And there, in a glorified NAAFI building looking down on one of the United States' most strategic airbases, gathered Prime Minister Blair, President George W. Bush, Spanish premier Jose Maria Aznar and their host, Portuguese Prime Minister Jose Manual Barroso on Sunday 16 March 2003.

They were making their final preparations for a war about to be unleashed four days later against Saddam Hussein's regime in Iraq.

On board Blair's chartered British Airways 777 jet on the way over, his civil service official spokesman Tom Kelly had told reporters: 'These are difficult times for the diplomatic track. Time is short.' And he added: 'The Attorney General will want to let it be known that under existing resolutions there is a legal basis for action.'

The following day, 17 March, the Attorney General Lord Goldsmith published a parliamentary written answer doing just that. It said:

> Authority to use force against Iraq exists from the combined effect of Resolutions 678, 687 and 1441. All of these resolutions were adopted under Chapter VII of the UN Charter which allows the use of force for the express purpose of restoring international peace and security:

1. *In Resolution 678, the Security Council authorised force against Iraq, to eject it from Kuwait and to restore peace and security in the area.*

2. *In Resolution 687, which set out the ceasefire conditions after Operation Desert Storm, the Security Council imposed continuing obligations on Iraq to eliminate its weapons of mass destruction in order to restore international peace and security in the area. Resolution 687 suspended but did not terminate the authority to use force under Resolution 678.*

3. *A material breach of Resolution 687 revives the authority to use force under Resolution 678.*

4. *In Resolution 1441, the Security Council determined that Iraq has been and remains in material breach of Resolution 687, because it has not fully complied with its obligations to disarm under that resolution.*

5. *The Security Council in Resolution 1441 gave Iraq 'a final opportunity to comply with its disarmament obligations' and warned Iraq of the 'serious consequences' if it did not.*

6. *The Security Council also decided in Resolution 1441 that, if Iraq failed at any time to comply with and cooperate fully in the implementation of Resolution 1441, that would constitute a further material breach.*

7. *It is plain that Iraq has failed so to comply and therefore Iraq was at the time of Resolution 1441 and continues to be in material breach.*

8. *Thus, the authority to use force under Resolution 678 has revived and so continues today.*

9. *Resolution 1441 would in terms have provided that a further decision of the Security Council to sanction force was required if that had been intended. Thus, all that Resolution 1441 requires is reporting to and discussion by the Security Council of Iraq's failures, but not an express further decision to authorise force.*

The trail from Lajes Field ended in the City of London this morning, as Blair, Brown and Industry Secretary Hewitt faced industry leaders and reporters, ostensibly to launch Labour's business manifesto. But all the media really wanted to talk about was the leak last night first to Channel Four, then to the BBC, of the conclusions of the Attorney's earlier, 7 March 2003 thirteen-page note to the Prime Minister – first revealed in the *Mail on Sunday* – which made reference to the detailed legal argument involved in sanctioning military conflict.

The TV coverage the night before had generated more front-page 'Liar' headlines, based on the fact that Blair had said Goldsmith's advice had not changed between 7 March and 17 March. The leak appeared to show it had. In fact, on objective reading the advice had not changed. But to read objectively, you needed to see the full document.

Blair had so far steadfastly refused to publish the note, classified 'Secret', citing precedent that legal advice to ministers should remain private and privileged. But there is a tide in the affairs of election campaigns which, if taken at the flood, can swamp your opponents. Blair was about to try to catch the tide.

But first, the Tories had their own morning news conference, supposed to focus on plans to tackle indiscipline in schools. Howard made a token reference, then went straight onto the offensive:

> *Last night we received devastating new information which exposed that when Mr Blair said 'I have never lied', he was not telling the truth.*
>
> *The questions that this new information raises are serious and profound.*
>
> *It's important for the British people to understand what has happened and what the implications are.*

Howard said that the Prime Minister had told the public that the Attorney General's advice had made it 'very clear' that an invasion would be legal.

Last night, official documents obtained by the media proved that on 7 March the Attorney General gave legal advice that was full of qualifications and warnings.

We've been told by Mr Blair that on 17 March – just ten days later – the advice given by the Attorney General to Cabinet was clear and it hadn't changed.

We now know beyond any doubt that it had changed.

So the first question Mr Blair has to answer is, why did he say advice hadn't changed when we know it had?

The second question that needs to be answered is, what or who changed the Attorney General's legal advice?

The Tory leader stressed: 'The issue of Iraq boils down to one very simple question: if you cannot trust Mr Blair on the decision to take the country to war, the most important decision that any Prime Minister can take, how can you trust Mr Blair on anything else, ever again?'

Faced with a barrage of questions about his own position on the war, the Conservative leader insisted it was Tony Blair, and not him, who should be put on the spot.

He said: 'What is at issue here is not my conduct – it was Mr Blair who took the country to war; it is Mr Blair who has to answer these questions; it is Mr Blair's character that is an issue and the extent to which the people can trust him.'

Blair, Brown and Hewitt, at the HQ of the Bloomberg financial wire service, staged their set-piece mini-manifesto launch, the PM openly acknowledging at the start that reporters would probably have other things on their minds. He was not disappointed as he was bombarded with questions about how Goldsmith came to present to the Cabinet, parliament and the public, a far more emphatic opinion that the war was legal, within a few days of having apparently written a document which suggested that he would have preferred to have seen a second United Nations resolution specifically authorising the use of force.

The PM hit back: 'Let us just be quite clear about this. The key thing was, was the Attorney General advising it was lawful to proceed.

'This so-called smoking gun has turned out to be a damp squib, because he did advise it was lawful to proceed.'

Brown and Hewitt rallied to the cause. And if anybody doubted that for the duration of the campaign at least it really was 'Team TB-GB' they soon had those doubts dispelled.

Mr Brown, asked if he would have proceeded with the war in the same way as Mr Blair, replied simply: 'Yes' – which attracted, bizarrely, a round of applause from the businessmen.

He went on: 'I not only trust Tony Blair but I respect Tony Blair for the way he went about that decision.'

Ms Hewitt added: 'When the Attorney General came to the Cabinet meeting, he gave us his advice that conflict would be lawful and he spelt out to us that although a second resolution would have been preferable, it wasn't essential. Its absence did not make the conflict unlawful.'

And Blair had something up his sleeve.

Challenged to publish, at last, the partially leaked thirteen-page Goldsmith note, he stunned reporters, who had expected his stock reply. Instead, with a casual wave of a hand he told them: 'You have probably got it all anyway. I see no reason not to publish it.'

Within an hour it was posted on the Downing Street website, after civil servants – normally neutral observers during an election campaign, safe in early-cut, long-lunch purdah – had been sent scuttling into action.

Labour can fix most things, but the release of a classified document from the Attorney General to the Prime Minister is not yet among them. Blair had decided that rather than wait for more drip-drip revelations based on partial sightings of the note, he might just as well seek to close the issue down by publishing the whole thing.

It was headed 'Secret' above the seal of the Attorney General, who laid out a 36-point summary of argument and conclusion. It was headed 'Iraq: Resolution 1441', and began: 'You have asked me for advice on the legality of military action against Iraq without a further resolution of the Security Council.'

He advised that there were three possible bases for the use of force – self-defence, action to avert overwhelming humanitarian catastrophe, or authorisation by the Security Council acting under Chapter VII of the United Nations Charter.

On self-defence, he argued that there must be 'some degree of imminence' to the threat to justify action. He acknowledged that the United States had been arguing for 'a broad doctrine of a right to use force to pre-empt danger in the future'.

But Lord Goldsmith said: 'If this means more than a right to respond proportionately to an imminent attack (and I understand that the doctrine is intended to carry that connotation) this is not a doctrine which, in my opinion, exists or is recognised in law.'

On action to avert an overwhelming humanitarian catastrophe, he said that he knew of no reason why it would apply in the prevailing circumstances.

On Security Council authorisation, he said that the question was whether Resolution 1441, which gave Iraq a final opportunity to cooperate with the UN weapons inspectors (UNMOVIC), revived the explicit authorisation to use force in Resolution 678 which was passed in 1990 after Saddam Hussein invaded Kuwait.

Lord Goldsmith said that the 'revival argument' had been used to justify air strikes by Britain and the US against Iraq in 1993 and 1998.

'The revival argument is controversial. It is not widely accepted among academic commentators. However, I agree with my predecessors' advice on this issue,' he said. 'I disagree, therefore, with those commentators and lawyers who assert that nothing less than an explicit authorisation to use force in a Security Council resolution will be sufficient.'

On the issue of whether 1441 was sufficient to revive the authorisation for the use of force, he said that the text made clear that if Iraq failed to comply with its requirement, there had to be further discussion in the Security Council.

'The text is, however, ambiguous and unclear on what happens next,' he said. There were two competing arguments – that if the Council failed to reach a conclusion the authorisation to use force remained OR that nothing short of a new resolution would provide a legitimate basis for the use of force. He noted that in the negotiations which led to 1441, it had been an 'essential negotiating point' for the US that they should not concede the need for a second resolution and that they were convinced that they had succeeded.

'I was impressed by the strength and sincerity of the views of the US administration which I heard in Washington on this point,' he said. However, the difficulty is that we are reliant on their assertions for the view that the French (and others) knew and accepted that they were voting for a further discussion and no more.

'We have very little hard evidence of this beyond a couple of telegrams recording admission by French negotiators that they knew the US would not accept a resolution which required a further council decision.

'A further difficulty is that, if the matter ever came before a court, it is very uncertain to what extent the court would accept evidence of the negotiating history to support a particular interpretation of the resolution, given that most of the negotiations were conducted in private and there are no agreed or official records.'

In his summary, Lord Goldsmith said that the language of 1441 left the position unclear. In these circumstances, I remain of the opinion that the safest legal course would be to secure the adoption of a further resolution to authorise the use of force,' he said.

'Nevertheless, having regard to the information on the negotiating history which I have been given and to the arguments of the US administration which I heard in Washington, I accept that a reasonable case can be made that Resolution 1441 is capable in principle of reviving the authorisation in 678 without a further resolution.'

He emphasised that the argument was only sustainable if there were 'strong factual grounds' for concluding that Iraq had failed to take its final opportunity to comply. In other words, we would need to be able to demonstrate hard evidence of non-compliance and non-cooperation. Given the structure of the resolution as a whole, the views of UNMOVIC and the IAEA [International Atomic Energy Agency] will be highly significant in this respect,' he said.

'In the light of the latest reporting by UNMOVIC, you will need to consider extremely carefully whether the evidence of non-cooperation and non-compliance by Iraq is sufficient to justify the conclusion that Iraq has failed to take its final opportunity.'

He said British action against Iraq in 1998 and in Kosovo in 1999 had been sanctioned by his predecessors on the basis that the case for legality was no more than reasonably arguable. But he cautioned:

'A "reasonable case" does not mean that if the matter ever came before a court, I would be confident that the court would agree with this view.

'It must be recognised that on previous occasions when military action was taken on the basis of a reasonably arguable case, the degree of public and parliamentary scrutiny of the legal issue was nothing like as great as it is today.'

He also warned that there was 'no basis in law' for arguing that an 'unreasonable veto' by the French in the Security Council would entitle Britain to proceed on the basis of 'presumed Security Council authorisation'.

'If we fail to achieve the adoption of a second resolution, we would need to consider urgently at that stage the strength of our legal case in the light of the circumstances at that time,' he said.

Lord Goldsmith warned that there were a number of ways in which opponents of military action could seek to bring a legal action – either internationally or through the domestic courts – against the UK, members of the government or British military personnel.

'Some of these seem fairly remote possibilities, but given the strength of opposition to military action against Iraq, it would not be surprising if some attempts were made to get a case of some sort off the ground,' he said. 'We cannot be certain that they would not succeed.'

He emphasised that any military action must be 'proportionate' to the objective of securing Iraqi compliance with its obligations to disarm.

'That is not to say that action may not be taken to remove Saddam Hussein from power if it can be demonstrated that such action is a necessary and proportionate measure to secure the disarmament of Iraq,' he said.

'But regime change cannot be an objective of military action. This should be borne in mind in considering the list of military targets and in making public statements about any campaign.'

Goldsmith had been consistent. He had said from the outset that 1441 revived the authority for military action in 678 and that no further Security Council resolution was needed to make a reasonably arguable case in international law that the conflict would be legal.

Asked to harden his advice into an opinion on 17 March with war three days away, that was the opinion he gave, following the precedent of Operation Desert Fox in 1998 and Nato's Kosovo campaign.

But the publication of the document was still a campaign bombshell, genuinely wiping away media coverage of any other issue for the first time since the announcement of polling day.

Journalists and opposition politicians pored over the densely typed A4 pages, revelling in the sheer novelty of holding documents marked 'Secret'. Shadow Attorney General Dominic Grieve told BBC Radio 4's *World at One* programme:

'Parliament and the Cabinet were deceived.

'The Prime Minister has repeatedly said that what parliament and the Cabinet saw was a fair summary of the Attorney General's formal, legal opinion. It was no such thing – by no stretch of the imagination can the one be equated with the other.

'That appears to be a fabrication by the Prime Minister.'

Liberal Democrat foreign affairs spokesman Sir Menzies Campbell said he had never argued that the Prime Minister lied 'but I do think that the Prime Minister may, as a strategy of staying close to the Americans, have persuaded himself that military action was the only course that was open to the government.

'As a consequence his judgement, and his competence in these matters, was affected to the extent that obstacles or inhibitions had to be discarded by whatever means were available.'

Kennedy said: 'What is clear from this – and it seems to be a very well argued and balanced legal advice – is that there is a good 50 per cent of doubt of legality in the absence of a second UN resolution.

'What we don't know is what further advice was then given, from the Foreign Secretary, from Sir Jeremy Greenstock, from No. 10 itself, based on what Dr Hans Blix was telling them, that led him to his final conclusion. I think those facts will have to be put in the public domain as well.'

Speaking on a visit to Rochdale Infirmary, Kennedy criticised the Prime Minister for dismissing the leak as a 'damp squib'. He said: 'I think the fact the Prime Minister had used such an unfortunate phrase as damp squib shows just how out of touch and cocooned he has become.

'This is not a damp squib for those who have lost loved ones in the service of the British armed forces or for the families of thousands of Iraqi innocents who have been killed.

'It is not a damp squib in terms of legitimate public opinion in this country. I think Mr Blair needs to put things back in perspective.

'I think also there is a genuine question to be answered in the conclusion in the Attorney General's advice that we have now seen in full. That is, he talks about the need to use proportionate force in terms of influencing or taking punitive action against Saddam Hussein and his regime. Was the invasion and the slaughter of thousands of Iraqi civilians proportionate force? I think the court of world opinion will be very harsh in judging that.'

The three party leaders were booked for a unique event tonight. For years, the Holy Grail of TV election coverage has been to secure a televised debate between the main contenders. The prime minister of the day, Tory or Labour, has always declined. Only the challenger really has anything to gain from a showdown.

However, on this occasion all three did agree to be questioned consecutively, for 30 minutes each, in the same studio by a BBC1 *Question Time* audience, moderated by David Dimbleby. It was a genuine first in that tiny world where TV people live. The leaders had had to blank off most of their diary for the day to prepare.

Kennedy began in the hot seat, in the east London theatre chosen as the venue. Reporters were kept away and not told the location in advance, although the Stop the War coalition somehow discovered it.

Iraq still dominated most of the questioning. Kennedy said: 'We can't even turn round as a country and say how many innocent

Iraqis did die because we've never bothered to do the body count.

'When I say "not in my name, Mr Blair", it's not just that I disagreed with the government and the policy; I am ashamed of what the government did in the name of our country,' he added to applause.

Kennedy appeared relaxed and at ease. Howard, next up, sat forward uncomfortably in his chair, looking nervous.

He immediately faced questions over his controversial focus on immigration in the campaign so far. Asked whether he would allow his family into the UK if they were still in Romania, Howard replied: 'I would do what I do on every question that faces me – I would do what's best for Britain.

'What I think is best for Britain is that we have a system of immigration control which works, which is fair and one which that has limits on it.

'My father came to this country as an economic migrant, he came to do a job, and we would make provision within our limits for people whose skills are needed in this country.'

Another questioner asked: 'What about the people who would be murdered if they went back? What about the people who would be tortured?'

On the war, his position seemed confused. Asked if he would have supported it even if he had known Saddam Hussein had no weapons of mass destruction he replied: 'Yes, I would have supported the war, because I think it was the right thing to do.'

He rejected the suggestion from Dimbleby that this amounted to an illegal policy of regime change, describing it instead as 'regime change plus'.

'Saddam Hussein had been in breach of many UN Security Council resolutions, I think he was a threat to the peace of the region and a threat to the wider peace in the world,' said Howard. 'But I think it was possible to go to war and tell the truth, and I don't think Tony Blair did that. And I think it was possible to go to war and have a plan.'

He added: 'It would be politically much more convenient for me to say I think it was a terrible mistake and I wouldn't have done it, but I'm afraid I have got to be straight about it and the truth as I see it was that it was the right thing to do.'

The 'plus' in regime change, explained Howard, referred to the breach of UN resolutions. But those resolutions, relating to the ceasefire conditions imposed by UNSC 678, were about Saddam's obligation to comply with the UN weapons inspection regime. If you knew Saddam had no WMD there would self-evidently be no inspection regime for him to comply with.

Blair gritted his teeth for his sweaty, sometimes awkward encounter. But he scored points, too. Whoever follows him as Labour leader will quickly learn that the gig is not as easy as he makes it look sometimes.

Facing a barrage of hostile questions on Iraq Blair said: 'I totally understand why there will be people in this audience tonight who very, very strongly disagree with my decision to take this country to war in Iraq.

'All I can say to you is this: it's not a matter of the Attorney General's advice because it's been shown he advised it was lawful.

'Neither is the matter of misusing the intelligence, there have been four inquiries into that.'

But he added: 'It is, however, a question of a difficult decision I had to take. Was it better to leave Saddam in power or put him in prison? I think it was better to put him in prison.' The audience burst into spontaneous applause. Defending his earlier refusal to publish the advice, Blair said the Attorney General's advice to parliament had only been published three times in the last 100 years.

Away from Iraq Blair had an illuminating brush with the real world, which often genuinely baffles him.

He was caught off guard by a complaint that GPs were refusing to make appointments more than 48 hours in advance, in order to meet government targets.

'I'm absolutely astonished at that,' he said. 'I would be absolutely astonished if you tell your GP "I don't need to see you for four days" and he's insisting he sees you in two.'

But a woman spoke out to say she had had the same experience trying to make an appointment for her son.

'You have to sit on the phone for three hours in the morning trying to get an appointment because you are not allowed to ask for the appointment before that, because by making it 48 hours before-hand they are missing the government target,' she said. 'The only way to get a doctor's appointment is to turn up outside at 8 o'clock in the morning.'

Several other members of the audience shouted their agreement, some saying their GPs would accept appointments only on the same day.

'That is news to me,' confessed Blair. 'The whole purpose of this was that people used not to be able to get an appointment within 48 hours. Obviously, it shouldn't work that way, because it would be absurd.'

Yes, but a patient booking on Monday an appointment for Friday, because it is their day off work, can look like a patient waiting four days for an appointment. And that's not the target.

It is that absurd world, rather than the world of secret files, that voters have to live in.

7

War, war, jaw, jaw

Friday 29 April

It was what passes for their real world that the politicians chose to return to, as Britain prepared for a lazy bank holiday weekend. Was Iraq so important? Yesterday, yes. Today? No.

Brown and Blair went to Battersea, west London, to take the wrappers off a poster. It said: 'Forward with Blair & Brown' on a red arrow pointing right, and 'Back with Howard & Letwin' on a blue arrow to the left. A slogan underneath read: 'Economic stability. If you value it, vote for it.' The duo made a straightforward appeal. Blair said:

> *Today we return to the big and fundamental choice facing the country – forward or back, the Labour government with a strong economy, economic stability, or back with a Tory government that will put that economic stability at risk.*
>
> *It's only if people come out and support us that that strong economy with investment in health and education and law and order continues.*
>
> *There's a fundamental choice. On 6 May people will either wake up with a Conservative government with Michael Howard and Oliver Letwin or with a Labour government with me and Gordon.'*

Asked if he was feeling under pressure, Blair replied: 'No, but I do think it's important that people understand how big and fundamental the choice is.'

The big choice, in reality, appeared to be how big a majority the PM would be returned with, and how big a message disgruntled supporters wanted to send him. That really was important and the message had to get through to Labour supporters that they had to walk out of their front doors next Thursday and vote. Blair stressed: 'It only takes one in ten of our voters to drift off to the Liberal Democrats and you end up with a Tory government.' Unfortunately, the couple walked off in the direction of the blue arrow, pointing to the way back with Howard and Letwin.

Blair, Brown and Howard all headed for Wales today, while Kennedy was off to Leeds after his morning press conference.

The Blair-Brown double act was starting to take on a curious dynamic. It was as if the Chancellor was wearing a suit lined with kryptonite, ensuring that even as the Prime Minister soundbite superhero stood beside him, the premier's power seemed visibly to drain away.

At the Barry Memorial Hall, Gladstone Road, the two each made unscripted stump speeches. But it was Brown this time whose phrases gripped the attention, if not the imagination. He appeared more animated and eager than Blair, whose body language seemed anxious and defensive, almost as if appealing for one last chance.

'I believe there is a majority in this country for stability and for low mortgage rates,' said Brown. 'And let that not be a silent majority.

'Let it be, in this constituency and every constituency in this country, a voting majority.

'There is a majority in this country for full employment, the New Deal, the minimum wage. Let that not be a stay-at-home majority, let that be a voting majority for Labour.

'And there is a majority in this country for investing in our schools and hospitals, and for fairness to pensioners and hard-working families.

'Let that not be a sit-it-out majority, let that be a voting majority, a majority for Tony Blair to be our Prime Minister, not only on 5 May but on 6 May and afterwards, too.'

The bigger the Labour majority, of course, the smoother the handover of the keys to No. 10.

Blair, in his speech, stressed again the vital importance of Labour getting its supporters to the polls next Thursday.

He said: 'I think this next six days is about telling people how fundamental the choice is.

'Only one of two things is going to happen when people wake up on 6 May: either I will be back in No. 10 Downing Street, Gordon in No. 11, or we will have Michael Howard in No. 10 and Oliver Letwin in No. 11.

'If people believe that it is not sensible to put the Conservative Party in, then they are going to have to come and vote to make sure it does not happen.'

Blair was forced to address the problems that had arisen for him by the way he handled Iraq and other difficult issues.

He said: 'Of course there are disappointments and disillusions and problems, that is life. It is difficult when you take decisions when you are in positions of leadership. Of course there are difficult issues that come up and difficult decisions that have to be made.

'But taking everything together I believe this country is stronger, better, fairer, than the one we inherited from the Conservatives in 1997.'

Blair added: 'We have got in these last six days to get out there, explain the choices to people . . .

'Labour's economic plan versus the Tories' economic plan; Labour's plan for the NHS versus the Tories' plan for the NHS;

Labour's plan for our schools versus the Tories' plan for our schools; Labour versus Tory – the choice for 6 May.

'Let us make sure that we are re-elected so that we can carry on changing this country for the better.'

Earlier in the campaign, Blair – with Brown standing nearby – had confided to friends that while voters might think there was some kind of choice between himself and Howard, when it came to choosing between Brown and Letwin, 'you'd have to be a lunatic' to choose Letwin. It was an interesting insight into how far Blair thinks he might have slipped in the public esteem.

Howard hosted a press conference in Cardiff and tried to set the tone for his next campaigning phase. 'We're in the last few days now of the campaign in this general election and it's time to focus on the wider choices people face in this campaign.

'Conservatives are taking a stand on the issues that matter. Character is an important issue for the British people but now they want to hear about something better – that is our approach to you.'

Howard went on: 'As people prepare for a long bank holiday weekend, it's time to remind people what we are going to do and how we are going to do it.'

He said that as Prime Minister he would not 'hang around', particularly on the issue of immigration, adding that, in the early days of a Conservative administration, he would call together business leaders to discuss how to implement his policy of a quota system.

The Conservative leader, sounding even as he spoke as if he recognised such a scenario was now increasingly an imaginary one, said: 'I would remind all those people what had just happened, that the British people had just voted for action and our clear and specific set of priorities, one of which is immigration.'

And he trailed a speech he was to make tomorrow where he would set out his own personal 'vision of the Britain I believe in' and promised on Monday reveal the eight priorities for the early days of a Tory government. He added that the British people would be able to 'mark on a calendar' when these points had been achieved.

Clearly he was banking on a sizeable Commons majority, since if any of them required legislation and the Conservatives enjoyed only a slender grasp on power, the timetable would not be in Howard's gift.

In his remarks in the principality's capital Howard borrowed a prime ministerial phrase he had previously mocked and said it was time to move on. 'We have had a week of Labour spinning, justifying the past, watching their own backs, not being straight,' he said. 'The British people want to move on now from the debate of the last few days.'

Kennedy sought at his morning news conference to quash speculation his party's plans would mean tax hikes. Seldom can a party leader be as confident as when the Lib Dems' boss assures the voters that his Chancellor of the Exchequer will not have to plunder their wallets too much. He said: 'Our starting point here is that we do not share, as a party, some of the more apocalyptic views about this supposed black hole.' Treasury forecasts over the last eight years had been 'broadly pretty accurate', he added.

'If, either for domestic reasons or unpredictable international reasons . . . you were to find a difficult set of economic circumstances in the years to come, having set out our shop stall at this junction where tax and expenditure is concerned, our inclination and instinct would not be to go for more tax.

'So you would have therefore to be prudent about what you do in terms of expenditure.'

However, Liberal Democrats had – as the Institute for Fiscal Studies recognised – built 'very significant cushions' into their projections, Kennedy continued.

'Even if we come across choppy waters economically, for whatever reasons, those cushions still leave, plus the tax base that we have identified, an ability to fulfil the promises that we make. We are not entering this in some kind of rose-spectacled way, we are being hard-headed and realistic.' He also argued that, because the tax burden would fall more fairly under Liberal Democrat policies, the income would come in.

'You can maintain the expenditure that our ambitions and aspirations detail in this manifesto, but if you have to curtail spending of course that is something that any government has to do in response to the events round about it.

'I don't anticipate that is going to be as much of an issue for us as it would be for any of the other parties.'

Kennedy , up in Leeds on the campaign trail later, sought to combat Labour's claims that a vote for his party would let in the Conservatives. Kennedy said Blair's maths were all wrong, he added:

> There is no chance whatsoever of the Conservatives getting in by the back, the side or any other door because they have lost this election and people know they have lost this election.
>
> What Labour are worried about as we have seen with the by-elections this parliament is, even if we are in third place, never mind challenging for second place, if people vote Liberal Democrat, they can elect Liberal Democrats and I think that is what millions of people want to do.
>
> After eight years in power with three-figure majorities and quite a benign economic backdrop, if the best you can turn round to the country and say is: 'Well, you must not vote for the Liberal Democrats for fear of something worse,' that just shows you what thin ice Tony Blair is now skating on.

Blair's clash on TV over GP waiting times refused to die down, and gathered pace as the day wore on. It had been Diane Church who had initially confronted Blair, and like others before her she now found herself in the limelight. Mrs Church, who lives with her husband Tony and children Gerard, ten, and Kieran, eight, told reporters today:

> I'm very angry that we have to spend so much time getting an appointment.
>
> The doctors are great once you get an appointment but it's the process of getting the appointment that's the problem.
>
> As far as Mr Blair's response goes, I think if he's seriously going to look at it and look at the way these targets produce absurd results, then I think that's fair.
>
> I didn't expect him to fix the problem at 10 p.m. last night.

Mrs Church had gone to her local surgery, the Limes Medical Centre, more than two weeks ago to see her GP because Gerard had been wheezing and feeling poorly.

The doctor gave him some medication and told Mrs Church to come back immediately if he did not get better, and return in a week's time for a check-up. Mrs Church said:

> A week last Monday I tried to call to get the advance appointment because he was not any better and the doctor had said it could be asthma.
>
> I was on the phone on and off from 8.30 a.m. to 10.30 a.m., having rung several times and either getting the engaged tone or it just ringing out. When I got through all the appointments had gone for the Monday. At the time I just accepted it and thought that was the system.
>
> But he didn't get much better and so I decided to queue up this

Monday at 8 a.m., I just thought: I cannot bear being on the phone again.

Aidan Thomas, chief executive of Epping Forest Primary Care Trust, said it was necessary for practices to 'hold back' some appointment slots to meet the targets.

'Patients may sometimes find it difficult to see a particular GP or nurse or get an appointment at a particular time,' he added.

'All the practices wish and endeavour to provide continuity of care, and, wherever possible will accommodate the patient's choice of clinician.'

Dr Mayur Lakhani, chairman of the Royal College of General Practitioners, said the RCGP wanted a review of the targets, which had become 'more important' than patient care. 'The current target system is not delivering according to patient needs and assumes that all patients are the same. This has the risk of distorting clinical priorities.

'GPs are determined to improve access and the RCGP urges policy makers to empower them to develop and implement flexible appointment systems in their localities that meet the clinical needs of patients.

'The RCGP believes that targets have become more important than genuine, patient-centred care.'

The chairman of the British Medical Association's GP committee, Dr Hamish Meldrum, said it had never liked the target, which was putting pressure on practices already struggling with a shortage of doctors.

'We have always felt that this has been a crude target which has distorted priorities,' he said. 'We are trying to get patients longer appointments, we are trying to give them more time.

'You have only got so much time in the working day and it's a fairly simple arithmetical fact that if you have to keep more appointments free for booking on the day, there will be less appointments available for patients to book in advance.'

Shadow Health Secretary Andrew Lansley accused the Prime Minister of being out of touch and promised that a Tory government would scrap NHS targets. 'After eight years in government, Mr Blair simply doesn't know what his government is doing or the impact their political targets are having on the NHS,' he said. 'Government targets do not make it easier to see a doctor, they result in reducing a GP's flexibility to manage patient demand.' The row was threatening Labour's sacred turf of the NHS.

Blair was stung into a BBC interview:

> I think that in the health service and in schools, targets are important, but there has been a danger, if I am frank about it, that they have been too crude.
>
> What we need to do is to keep them but make them sufficiently flexible and not to have so many of them that they overburden the system.
>
> The purpose of having a target in order that people should see their GP quickly is that for years and years people weren't able to go and see their GP. Same with accident and emergency, where people used to wait for ages and ages. Same with waiting lists.
>
> Where I think we as a government, though, have got to respond is that targets are good, they are necessary to engineer change in public services, but they shouldn't become an end in themselves.
>
> Whereas at the beginning I think they were necessarily somewhat crude and blunt, I think over time we can make them more flexible and make them work in the right way for the people who've got to implement them as well as for the consumer of the service.

Blair said it would not be right to scrap all targets, as the Tories were suggesting.

'If you got rid of them altogether, you would start to go backwards,' he said.

> We are very clear, the reason we have got waiting lists substantially down in the health service, accident and emergency improved, people able to get to see their GP within 48 hours, is precisely because there has been performance management of the system for the first time, along with the extra investment.
> But you need to make sure the balance is right.
> I think you need to strip the targets down to the essential ones you need. I think they need to be more flexible.

It remained to be seen whether Blair had done enough to damp the row down. His previous attempt at 'closure', publishing the Attorney General's thirteen-page legal note, seemed to have worked. Although it demonstrated the perils of publishing secret documents. Goldsmith's office was forced to circulate an email to the media warning of a forgery being passed around news organisations.

Goldsmith's spokesman said: 'A document has been sent to news desks today claiming to be a minute from the Attorney General to the Prime Minister, dated 1 March 2003. The document is a complete forgery and the matter has now been referred to the Metropolitan Police for investigation.'

The forged note carried the same seal as the real document posted on the No. 10 website, which had instantly made it available to every downloading no-good fraudster.

But the Attorney's office evidently did not have too high an opinion of media savvy. The note was an obvious forgery. It was marked Top Secret – the forgery was more classified than the real thing – and in part read:

It is important that the implications are understood before proceeding with our American partners in their doctrine for regime-change, I will be justifying what in essence may well turn out to be an illegal war.

However, this is why it is necessary to grey the lines as much as possible.

As agreed, I will be drafting this justification and it should be ready in one week.

If we succeed in this argument it will set a precedent for planned future conflicts that have been discussed, like Syria, Iran and Saudi Arabia.

I trust this will satisfy your requirements as well as those of our partners.

It was complete with fake Lord Goldsmith signature.

Meanwhile there was nothing fake about the first stirrings of the internal turmoil Blair hoped would not – and others had predicted would – accompany his pre-resignation announcement.

Bob Marshall-Andrews, fighting to retain his Medway seat for Labour, a frequent critic of his leader, never afraid to speak his mind, said in comments to the *Morgan and Platell* TV show released tonight:

I think if it looks as though the Prime Minister is going to stay for very long – and by that I mean more than a year – then there will be serious movements within the Parliamentary Labour Party in order to take effect of the machinery that we have in order to change our leader.

And I see absolutely no reason why that shouldn't take place. Indeed, I suspect confidently that it will.

Saturday 30 April

Brown, looking increasingly like Labour's own 'dog whistle' Prime Minister-in-waiting (Vote Blair – Get Brown), sent a subtle message of his own to disaffected Labour voters this morning over Iraq. In an interview with the *Daily Telegraph*, he promised to lock in the need for parliamentary approval for any future conflict.

Brown said: 'Now that there has been a vote on these issues so clearly and in such controversial circumstances, I think it is unlikely that except in the most exceptional circumstances a government would choose not to have a vote in parliament.

'I think Tony Blair would join me in saying that, having put this decision to parliament, people would expect these kinds of decisions to go before parliament.'

There had, of course, been three debates and votes in parliament over what became Operation Telic in 2003. The real controversy now was whether MPs had been given an accurate picture of British intelligence and Saddam's WMD capabilities when they voted.

But Brown's comments were presented as subtly going further than Blair's usual line, which was that it would be inconceivable for a prime minister to go to war if parliament had voted against it.

Blair himself was absent from the campaign today for the first time since hitting the trail in earnest on 11 April. He was said to be writing three speeches for three rallies tomorrow.

In his stead, Health Secretary John Reid hosted his party's morning news conference, attacking the Conservatives' health plans again.

When Brown's Iraq comments were thrown at him, a flicker of irritation may have passed across his face. Or it could just have been his usual expression.

'This is already our policy, of the whole Cabinet, since we did it. The Prime Minister decided that some time ago,' said Reid. 'That's why we had three debates on substantive motions before going into Iraq.

'This is and has been for some time the policy of the whole Cabinet led by the Prime Minister.'

Asked if he would serve in a Brown Cabinet, Reid – fiercely loyal to Blair, and sometimes spoken of as a possible anti-Brown candidate for his job – replied that it was up to the voters to decide who would win the election. He added: 'As Gordon says, the more we are in this game, the more we recognise it's not the job you hold, it's what you do for the country that's important. I entirely agree with Gordon.'

Reid was in feisty mood, too, when the issue of waiting times for GP appointments was raised with him, the issue that had appeared to flummox Blair during his *Question Time* session. Family doctors were plain wrong if they refused to let patients book ahead, citing the government's 48-hour target as the excuse, he said.

It was aimed at addressing the fundamental priority and biggest patient complaint ever, which was that they couldn't get to see a doctor within a week.

Most people had to wait in 1997 eight to ten days to see a doctor. That has now been completely transformed.

In the course of last year we discovered that, mistakenly, some GPs, a very small number of GPs, about 3 per cent, believed either that they had to see everyone within 48 hours, mistakenly, or believed they couldn't run a system that had forward bookings and a 48-hour priority. In both of these cases they were wrong.

He said Primary Care Trusts had been contacted where the problem had been identified. If GPs were still running the wrong system 'it's not for want of trying'.

Reid promised to double the amount spent on palliative care, allowing patients with terminal illnesses to 'die with dignity' in their own homes should they wish. And he offered expectant mothers greater choice over how and where they would have their babies.

Labour also produced three 'endorsers', NHS professionals who were supporting the party – south London GP Tom Coffey, surgery professor Ara Darzi and cancer nurse Annie Young.

'Labour created the NHS, Labour has revived the NHS in recent times and Labour will keep the NHS alive. That is why I will vote for the NHS and for Labour,' said Mr Darzi.

Nurse Young, working in the Cancer Network, welcomed Labour's promise that any woman with breast cancer symptoms would be seen by a specialist within two weeks.

With the job of reforming the health service 'half done', she said the goals of further improvements in waiting times and cutting health inequalities would be best achieved under a Labour government.

Dr Coffey said there had been a 'transformation' in the accident and emergency department where he also worked, with suspected heart attack patients seen and treated within 30 minutes.

'Eight years ago, half the patients who came in at the start of my shift were still there when I left at the end. Now they are all admitted, treated or discharged when I leave,' he said.

Away from London, Kennedy was back in Scotland again, up in Inverness, and still in buoyant mood. He said: 'We're going in to the final furlongs now very optimistic indeed.'

'I can't predict what this perverse voting system will throw up in terms of actual parliamentary seats but I am confident of a big increase in share of the vote for the Lib Dems. How much that transfers into more seats, frankly, is a bit of a roll of the dice, but I hope a lot more MPs.'

He dismissed Labour's argument that voters switching to the Lib Dems risked letting the Conservatives into power by the back door.

'Clearly, Labour are rather worried about the Liberal Democrat challenge,' he said.

'There is no danger of a Michael Howard Conservative government.

'People can go out there and vote for what they believe in and agree with, confident in the knowledge that he's not going to be Prime Minister and that Tony Blair should certainly not enjoy another three-figure majority.'

He argued that it was not possible to generalise about the effect of more people voting Lib Dem because the election was throwing up a 'mixed picture' across the country.

In the north east, for example, the Lib Dems were challenging Labour in areas like Newcastle and Durham, following on from successes in local elections. In the south they were targeting the seats of prominent Tories. 'It is a real patchwork quilt of a general election but I think the common theme is we are clearly coming up at the expense of both the others.'

Asked how he was managing to juggle a hectic campaign with helping to look after his newborn son, Kennedy added: 'On the domestic side, things are very happy indeed and the arrival of Donald has really helped keep all of this in perspective and keeps your feet on the ground.'

Later Kennedy travelled to his family croft in Fort William to pose for TV pictures with wife Sarah and baby Donald. Kennedy's parents Ian and Mary, who live in the croft next door, joined them in the garden to complete the happy family shots.

Howard, meanwhile, was making his now routine Saturday 'vision' speech, close to his constituency, this time in Ashford, Kent.

After eight years of Labour government, people have 'forgotten what it's like to have a government that actually gets things done', he said.

'I'm not going to hang around – and I won't. I will be a Prime Minister who rolls up his sleeves and gets things done.' On a walkabout later he had to be prompted by a photographer actually to roll his sleeves up.

Howard said the Tories would announce their 'priority tasks' for an incoming Conservative government on Monday.

Identifying the fight against crime as one of them, he said: 'They're not ploys to win an election. I don't believe in empty promises.

'I believe in rolling up your sleeves and getting on with the job.

'The only way a politician can make life better is by taking a stand, and focusing on the specifics.'

Howard told his gathering of Conservative candidates and activists that Britain could be 'waking up to a brighter day' on 6 May – 'The first day of a government that starts taking action on the things that matter to our country: a government that never stops taking action on the things that matter, because that is what government is for.

'It's not about talking: it's about doing. It's not about promising: it's about delivering.'

He told those who doubted his determination to get things done:

I'm 63 years old and I'm an incredibly lucky 63-year-old.

I have a wonderful family. I've had a fascinating and rewarding career. But most of all, I'm lucky because I can call this country home.

This country; this place called Britain; these islands of beauty and wit, common sense and splendour, quirky individualism and instinctive togetherness in the face of challenge.

What a country. What a privilege to be British. And what a chance we now have to serve again in government, to apply all our will and all our energy to the noble task of making this country a better place to live for everyone.

I remember my roots. I'm not ashamed of them: I'm proud of them. I started out in a State school in a small town in South Wales. I've learnt that if you work hard, apply yourself and stick at it – whatever your background - you can make a success of your life.

So to all of you watching at home – don't be in any doubt about my determination to fight for a better life for you.

I could easily decide to call it a day, enjoy my retirement, and spend time with my wonderful grandchildren. But I'm not going to do that.

I love my country, just like you do. And I know, just like you do, that it could be doing so much better. Your life could be easier. Your prospects could be brighter.

And that's what I am determined to deliver. To serve you to the best of my ability. To give back all I can to the country that has given me everything.

It was Howard's attempt to answer critics, led by Lord Tebbit, that he had been lacking in 'the vision thing' stakes. But it was a familiar, slightly nostalgic, line that left as many heads shaking as nodding in agreement. Why paint a picture of yourself as a grandad who should really be sitting at home dangling babies on your knee?

As if to counter that image, Howard later combined canvassing with a spot of keep-fit by running between homes on Downs Road in Hythe, in his constituency.

He displayed a startling turn of speed as he sprinted along pavements and up steps of the comfortable semi-detached properties, pausing only to hand out leaflets and talk to residents.

Without a suit jacket and wearing – finally – his shirt sleeves rolled up, he appeared far less out of breath than the photographers trying to keep up with him.

Howard's wife Sandra joined in the canvassing after asking him whether she had to run as well. He replied: 'I don't think it's compulsory for you.' However, Sandra did eventually, and elegantly, jog, albeit at a slightly more leisurely pace.

Retired British Rail employee Alan Birch, 66, accosted the Tory leader as he dashed past his house, saying: 'I remember what you did. You got rid of all the nurses.'

As Howard made to move on, Mr Birch, wagging his finger, added: 'It'll be doomsday if you get in. Doomsday.'

Up in Blair's Sedgefield constituency, the PM's anti-war opponent Reg Keys, whose son Tom was killed in Iraq, was wheeling out his own celebrity 'endorser' – novelist Fredrick Forsyth. He laid a large bouquet of lilies at the town's war memorial before telling reporters:

> We were told over and over again by the Prime Minister that Saddam Hussein had a massive industry producing weapons of mass destruction that could be launched in 45 minutes.
>
> He went to the House of Commons that day and he made it up. That is why Thomas Keys had to die.
>
> He died so that this man could have a standing ovation in Washington and his place in history.

Blair had a majority of more than 17,000 at the 2001 contest, but his seat was a magnet for all manner of protest parties. A total of fifteen candidates had been validly nominated:

Berony Anne Abraham (Independent);
John, alias John Bradfield Barker (Independent);

Anthony Charles Lynton Blair (Labour Party);
Cherri Blairout-Gilham (Pensioners Party);
Julian Fraser Brennan (Independent);
William John Brown (We Want Our Country Back);
Robert Woodthorpe Browne (Liberal Democrats);
Jonathan McQueen Cockburn (The Blair Must Go Party);
Mark Neville Farrell (National Front Britain For The British);
Helen John (Independent);
Reginald Thomas Keys (Independent);
Alan John Lockwood (Conservative Party);
Fiona Chistina Luckhurst-Matthews (Veritas);
Terence William Pattinson (Senior Citizens Party);
Melodie Elizabeth Staniforth, commonly known as Boney Maloney (Official Monster Raving Loony Party).

Gordon Brown was on a constituency visit too – but not to his own Dunfermline East patch. He was making his third visit to Edinburgh South West to campaign for Alistair Darling, Transport Secretary and Scotland Secretary.

In an aggressive speech, Brown turned all his fire on the Tories, virtually ignoring the Lib Dems and the Scottish Nationalists.

'There are three ways of getting a Tory government,' warned Brown.

'You can vote Tory, you can vote for a third party and let the Tories in. Or you can fail to vote at all, and let the Tories in.'

Election coordinator Milburn picked up the theme in a TV interview: 'This is a real contest. It's a tight fight, particularly in the marginal seats. That's why over the next few days we will be going out there with renewed momentum, more zest – seeking to win every single seat and fight for every single vote.'

He said: 'This is a turn-out election. It depends on who turns out.'

The Conservative strategy was to 'play dead and say it is all a foregone conclusion'.

> *They have worked out they can't positively ask people to vote Conservative because they have an unattractive set of policies and a pretty unattractive leader.*
>
> *The best way, they think, of getting into power isn't through the front door but by the back door.*
>
> *Their strategy, by running this grievance-based campaign, is to depress the Labour vote, in the hope that Labour voters stay at home or switch to the Liberal Democrats, Conservative voters turn out and then it will be Michael Howard walking up Downing Street.*

The Sunday newspapers first editions began to drop in media newsrooms. Their polling still showed Blair on course for No. 10. The Tories received the backing, sometimes grudgingly, of the *Sunday Times*, *Sunday Express* and *Sunday Telegraph*. But Guy Black had won over neither the *News of the World* nor the *Mail on Sunday*. The *MoS* advised its readers to vote for anybody but Tony Blair.

Other newspaper stories made less comfortable reading at Labour HQ . . .

Sunday 1 May

Iraq was back in the headlines for the second Sunday in succession, and an alarming number of secret documents seemed to have found their way into the willing hands of Fleet Street hacks. If Alastair Campbell had believed the Attorney General episode had sated the media appetite, he was to be sorely disappointed.

The *Sunday Times* had obtained a secret minute of a Downing Street meeting held on 23 July 2002, seven and a half months before the war, which had been attended by the most senior military and intelligence top brass. It bore the – for hacks – mouth-watering warning: 'This record is extremely sensitive. No further copies should be made. The paper should be shown only to those with a genuine need to know.'

The story it told was not, of itself, that sensational. But it confirmed deeply-held suspicions that Blair had promised George Bush, on a visit to his 1,600-acre Prairie Chapel ranch in Crawford, Texas, on 6 April 2002, that the UK would join US military action against Iraq.

In fact, Blair had made a speech on that visit at the George Bush Senior Presidential Library in College Station, Texas, that all but declared for 'regime change' and military action against Saddam unless he disarmed his WMD.

The minute in the *Sunday Times* was written by No. 10 foreign policy aide Matthew Rycroft to David Manning, Blair's then chief foreign policy adviser (now Sir David, UK Ambassador to Washington) and its conclusions said: 'We should work on the assumption that the UK would take part in any military action.'

It also said the then Chief of the Defence Staff Admiral Sir Michael Boyce 'would send the Prime Minister full details of the proposed military campaign and possible UK contributions by the end of the week.'

Downing Street said it contained 'nothing new' and had already been seen by the Butler Review into the use of intelligence in the run-up to war. Lord Butler's published report referred obliquely to the meeting.

The question of just when Blair signed up to military action to enforce regime change has seen commentators agonise. But here is my PA report of Blair's speech, which he made on 7 April 2002 after supper at the ranch and lunch the following day with Bush:

> *Prime Minister Tony Blair tonight threatened military action to topple Iraqi President Saddam Hussein's 'brutal' regime.*
>
> *Mr Blair pledged there would be no 'precipitive action' but delivered a blunt warning to Saddam that he had to allow weapons inspectors back into his country 'any time, any place that the international community demands'.*
>
> *The Prime Minister's toughest talk yet on Iraq came in a speech at the George Bush Senior Presidential Library in College Station, Texas, after two days of talks with the present President, George W. Bush.*
>
> *Mr Blair said: 'We must be prepared to act where terrorism or weapons of mass destruction threaten us.*
>
> *'The fight against international terrorism is right. We should pursue it vigorously, not just in Afghanistan but elsewhere . . . Since September 11 the action has been considerable, in many countries, but there should be no let up.*
>
> ***'If necessary the action should be military and again, if necessary and justified, it should involve regime change.***
>
> *'I have been involved as British Prime Minister in three conflicts*

involving regime change – Milosevic, the Taliban and Sierra Leone, where a country of six million people was saved from a murderous group of gangsters who had hijacked the democratically elected government.'

Mr Blair said the international community could not intervene in all cases 'but where countries are engaged in the terror or weapons of mass destruction business, we should not shirk from confronting them'.

Mr Blair said he hoped that Syria, Iran and North Korea could be persuaded to reform. But he went on: 'As for Iraq, I know some fear precipitive action. They needn't. We will proceed, as we did after September 11, in a calm, measured, sensible but firm way.

'But leaving Iraq to develop weapons of mass destruction in flagrant breach of no less than nine separate United Nations Security Council resolutions, refusing still to allow weapons inspectors back to do their work properly, is not an option.

'The regime of Saddam is detestable, brutal, repressive; political opponents routinely tortured and executed. It is a regime without a qualm in sacrificing the lives of its citizens to preserve itself, or starting wars with neighbouring states and it has used chemical weapons against its own people.

'The moment for decision on how to act is not yet with us. But to allow weapons of mass destruction to be developed by a state like Iraq without let or hindrance would be grossly to ignore the lesson of September 11 and we will not do it.

'The message to Saddam is clear: he has to let the inspectors back in, anyone, any time, any place that the international community demands.'

The message had seemed clear enough to me, too.

Today's publication of the secret minute confirmed Blair had gone back with a clear view of the likely outcome of the showdown with Saddam. The *Independent on Sunday*, too, had a 'secret' document, in this case Foreign Office legal advice marked 'Secret UK Eyes Only', sent in March 2002, which made clear the worries in Whitehall about the legality of a future war against Saddam.

The *Observer*, meanwhile, had comments from Chief of the Defence Staff Sir Michael, expressed in down-to-earth sailor's language, giving the context in which he had sought crystal-clear guidance about the legality of a war in Iraq from Attorney General Goldsmith.

He told the newspaper's reporter: 'I just wanted to make sure that if my soldiers went to jail, and I did, some other people go as well with me. Not to be facetious about it. And that's what I had. I had a perfectly unambiguous black-and-white statement saying it would be legal.

'I wanted to make sure we had this anchor which has been signed by the government law officer. It may not stop us from being charged, but by God it would make sure we brought other people in the frame as well.'

Question: 'So if you were called to account it would also be Lord Goldsmith and the Prime Minister . . .'

The admiral: 'Too bloody right!'

It was against this backdrop that Blair was due to appear on BBC1's *Breakfast with Frost* this morning. Aides had already flagged up he believed it was time to take the 'leadership' and integrity' issues head on. Now he had no choice anyway.

'I took a difficult decision there. You have got a situation where last week Mr Howard eventually had to admit that he would have taken the same decision and Charles Kennedy advanced the extraordinary proposition that if only we'd let the weapons inspectors stay a little bit longer in Iraq, the Iraqi people would have risen up and deposed Saddam,' said Blair.

'This isn't the real world. The real world was you had to take a decision to take Saddam out, put him in prison or leave him in power. I decided to put him in prison.' Thereby, some felt, confirming the policy of regime change which the Attorney General had warned so clearly against pronouncing publicly on.

Blair said that on 5 May voters would have to decide who they believed was the best person to lead the country.

'When you do this job you take difficult decisions and there is a wear and tear that comes with that but in the end the question people have got to ask themselves is: Who do you trust to run the economy, who do you trust to deal with the big issues that confront this country?'

He rejected the suggestion that Britain could have left the United States to go it alone in Iraq.

'So we the British, at the moment of decision, would have faltered and backed off? That is not my conception of Britain.'

He played down the *Sunday Times* leak: 'What happened subsequent to that meeting is that we went the United Nations route. We went back to the United Nations in November to give them a last chance.

'The idea that we had decided definitively for military action at that stage is wrong and disproved by the fact that several months later we went back to the United Nations to get a final resolution and actually the conflict didn't begin until four months after that.'

TB then had to be quizzed about GB. But he refused to be drawn on the arrangements for the transition, or reports that he had already anointed Brown as his successor.

'I don't think it helps him, let alone me, if I start speculating on what happens when I step down,' said Blair.

'I have always said that he would be a fantastic prime minister but it doesn't really help anyone to go in and out of all the permutations that could happen in the future.

'It doesn't actually help him, but it is not a bad recommendation on your CV to have been the most successful Chancellor in this country for decades.'

Blair also went out of his way to praise Foreign Secretary Jack Straw who, according to some reports, is facing a demotion in a post-election reshuffle. I think Jack Straw has done a fantastic job as Foreign Secretary. He is also a major player in the government,' he said.

Canny Sir Menzies Campbell said the latest Iraq revelations simply underlined the case his party had been making against the decision to take military action.

'In the Attorney General's well-argued document of 7 March which we've now at last seen the whole terms of he says, right at the very end . . . you can only use military force to the extent that is necessary to achieve your objectives, and military force for the purpose of regime change is illegal.

'In a sense what we have seen in the last 24 hours simply confirms what we had been inferring before,' he told the *Sunday with Adam Boulton* show on Sky News.

While Iraq may come low down in opinion polls of voters' top priorities, it was 'for many people the context, the background against which this election is being fought', he insisted.

And it continued to dominate the headlines and public grillings of the Prime Minister because 'trust and credibility lies right at the very heart of this election'.

'When the Prime Minister, as he has done already, argues that this is all about leadership, then I think it is inevitable that trust and credibility and leadership becomes a significant issue.'

Blair came under more pressure over Iraq when all three leaders separately joined a UK-wide commercial radio phone-in. He said that the deaths of British soldiers was 'a deeply heavy responsibility' but said he could not apologise for taking the country to war.

'Yes, we do say sorry for all those people who have died, but I can't apologise for having taken the country to war in circumstances where I believe that if we had not done so then the hundreds of thousands of people – we just had another mass grave in Iraq uncovered today – who died under Saddam would have carried on dying.'

Asked how many British soldiers had died, he said: 'It's 70 to 80 people who have died.' In fact, it was 86 as he spoke – not counting one death from natural causes on board a ship in the Gulf region but not assigned to Operation Telic. Blair said he had met their families, adding: 'If what you are saying to me is that it is not a heavy responsibility, it is a deeply heavy responsibility. Yes, it is. Very, very heavy indeed.

'But I had to decide what was the right thing to do for our country and I genuinely believe that the world is a more secure place now that Iraq has the prospect of becoming a democracy.'

Kennedy, during his grilling on *UK Leaders Live*, said: 'I don't think that by and large the Iraq situation is one which I've ever seen as electoral collateral.

'We took a decision as a party, I took a decision as a person, on principle. I did not think this was the right way to proceed.

'We have maintained that and people forget two years ago how much flak as Liberal Democrats we came in for taking the stand that we did.'

Asked why he had not accused Mr Blair of lying over the war, he replied: 'I think the Prime Minister persuaded himself as to the course of events that he wanted to pursue. I think he made the wrong judgement and it's as simple as that.'

Alastair Campbell decided to intervene, briefing lobby correspondents en masse for the first time since he stepped down from his post as the Prime Minister's official spokesman in 2000 to take a backroom role, as he summoned them to Labour's Campaign HQ.

But he was not about to talk on Iraq. He wanted to warn again of the Conservatives' 'Queensland' strategy. 'It is, from our perspective, quite dangerous,' said Mr Campbell. 'It is utterly unscrupulous. It is a completely novel development in British politics.'

He said that the Tories appeared to be pouring resources into the key marginals where the election would be decided – including both volunteers and paid workers – and admitted that Labour could not match their effort. The only resources Labour had were Blair and Brown, and Cabinet tub-thumpers such as Reid.

Blair whizzed to Watford with Reid. Blair: 'There isn't going to be a Liberal Democrat government, but what there could be is Liberal Democrat votes that let the Tories in.' Reid: 'You may think you are voting for Mr Nice – Mr Kennedy – but you will get Mr Nasty in Downing Street.' Next stop Enfield, north London. Blair: 'We have got a few days to go, and there is everything to fight for and everything to play for, because this is a fight for the future of this country.'

Then Blair in Hove: 'I don't need to mount an attack on Mr Howard's character. He has launched the most sustained assault on it himself that there possibly could be.'

Campbell, all the while, was hoping the party's focus groups, its private polling and the public national opinion polls were right: Iraq was now a neutral election issue. Minds were made up. Blair was not going to haemorrhage votes to the Lib Dems on the issue.

In one constituency, the general election was cancelled today. It was announced that Jo Harrison, 53, the Lib Dem candidate for the Staffordshire South constituency, died at her home in Kinver yesterday morning.

A party spokesman refused to reveal the exact nature of Ms Harrison's illness but said her death was not sudden. In a short statement the party's chief executive, Chris Rennard, added: 'Jo has been ill for some weeks and will be sadly missed. Our sympathies go out to her family.'

Because of her death, the constituency election had to be abandoned, with her name already printed on postal ballot papers, and a by-election will have to be called in a month.

Ms Harrison had polled in third place when she contested the seat in the 2001 general election, winning 4,891 votes.

The MP from that election, Conservative Sir Patrick Cormack, gained a majority of 6,881 votes over the second place Labour candidate.

He paid tribute to Ms Harrison this morning, saying: 'I am obviously extremely distressed at the death of my Liberal Democrat opponent, and very sorry indeed that I am not going to be in a position to return to Westminster on 11 May, but we will be doing everything possible to ensure we come back at the by-election.'

May 11 is the first day of the new parliament, when MPs begin swearing in. The national race, though, was definitely on and about to enter its final frenetic phase. For Campbell, that left just 72 hours to complete Project TB3, securing Blair's historic third term. For Howard, three days to pull off what would be the most stunning political coup of modern times. For Kennedy, three days until he could perfect his nappy-changing prowess with a little more constant practice; and find out whether his party had continued accumulating MPs at the expense of both his opponents.

8

One last heave

Monday 2 May

As Blair settled in for a routine press conference with Brown, in the south-west London marginal of Wimbledon, he was handed a sheet of notepaper. It told him that the Ministry of Defence had confirmed the death of a British solider in southern Iraq, caused by hostile action. The MoD was keeping back further details until the soldier's family could be informed.

Reporters were getting the same messages too, and eventually Blair was asked to comment on the death. 'First of all, I have literally just been passed a note about it. I send my profound condolences to the family,' he said. 'It underlines once again the extraordinary work and sacrifice that British soldiers are making in Iraq, to help Iraq become a stable and democratic country that's no longer a threat to its region and the world and we should be immensely grateful for the work they do.'

A little later, Howard, speaking in Manchester, added his sympathy to the – so far unknown – family, as did Kennedy in a one-line statement. And there the matter rested, for several hours, as details of the incident trickled out, along with the identity of the soldier who had died. For the politicians it was back to the grind of the final push for votes. It was becoming a physical grind now, too. The travelling became more intense, the same speech over and over again in different locations, the same message. Don't let up now.

In Wimbledon, Blair and Brown had been unveiling a poster with the latest refinement of their slogan: 'If one in ten Labour voters don't vote, the Tories win'. Asked to justify the slogan, Labour countered that the total Labour majority in the 158 swing seats the Conservatives would have to win to rattle the keys to No. 10 in their pockets was 581,000. Labour had received 10.7 million individual votes in 2001 so if 10 per cent failed to support the party that would equal a million votes – enough to make those seats change hands. It was the most tortuous electoral arithmetic.

Blair said only Labour had a serious programme for government and only Labour would build on and preserve economic stability. The Conservatives' economic plans collapse under scrutiny. The Liberal Democrat plans simply do not stack up,' he told the news conference, which followed the poster launch. Everything we do and everything we want to do in the future depends on the economy staying strong. Stability was hard-won and we will do nothing to put it at risk.'

Brown slightly startled reporters by disclosing much of the contents of the Queen's Speech, should Labour be re-elected, re-affirming the impression that in at least one parallel universe somewhere he had already taken over from Blair.

'Labour's economic plan starts from the foundation of economic stability – to do nothing that will put stability at risk.

'In the first Queen's Speech we will boost home ownership so that in the coming parliament Britain will have more home owning families than at any time in our history – moving from one million extra homeowners since 1997 to a million more homeowners by 2010.'

Brown said Labour would also use the first legislative programme to boost employment, boost childcare and raise spending per pupil in schools to £5,500 by 2007.

> *Both the Conservatives and the Liberals will abolish the New Deal and leave young men and women and redundant workers without hope.*
>
> *But the biggest risk to stability is that the Conservatives now have £15 billion of spending commitments for the first three years of their government that they cannot fund and which they cannot deny.*
>
> *As a result of promising to spend more, tax less and borrow less, the Conservative black hole is already £6 billion in year one, £16.2 billion in year two and £14.1 billion in year three.*

He said since the election began the Tories had dug themselves deeper into this black hole with dozens of further local spending commitments by Conservative candidates, including shadow ministers. He said these extra spending commitments, beyond the national published plans, had now been costed by Labour as amounting to an extra £1 billion.

'If, as shadow Chancellor, I had allowed discipline to collapse in this way, I would rightly have been accused of being reckless, of an irresponsible spend, spend, spend approach.'

Wimbledom was the first in a series of stops in marginals around the south-east, Blair and Brown all the while pumping the sound bite. It being a sunny bank holiday, Blair eschewed a tie for much of the day. Brown retained his neckwear. Split, or cunningly going both for the tie and no-tie vote? Howard went for no tie and pink open-necked shirt, as he sprung his campaign 'surprise': an endorsement from *Coronation Street*'s Ken Barlow, no less – actor William Roache. The Conservative leader revealed that focus groups had named the soap character as the one he most resembled.

'I think it was not as fulsome a compliment as I take it. I think it was a wonderful compliment,' he preened.

Howard was asked whether he would stay on as Tory leader if, as polls suggest, he were to lose on Thursday. Answering questions in front of a parade of activists and candidates he replied: 'I am very, very confident about the outcome.

'I believe our message is getting across. People know what is needed for the future of our country and they have a very clear choice on Thursday.' Howard offered no explanation of why polls appeared to show him heading for defeat and insisted that he was not thinking beyond polling day and a Tory win. 'All my thoughts and my actions are focused entirely on that objective.' Blair was trying to 'cling on to office . . . That's the limit of his vision,' he said.

'My hope is for a better Britain. A new chapter. A chapter of hope. A chapter of action. A chapter of achievement.'

Kennedy, meanwhile, expressed his now customary scorn for Labour's scare tactics and instead presented his new convert Greg Dyke at his morning news conference.

The former BBC director general was blunt:

> I do genuinely believe that our democracy has been undermined in the years since the Blair government and I think another Blair government would pose further dangers to our democracy. I am unable to support a Labour Party led by Tony Blair.
>
> It's now, I think, very clear that the Blair government tried to do to the legal opinion exactly what they did to the intelligence. They chose the bits they liked and they ignored the rest.
>
> I don't think that is acceptable.
>
> The thing that's haunting me and should haunt all of us is what if it had been one of our children going to war?

He said the system of Cabinet government which existed 30 years ago did not exist now. 'I believe what we have seen over eight years is the destruction of Cabinet government. Instead we have replaced it with a presidential system of government.

'I think that was made very clear by Mr Blair last week when he made it very clear it was his decision to go to war in Iraq, not his Cabinet. That's not the democracy I've ever voted for.'

Kennedy was asked if voters in constituencies where Lib Dems could not win should vote Labour to stop Conservatives.

He replied: 'If there was ever a tacit understanding in days gone by, and I am not sure about that, that is certainly terminated.

'Forget what the starting point might be. I don't think the last election is the most reliable guide to this election – quite unlike elections that I have participated in up until now. I think people are looking at a blank sheet of paper and saying: "Who do we want?"'

Blair and Brown continued their holiday trip together, a couple of chums on an outing, by visiting the Ikea furniture superstore in Croydon, Surrey, where they joined manager Goran Nilson and shop workers for breakfast in the staff canteen.

They queued at the breakfast counter, where Blair ordered baked beans and bacon and his more cautious pal fruit salad, orange juice and a croissant. Brown even attempted to pay for the meals with a £20 note but was told they were on the house.

Tony and Gordon then went to a barbecue in the garden of a church hall in the marginal constituency of Gillingham, Kent. Both gave activists their 'complacency' warning. Brown urged voters to 'put Tony Blair in Downing Street on Friday', while Blair hailed his colleague as 'Gordon Brown, my friend, our Chancellor, a fantastic asset for our country'.

When Tony bought an ice cream from a passing van, he bought one for Gordon, too. See, they really were friends. ''Ere, Gordon!' said Tony as he passed the cornet over.

Next the gang of two visited the Colney Fox pub in the village of London Colney in the marginal St Albans constituency to meet local Labour supporters. The two men were greeted by loud applause and cheering from activists, who had been told they were being invited for a drink to thank them for volunteering to work in Labour candidate Kerry Pollard's campaign, but had no idea they were expecting such famous chums.

They really enjoyed their mineral waters. But it was getting late by now. Time to go home for tea.

Alastair Campbell was out to play too, for the second day running. He claimed Labour had got its hands on internal Conservative campaign documents which showed the Tories believe they need to target just 838,000 voters in 165 key marginal constituencies to overturn Labour's majority. Using the Voter Vault computer system imported from the USA – where it was successfully used by the Republicans in the 2002 Congressional elections – Tories had individually identified potential swing voters in the marginals, he maintained.

Solid Labour or Tory voters are ignored while waverers are bombarded by the Conservatives with election leaflets and doorstep calls, said Campbell. Particular attention was being paid to key groups such as the over-65s, young professionals and people concerned about Europe. The leaflets being sent out feature Mr Blair's image, alongside slogans including 'Labour think they've got your vote in the bag' and 'It's now or never to tell him what you think'.

'They're not even saying Vote Conservative,' moaned Campbell. 'They are just trying to depress our vote.'

Campbell said the Tories had hired large numbers of workers to distribute the leaflets. 'They have bought a campaign organisation,' he said. 'We are using activists for these sorts of jobs. We haven't got the same money as them.' Why can't they play nicely like Tony and Gordon?

Howard had flown back to London from Manchester for his biggest rally of the campaign so far. Daughter Larissa, 27, stepson Sholto, his wife Alex and their children Louis, aged six, and Tallula, four, met him and wife Sandra at City Airport, where they boarded a campaign bus heading for Docklands. There at the Excel Centre, Howard delivered his 'Eight Commandments' speech, outlining the specific commitments he had promised he would detail for the first months of a Conservative administration.

> *Here's what we'll do. If you elect us on Thursday, the action starts on Friday. Here is a timetable of eight specific tasks that will be my personal priorities.*
>
> *First, on 9 May 2005 we will set out our plans to prevent police officers having to fill in a form every time they stop a yob in the street.*
>
> *Second, by 6 June 2005 we will have signed up hospitals to put matron in charge of delivering cleaner hospitals.*
>
> *Third, by 6 June 2005 we will have set in train a new 24-hour surveillance scheme to secure our borders. By 6 April 2006 we will make sure that all 35 major British ports of entry will be operating under the scheme.*
>
> *Fourth, by 1 December 2005 classrooms will benefit from unruly pupils being expelled under our plans to give headteachers complete control over expulsions.*
>
> *Fifth, by 1 April 2006 up to five million pensioners will have received their new council tax bills showing a discount of up to £500.*
>
> *Sixth, by 6 April 2006 the first young families will have benefited from our abolition of stamp duty on houses costing up to £250,000.*
>
> *Seventh, by 1 September 2006 students going to university will be freed from paying all tuition fees and Mr. Blair's planned top-up fees will not be introduced.*

Eighth, by 31 December 2006 we will have created a single body to fight illegal immigration – the British Border Control Police – and their 7,400-strong force will be under one unified control.

You can hold us to account. We've taken a stand on school discipline, cleaner hospitals, controlled immigration, more police and lower taxes. We've set out the specific actions we'll take.

We've given you a timetable. Now it's time for change. It's time for action. I love my country, just like you do. And, just like you, I know that Britain could be doing so much better. Your life could be easier. Your prospects could be brighter. And that's what I'm determined to deliver.

Howard went on to talk to party workers at their Campaign HQ and was caught up in one of those bizarre outbursts of over-enthusiasm that often afflicts political parties and most often when they think they are losing. The spirit of General Montgomery was invoked by party co-chairman Lord Saatchi as he introduced Howard.

The peer paraphrased the General who reversed the advance of Rommel's Afrika Corps. 'The great point to remember is that we are going to finish with Blair once and for all. It will be quite easy. There is no doubt about that.

'This chap Blair is definitely a nuisance. Therefore we will hit him with a crack and finish him.'

Saatchi compared the election to the battle of El Alamein which, he said, 'most historians think was the most decisive'.

When Montgomery took command of the Desert Rats he refused to accept any prospect of defeat, said Saatchi. There was laughter as the peer told the party workers: 'He said we will stand and fight here. If we can't stay here alive, we will stay here dead.'

Montgomery had ordered all plans for retreat to be burned immediately.

'This is exactly what Michael Howard said to me when he gave me this job. That he was going to advance.'

Speaking from the stage where chief strategist Lynton Crosby normally addressed staff meetings, Howard told the predominantly young audience he wanted to thank them from the bottom of his heart and ask for three more days of the same.

Unlike previous elections, activists on the ground had praised the 'fantastic' service they have had from those in headquarters.

> It is all down to you, you have been utterly fantastic. You are the best and the brightest.
>
> Anyone in any field of human endeavour would want to have you on their side and I am the luckiest person in the world, because I have you on my side and I appreciate it enormously.
>
> Your commitment, your unflagging energy, your enthusiasm, your cheerfulness, the absolute devotion with which you have approached every task you have been set has been a wondrous joy to behold.
>
> And so I just want to say from the bottom of my heart, thank you hugely for everything you have done so far.

It was a different war that returned to the forefront of Blair's campaign yet again. The MoD had now released details of the death of Anthony Wakefield, 24, of the First Battalion the Coldstream Guards. He had died today from injuries sustained when a roadside bomb, an Improvised Explosive Device or IED, detonated while he was on a routine patrol in a Land Rover just south of Amara.

And in his appearance on ITV1's Dimbleby programme Blair was again tackled on Iraq. 'I've had this election campaign where there have been some pretty fearsome attacks on my character and I'm not going to stand here and beg for my own character.

'People can make up their minds whether they trust me or not and that's their decision on 5 May.' Blair said he had given up believing he could persuade people he took the right course of action over Iraq.

> The relevance of the regime, as I said at the time before we took the action, was that if we had to remove him we should do so with a clear conscience, because he was a monster and a dictator who murdered hundreds of thousands of his own people.
>
> The reason has never changed – not before the war, not during it, not afterwards – that's still the reason.
>
> I've been through these arguments over and over and over again.

Guardsman Wakefield, from Newcastle, had been separated from his wife, Ann Toward, and the couple had two children together.

Ms Toward angrily blamed Blair for the death of her children's father:

> He sent the troops over and he should not have done that. If it was not for that, their dad would have been here today.
>
> He was such a brave man. I had two children with him and I am trying to explain to them that their dad won't be coming home. It is very hard.
>
> My son Scott has been talking about his dad and wants to write him a letter to tell him how proud he is that he fought and died for his country.

Tuesday 3 May

Fractious, fraught, frantic. It was the day the campaign got up close and all too personal, not least for Howard – who had to contend with Rory Bremner, the rain, an out-of-date tax disc on a campaign bus and hecklers galore, with only an inner belief that political miracles really do happen to sustain him.

On one of the last campaigning days of the 1987 general election, Neil Kinnock's then chief of staff was confronted by a young reporter who argued Labour had run such an effective campaign, in PR terms, that given another few weeks the party might even have pulled off the seemingly impossible and won.

'Sticking plaster only goes so far,' the substantial bat-eared bearded figure replied, shaking his head. His name was Charles Clarke, later Education and Home Secretaries in Blair's government.

Howard's campaign has, by the very nature of its guerrilla strategy, not been so obviously effective in headline terms, but his team must have begun with some sense of hope. Now all that was left was faith. 'I believe for every drop of rain that falls, a voter grows.' Howard's stock: 'I will give every one of my opponents every opinion poll between now and 5 May provided I can have the one that counts then,' is a soundbite answer to an awkward question, not a political philosophy.

Today's Mori poll for the *Financial Times* found that among people absolutely certain to vote, Labour was on 39 per cent, a ten-point lead over the Conservatives on 29 per cent, with the Liberal Democrats on 22 per cent. The Tory figure had dropped five points since the *FT*'s poll a week earlier.

If those figures were replicated in 48 hours' time, and assuming a uniform national swing, Blair would be returned to Downing Street with a 146-seat majority. The poll also claimed some 36 per cent of people said that they may still change their minds even now.

This is far higher than was registered at the same stage of the 1997 and 2001 campaigns, when 21 per cent of people said they might change their minds in the final days of the campaign.

The bulk of the work for the poll was done on Saturday, and one factor which may have influenced the relatively poor Tory showing was party leader Michael Howard's attack last week on Mr Blair as a 'liar', an accusation whose fierceness may have alienated older voters. Just 36 per cent of people over the age of 55 said they would vote Conservative, a seven-point drop from an identical Mori poll for the *Observer* conducted earlier in the week.

The *FT* quoted one, un-named senior Conservative as criticising Mr Howard's attack. 'The "liar" line was too brutal; we lost ground and we very quickly had to switch on to other messages,' the Tory said.

'The 2005 campaign is the last gasp of the one-more-heave brigade,' one senior party figure told the newspaper.

'The language has been too narrow. It has reinforced our support but failed to broaden it. The whole composition of this campaign has been weak.'

The poll also found that Iraq continued to plague Blair – but not enough for the Tories to profit. Asked whether last week's dispute over the disclosure of the Attorney General's legal advice had changed the way they intend to vote, 11 per cent said yes, while 86 per cent said no. Mori also found that a majority of people – some 62 per cent – believed that Mr Blair had at some stage misled them about the war.

The polling industry will be one of the biggest casualties if Howard's revolution happens. And it was already becoming clear that the Conservatives' own favourite blood sport – hunting the scapegoat – would commence very swiftly if it does not.

Howard got his '*Je ne regrette rien*' moment in early, on GMTV today. Asked if he would have run the campaign any differently, Howard declared: 'I would not change anything.'

The Conservative leader rejected any suggestion that he might now regret denigrating the PM personally. 'What do you think is worse – calling someone a liar or taking us to a war on a lie?' He shrugged off Labour's peskily consistent poll lead and insisted he had not contemplated the future if he fails to win.

'It is not the polls or the pollsters who are going to decide this election, it is real people out there,' he said.

Asked if he would resign following a defeat, he would only say: 'I'm concentrating on telling the people of our country, the people who will decide our election, that they still have it in their power to change direction, to elect a government that will make their lives better.'

Pressed on the point, he added: 'I'm concentrating on between now and Thursday doing everything to make people see that we can deliver a better, brighter Britain.'

Howard insisted he was 'really enjoying' the campaign. 'The last two days have been terrific because the sun has been shining. It makes such a difference.' But Howard's day had yet to unfold in all its misery.

One man who had a plan and genuinely believed it was working was Kennedy. The only party leader to hold a morning news conference, he told reporters: 'It's now clear that a large part of the story of this general election has been the growing support for the Liberal Democrats.

'People out there have made their minds up that the Conservatives are not going to win this general election.

'They can't break out of their core vote.

'Labour and Tony Blair, self-evidently, are running scared of the Liberal Democrats.'

He was heading for Howard's own constituency of Folkestone and Hythe, part of the decapitation plan. It's a moot point whether the plan was ever actually intended to succeed in its own self-explained terms, or whether simply by highlighting the relatively low majorities enjoyed by the only senior Conservatives most voters had heard of it was designed to reinforce the Tories' fragility and the point Kennedy had just made: The Tories can't form a government.

Kennedy ended his news conference underlining the ten key messages which the party launched at the outset of the campaign, including pledges to scrap student fees, provide free personal care for the elderly and replace council tax with a new local income tax.

But he also stressed that only his party had stood up to the Prime Minister over 'the seminal issue' of Iraq.

Kennedy was asked if, like the family of the Coldstream Guardsman killed in Iraq yesterday, he blamed the Prime Minister for such deaths.

He replied: 'I think it would be completely wrong for any competing party politician or party leader to try and score any sense of campaign points out of the loss of life of any British serviceman killed in action this way.'

Guardsman Wakefield's widow had repeated her criticism of Blair again today, and other families of servicemen killed in Iraq were making their own protest.

They delivered a letter to 10 Downing Street, officially launching their attempt to take legal action against the government and the Prime Minister. Several families were represented in a delegation which gave notice to Blair that a challenge against the legality of the war was, they hoped, going ahead.

The relatives said their determination to take action had been fuelled by last week's publication of the advice given to Blair by the

Attorney General just before the conflict started. The Stop The War Coalition, backing the legal action, said today's move was the first step in challenging the legality of the war and the role of the Prime Minister.

The letter outlined the legal case which the families hoped to take under the European Convention on Human Rights. A spokesman for the Coalition said there were also plans to take a private prosecution against the Prime Minister.

'We have been told by senior barristers that we have a very strong legal case,' he said.

Brown was fielded early on to defend the Prime Minister. He said that he understood Ms Toward's feelings of grief over the death of her husband. He told BBC1's *Breakfast* programme: 'Anybody who has suffered grief and loss will understand the feelings and the difficulties that this family is facing today and our thoughts must be, initially, with them.'

But in an unfortunate slip of the tongue, he added: 'We believed we were making the right decisions in the British national economic interests.'

Brown went on: 'Of course we have lessons to learn, as Tony Blair has said, about the way things were done, like the dossier, but at the end of the day we wanted the security of Britain and the British national interest to be advanced.

'Iraq, of course, being a democracy means that the Middle East is a safer place.'

Howard – who had said he would have taken Britain to war with Iraq even if he had known there were no weapons of mass destruction – muddied his position in the minds of voters further, saying that he would be prepared to launch military action, even if the legal case was not clear-cut.

'If it was clear that going to war in those circumstances was illegal, I wouldn't do it,' he told the *Today* programme.

'But as the Attorney General himself recognised in the opinion that we were at last allowed to see last week, it is possible to hold different views on the legality of questions like that. International law is not precise. There is room for more than one opinion.

'If I had honestly held the opinion that it was legal to go to war, I would have taken the same action but I would have told the truth about it and I would have had a plan.'

Asked whether in future, if he was Prime Minister, he would present at least to the Cabinet the Attorney General's advice on the legality of possible military action, he replied simply: 'Yes.'

As Kennedy headed for the Conservative leader's constituency Howard made his way to Tamworth, once the constituency of Robert Peel.

Here, in 1834, Peel had proclaimed his 'Tamworth Manifesto', a more enlightened form of Conservatism, supporting the Reform Act extending the franchise, and hailed by some as the founding document of the modern Conservative Party. It was presumably this sort of resonance Howard had in mind, rather than the fact that later Peel introduced income tax – at seven pence in the pound – and repealed the Corn Laws at the cost of disastrously splitting his party from top to bottom.

Today, when Howard arrived for his 'really enjoyable' campaign Labour and Tory activists staged a fierce placard Battle of Tamworth as he struggled in the drizzle to deliver a stump speech to shoppers.

Conservatives used umbrellas, balloons and their own signs to cover up Labour placards warning of cuts.

Labour's own balloons were gleefully popped by the Tories as they sought to keep them out of TV pictures. There was also a lone supporter of Robert Kilroy-Silk's Veritas Party hovering, carrying a sign featuring the former chat show host's face.

As this went on around him, the Tory leader told voters they had a clear choice at the polls.

'All Mr Blair can say is "Vote for me, don't let the Tories in," he doesn't have anything positive to say at all,' he said. Whether anybody heard anything at all is not known.

Blair was not having things all his own way either, as he and Brown took their roadshow out and about.

As he arrived in Wellington, Shropshire, the PM was heckled by pro-hunting campaigner Otis Ferry, the son of rock star Bryan.

Ferry, 22, master of the South Shropshire hunt and one of those who ran into the House of Commons chamber piped up as Blair entered a church hall in the marginal Wrekin constituency: 'Tony Blair, you should be ashamed of yourself. You are ruining our countryside.

'Tony Blair, go back to the city. That's the only place you are welcome.

'Stop smiling. I haven't got words for you. Go away back to the city.'

Ferry was standing in a graveyard alongside the church hall and said that Labour officials had tried to move him away out of earshot. He said hunting protesters had been thwarted throughout the campaign for making their feelings known to Mr Blair by the secrecy surrounding his movements. He told reporters: 'I live ten minutes away from here and when I got a call and heard he was coming here I dropped everything.

'This is a fake campaign by Tony Blair. We never know where he is going to be. He would be mobbed left, right and centre if he made his campaigning public.

'It's a very sad state of affairs if the Prime Minister has to be shielded from the British people.'

Ferry said he had been canvassing on behalf of the Conservatives during the election campaign.

Earlier, in Gloucester the TB-GB show had got off to a smoother start as they unveiled a 'mortgage wheel', like a gameshow spinner, showing the financial difference for home-owners between the 11.35 per cent average mortgage rates between 1979 and 1997 and the 6.1 per cent average since Labour came to power.

Blair told party workers – and the cameras: 'What is at stake and at risk in this election?

'Your mortgage is at risk. Your job is at risk. The stable economy is at risk. The investment in schools and hospitals, they are at risk if the Conservatives are returned to government.

'Everything we have built up over these past few years, everything we can do for the future of this country depends on that choice.'

Brown said that one million people had been enabled to become homeowners as a result of low interest rates under Labour, and he set out plans to help a further million people on to the housing ladder within five years if Labour won on Thursday.

The party was proposing a new shared-equity scheme, under which prospective homeowners would buy part of a property if they could not afford to buy it all.

Brown also said the government would free up more public land for house building, work with house builders to develop a low-cost £60,000 home for first-time buyers, and develop shared-use estates, where expensive and low cost homes would be built side by side.

According to Labour's mortgage wheel-of-fortune, homeowners with a £75,000 mortgage were £266 a month better off with the average rate under Labour than the average during the Tories' time in power, rising to £444 for a £125,000 mortgage, £622 for £175,000 and £799 for £225,000.

Brown said: 'In the years from 1979 to 1997, mortgage rates averaged 11 per cent and famously went up to 15 per cent for a long period of time. Under Labour they have averaged 6 per cent.

'That's the reason why there are one million more homeowners in the country and many more homeowners in this constituency than there were in 1997. But we believe we can do better in the years to come. As Tony and I have gone round the country, we have been struck by how many young couples find it very difficult to get on the first rung of the housing ladder and how high house prices have made it difficult, even with low interest rates, for young couples to get the houses that they want and to make that start on the housing ladder.'

Blair was cornered as he left the venue by Mohammed Jaffer, who told the Prime Minister that he supported his domestic policies but was angry about the decision to take Britain into a war which had cost thousands of lives. Mr Jaffer insisted: 'Tony, can we trust you after Iraq?

'We have lost hundreds of lives, thousands of lives. We got the impression you were just following President Bush.'

Blair replied: 'In the end, you have got to try to do as Prime Minister what you think is right for the country and some of those decisions are very, very difficult.'

Earlier he had repeated his sympathy for Guardsman Wakefield's family, when asked about their anger, saying:

I have expressed my deep sympathy and condolences to the family.
I really don't think there is anything I can, or should, say more than that and I don't think it is right or appropriate to do so.
As I said yesterday, the British soldiers have done an extraordinary job in Iraq, helping that country become a stable democracy.
I totally understand the grief and distress of people who are bereaved by soldiers who lost their lives.

Kennedy was having a peaceful time in Howard's Hythe back yard. He said: 'I came to this constituency during the last general election because it was a prime target seat for the Liberal Democrats and I am here irrespective of who leads another political party and precisely because this is a prime target seat for the Liberal Democrats.

'It is all there to play for, we can win in this constituency and we can win big across the country as a whole.'

Kennedy was again asked if he blamed the Prime Minister for the death of the latest British soldier in Iraq.

He said: 'I think family emotions when there is a loss of life of one of our military personnel, understandably the grief must be absolutely terrible. And all our sympathies go out to them. I don't think it is right for somebody like me as a party political leader to seek to exploit that in terms of this election. People have formed their own views.'

Kennedy was again forced to pooh-pooh Labour claims that voting Lib Dem risked handing victory to the Conservatives.

He said. 'If it was me in Tony Blair's shoes with 48 hours to go before polling day, if I had been Prime Minister of the country for eight years, had a three-figure parliamentary maturity behind me for that period, I think I would like to say something a bit more positive and persuasive to the public when it comes to casting their vote.

'If that is the best he has got to say it shows you what thin ice he is on and what strength of territory we are on.'

Addressing Howard's campaign he said: 'I think it has been a very inward-looking, very backward-looking campaign. It is a campaign for an insular Britain when I think we need an outward-looking internationalist Britain and a Britain that does better in terms of the international order than this Prime Minister has delivered over his absolute crass misjudgement over Iraq.'

Hythe's Conservative candidate was continuing his enjoyable day's campaigning in Loughborough. Arriving in the town centre for his John Major soapbox-style speech Howard was first loudly and roundly booed in the rain. Labour activists then kept up a constant barrage of barracking, as Howard demanded to know whether they backed the government's early-release scheme for prisoners.

Others then arrived dressed in Death outfits, complete with scythes and wearing Michael Howard facemasks. They proceeded to chant 'Boom and Bust'. The Tory leader gamely completed his speech, repeatedly urging voters to 'send a message to Mr Blair'.

There were then scuffles as he left the stage and he was whisked away by car, leaving behind the handful of journalists whose organisations had paid £10,000-a-head for the privilege of travelling with him.

A short time later, it emerged that a tax disc on one of Howard's campaign buses, which he had been photographed smiling beside, had expired in April. At first flustered aides had no rebuttal to Taxgate.

A spokesman for Mr Howard later explained that the coach was 'perfectly legal'.

As long as a tax disc had been purchased, vehicle owners had a ten-day period of grace in which to display it, the spokesman said. The only reason the new disc was not on the coach was that the company did not know day-to-day where the vehicle would be.

It's all about accountability though, Michael.

The Tory spokesman was contradicted by DVLA spokesman Viv Sterl who insisted that coaches did not have any special dispensation. 'They fall into the same category of rules. They must display a disc at all times,' he said.

A few minutes later the Conservative Party leader moved into action and ordered the vehicle off the road. 'It is now parked up on private property and will not be driven any further until the tax disc has been properly displayed,' said Howard's spokesman.

Nothing else could surely go . . . TV impressionist Rory Bremner was waiting for Howard in Rushden, Northamptonshire.

Dressed as the Tory leader, he was lampooning him in front of activists gathered in the town centre in the pouring rain.

Howard was already around 90 minutes late arriving for the event, and those Labour activists dressed as the Grim Reaper were again on hand, after their own campaign bus had earlier toured the town urging people to vote Labour. The Tory leader delivered his speech to damp activists, with Bremner standing quietly by under an umbrella, before visiting a nearby cafe. Men made of less stern stuff would have been tempted to visit the pub instead.

Sandra Howard revealed to Radio 4's *PM* programme that she had 'calmed him down once or twice' during the campaign. 'Although he has been pretty good. He has not got uptight too much which is always a danger when you are at full stretch.' This afternoon could, possibly, have been one of those danger moments.

Blair meanwhile was chatting to photogenic 'concerned parents' at a community centre at Penwortham, near Preston and sent a message to those thinking of voting Lib Dem that the party was 'soft on drugs'. But hadn't he backed the decision to downgrade cannabis to a Class C drug? He told them:

> *We have said we will look at it again. There's actually been mis-understanding about this – what we really say to the police is, 'Go after the hard stuff'.*
>
> *I have thought about this a lot. I know people say cannabis is different from hard drugs – and of course it is – but I think there is a risk that you start with that and then get into other things.*
>
> *And also I think there is increasing evidence emerging that it isn't quite as harmless as people make out.*
>
> *So I take a very strong line on it, and a particularly strong line if there is any question of people dealing anywhere near kids and schools.*

With GB alongside, TB said he thought 'misunderstandings' now needed correcting. We'll get tough again on drugs unlike the wishy-washy Lib Dems was the signal.

Ending his hectic day with a rally in Huddersfield, Blair said:

> *The next couple of days are crucial. It is when we have to go out and persuade and we have to persuade by the strength and confidence in our case.*
>
> *I have that strength and confidence. I have that strength particularly when I think of the campaign the Conservatives have run.*
>
> *'Send him a message,' they said.*
>
> *I think the British people should send him a message – we have seen your campaign, we have seen your leadership, we have seen your Conservative Party and we don't want it back in charge of our country.*

Kennedy meanwhile ended his day with a rally in London. He told his fans: 'As we enter the last lap of this campaign it is now clear that the Liberal Democrats are set to go into the next parliament with significantly more MPs and with the highest level of voter support for a generation.

'We set no ceiling on our ambitions as a party. We are clearly set for a further major advance on Thursday. But I am determined this will not be the high watermark of Liberal Democrat or electoral success. It will be a further staging post – an important staging post – in our upward progress as a party.'

And Howard was eventually safe and sound too, in Hythe Town Hall, a traditional rallying point for his local supporters before polling day. At last, they cheered him to the rafters, more than 100 of them, cramped into the hall.

They cheered as Howard promised that he would deliver on his key pledges if elected Prime Minister.

They awarded a noisy round of applause when he tore into the Liberal Democrat-run local authority for mismanaging budgets, 'closing public toilets' and 'not mowing public lawns'.

But the room really came alive when a member of the audience shouted that Liverpool were beating Chelsea by a goal to nil in the UEFA Champions League semi-final second leg – a scoreline sending them through to the final in Istanbul.

Avid Reds fan Howard asked, nervously, if that was true, and on being assured that it was, said: 'This clearly means it's going to be a great week.'

Wednesday 4 May

It was possibly the most unusual interview a British Prime Minister has ever given. And it was to one of Fleet Street's most celebrated . . . photographers. The *Sun*'s royal photographer Arthur Edwards was taking the pictures for his paper's eve-of-poll chat with Mr and Mrs Blair, published this morning, where they talked about their personal life and their marriage. The paper had come out earlier in the campaign in support of Blair, saying it would give him one final chance in Downing Street. Political editor Trevor Kavanagh and editor Rebekah Wade sat down with the Blairs and their interview ran over three pages. But Arthur is an official 'character' – besides being a top-notch photographer – and has a habit of getting into a dialogue of his own with his subjects.

On this occasion, with Blair (TB), and wife Cherie (CB) it ran thus, after Arthur Edwards (AE) had asked Blair to remove his tie:

TB: *I'm not doing anything cheesy, Arthur, so don't ask.*
CB: *Oh, come on, Tony, strip off. Let's see that fit body we've been talking about.*
TB: *Keep your hands to yourself, Cherie!*
AE: *So how fit are you, Tony?*
CB: *Very!*
AE: *What, five times a night?*
TB: *At least. I can do it more, depending how I feel.*
AE: *Are you up to it?*
CB: *He always is.*

TB: Right. That's enough. Interview over. And I'm not doing any kissing pictures! Come on, woman, time to cook my dinner!

You're right, Tony. Pictures of you kissing your wife of 25 years would have been so tacky.

Today really was the final throw of the dice. All the campaigning, all the convoluted strategies, all the salaries of those extra staff, all the risks they took, all the miles they travelled, have 24 hours to pay dividends. From 7 a.m. tomorrow, the voters really are in charge.

Blair began his day with a rather more routine grilling on the by now familiar GMTV sofa.

'The point about a general election is it's fought constituency by constituency,' he said. 'Whatever the opinion polls say, in the key seats a few hundred votes or a few thousand votes can determine it either way. We are very much saying to people in those key constituencies, if you have got the Conservatives in second place and you want to keep a Labour MP you have got to get out and vote.'

He added: 'This is the moment when the people take control and the future of the country is in their hands.'

Off then to the BBC's Millbank studios across the River Thames for his John Humphrys grilling on the *Today* programme. It was, in the circumstances, a rather lightly done grilling for those hoping for a classic dust-up. Blair insisted, under questioning, that it was not the case that he decided to commit Britain to war against Iraq during discussions with Bush as early as Easter 2002, and that everything he did afterwards was designed to win the public's support for that secret decision.

He acknowledged: 'That is what people say,' adding 'and it is simply not right'.

The PM went on: 'Because if I had the ability to get a second United Nations resolution, as we tried very hard to do, we went back to the UN in the first place in order to try and resolve this peacefully.'

Blair dismissed the various leaks suggesting he had been committed to regime change from an early point: 'What happens with all these things is that they are just lifted out of context.'

He continued: 'I did support regime change, provided that it was impossible to get what we wanted through the United Nations route.

'Going down the UN route, and giving Saddam a final chance to comply, is completely inconsistent with the notion that we decided to go to war in any event.

'Because had Saddam complied fully, unconditionally, immediately with the UN resolution passed in November 2002 . . . then of course there would not have been a conflict.'

He insisted that 'within myself, I know that I have tried to do the right thing for the country'.

Pressed on how long he would remain at No. 10 Blair was phlegmatic: 'There is going to be a change at some point, you can leave the precise detail of it until later.

'People understand that there is a finite time for any political leader. The reason I want to carry on now is I believe passionately that there are things that we can do – I actually believe I too have something to contribute to this.'

Kennedy was not in a TV studio. He was fronting his routine early morning news conference. He argued, plausibly, that his party's 'positive' campaign had seen it reach record levels of support in the opinion polls. Liberal Democrats had 'set the pace' throughout the campaign, while the Conservatives' challenge had petered out and Labour were running scared, he said.

Kennedy also underlined his party's performance in recent by-elections as evidence that Liberal Democrat candidates could jump straight from third to first place.

And he kept the spotlight on Iraq, urging voters: 'Cast your vote to restore Britain's reputation on the international stage. Vote Liberal Democrat if, like us, you say never again to an episode like Iraq.'

Kennedy also continued habitually to rubbish Labour warnings that a vote for the Lib Dems could let in Conservative candidates. He said:

> *I think that at this election Liberal Democrats in many respects have set the pace.*
>
> *The Conservative challenge, if challenge it was, has petered out. They can't win and I think that most people have concluded they certainly don't deserve to win.*
>
> *Labour are now self-evidently running scared from the challenge that we represent.*

Kennedy pointed out that one in four voters in the Brent East by-election had switched to the Lib Dems and the party had won the seat.

'In Leicester South, one in five voters switched to the Liberal Democrats and the Liberal Democrats won in both cases. The Tories were relegated to a very poor third,' he added.

'So let's have none of this Tony Blair nonsense that we have heard at the conclusion of this campaign. He has cried wolf one too many times. No one believes his claims any more.'

Does anybody believe anything any more?

Howard took to the airwaves on BBC *Breakfast*. One more heave, everybody. He insisted he was not to blame for the negative tone of some of the campaign:

> *It is the actual untruths. It is not telling the truth that makes politics seem negative, that makes people think all politicians do*

> *not tell the truth. That is what contributes, I think, to the lack of*
> *trust in politics and politicians.*
> *I just say it as I see it, I'm afraid.*

Howard again insisted he had given no thought to what he might do in the event of defeat. 'I don't think about that. I think about what I can do today to show the people of this country they do not have to settle for second best.'

Blair, the one party leader who admits he will be out of a job in a few years' time at most, reproduced his manifesto launch for his final showcase press conference in Margaret Thatcher's old Finchley seat, now a Labour marginal with a 3,716 majority.

He took to the stage flanked by Prescott, Brown, inevitably, Jack Straw, unusually, and Margaret Beckett.

They stood at their 'Weakest Link' podiums with the rest of the Cabinet seated once again behind them. Was it accident or design that meant election coordinator Milburn was placed directly behind the PM? The consequence was that his face was never seen. It may sound trivial, but Kremlinologists made fortunes from analysing who stood next to Stalin on the Red Square balcony for the parade in celebration of the glorious revolution.

Blair said: 'The central question of this campaign is which party is best for the future of Britain – which party is best able to run and manage our economy in the interests of hard-working families.'

He said Labour had put forward positive policies throughout the campaign and had emerged as the 'one serious party with a serious programme for government'.

Blair said the choice tomorrow was very simple on the economy. 'Either we continue with economic stability . . . additional help for first-time buyers, pensioners and families. Or we return to the days of the past under the Conservatives with 15 per cent interest rates, high unemployment and boom and bust economics.'

He said the Tories planned to take money out of the NHS and subsidise private health care, contrasting this with Labour's plans for greater investment.

'So there are big choices on all the main areas of policy. There's only one choice in terms of government – a Labour government or a Conservative government.'

Blair warned that if Labour voters 'opted out or drifted off' by failing to vote, or making a protest vote for another party, they risked getting a Tory MP.

'The choice is fundamental between a Labour government or a Conservative government – forward with policies properly worked out for the future of this country or a return to the past,' he said.

'Between now and when the polls close we are going to be out in every single part of the country, making our case with conviction and confidence because we believe it is the right thing for the British people.'

Blair's message was forced home in a succession of speeches from the senior Cabinet ministers flanking him on the stage.

Brown said: 'Labour's pledge to the hard-working families of Britain is that economic stability will always come first and we will do nothing to put that stability at risk.'

A protest vote would not only allow the Tories into government 'by the back door', but would also 'by punishing Labour, end up punishing the people who most need Labour'.

He went on: 'So let us be clear, a protest vote in Labour-held seats is a vote to risk Michael Howard in Downing Street, to put economic stability and jobs at risk, tax credits for families at risk, investment in health and education at risk.

'So I ask people who share Labour's values to stand with Labour and help us do what is right and good to build a stronger, fairer, more prosperous society for the many and not just the few.'

Prescott said that he had got 'no sense at all' that voters wanted a return to Tory government as he had toured the country during the campaign. The question of leadership was highlighted by Beckett, who launched a direct attack on Howard. She said:

> *I believe Tony Blair has the leadership qualities that Michael Howard lacks.*
>
> *Unlike Michael Howard, Tony Blair does not duck the big issues, but confronts them. Unlike Michael Howard, Tony Blair does not exploit problems but tries to solve them. Unlike Michael Howard, Tony Blair does not pander to prejudice but challenges it. Unlike Michael Howard, Tony Blair does not blow in the wind but stands up for Britain.*
>
> *The central question is who is best equipped to run a country, to manage our economy and to prepare our country for the challenges of the future. I believe this team, with this Prime Minister, is the answer to the question.*

Straw said that as well as domestic issues, Britain 'takes seriously its responsibilities to the rest of the world'.

Promising to be 'strong' on defence, international terrorism and fighting world poverty he also briefly mentioned Iraq.

'We will work with our allies to help make the world a safer place including by building a democratic Iraq wanted by its people, and promoting a settlement in the Middle East with a viable and independent state of Palestine alongside a safe and secure state of Israel.'

It was formulaic, slightly stilted and somehow curiously dated. Maybe in 1997 it would have looked smooth, slick, modern and professional; but Blair's anxious appeal struck an awkward ill-at-ease note.

At the news conference following the presentation, Blair said he felt he still had much to achieve.

He told reporters: 'What moves me is very simple.

'We have made tremendous progress but there are still far too many children that do not get the right breaks, still far too many people that do not get the healthcare they need, far too many hard-working families that do not get support they depend on.

'We are creating, I believe, a better, fairer, stronger country but we have not achieved all we can achieve.'

As the questioning became circular Prescott said bluntly: 'I've had enough of this.'

Blair asked him, in a nervous jocular fashion: 'Do you mind if I take one or two more questions?'

On his Brent East walkabout, Kennedy stayed upbeat: 'We have stayed on the positive, we have put forward our case and I think we have really got through to people.

'Here we are in the closing 24 hours and people have got to make their minds up tomorrow. A lot of contests out there up and down the country, every vote for the Liberal Democrats, will matter and can make a difference.

'I think what we are seeing is support for the Conservatives disappearing like snow off a dyke, support for us coming up, and Labour very badly rattled by the Lib Dem challenge in the closing stages. It is a great optimistic feeling.'

Supporters and opponents competed to drown each other out as Howard arrived in Guildford.

As well as Labour activists, there were UK Independent Party members there to greet him for the first time since his campaign began. The Eurosceptics carried their placards on 30ft poles to keep them beyond the bunches of balloons Tory activists were using to mask their rivals' messages.

Howard was also heckled by a lone environmentalist who repeatedly shouted: 'Vote Green.' As the Tory leader delivered his stump speech from the steps of the Guildhall, a police officer filmed the crowd. After the scuffles of yesterday, just one UKIP supporter was led off by police for a ticking off for 'pushing in'.

Howard took it all in his stride.

> The British people can vote for things to stay as they are or they can vote for positive change.
>
> If they vote for positive change tomorrow, the country will wake up on Friday to a brighter, better Britain.
>
> We will have a government that will take action, action that really matters to the country, action that really matters to the people of our country.

In Norwich Howard drew on Liverpool's victory over Chelsea in the Champions League semi-final for inspiration: 'It may well be an omen, and I will use it to say to all Conservative candidates, to all Conservative activists, to everybody who wants to see a Conservative victory tomorrow, I would use the words of our wonderful Liverpool manager who said after the match that what you need is to work hard and believe to the end.'

In London it emerged that three Court of Appeal judges had yesterday quashed the findings of 'banana republic' Election Commissioner Richard Mawrey QC relating to Muhammad Afzal, one of three Birmingham councillors investigated for postal ballot corruption.

Lord Phillips said the ruling of Judge Mawrey would have to be changed to delete any reference to Mr Afzal being personally guilty of corrupt and illegal practices. But the Appeal Court said the rulings on the other two councillors stood. Mr Afzal said: 'I am glad I have been vindicated by the Court of Appeal. I have always believed in British justice.'

Meanwhile, back on the campaign treadmill: more marginals, more messages. Gordon Brown here, Tony Blair there, Michael

Howard here, Michael Howard there. Charles Kennedy every-
where.

Sky presenter Kay Burley brought a blush to the Prime Minister's
cheeks questioning him at Rawtenstall, Lancashire, about the 'five
times a night' claim.

KB: I just want to ask you very quickly . . . is it really five times a night?
TB: What?
KB: That is what Cherie said in the paper.
TB: I think that was a joke. I clearly hope so. At least you have made
me blush, anyway . . . first time in the campaign.

And well might he blush.

The BBC gave all three leaders the chance, in effect, to have a final
two- to three-minute party election broadcast putting each life into
the *Six O'Clock News*. Although technically being questioned by the
presenter they simply chanted their slogans off pat.

Kennedy said Labour were rattled. Howard promised a brighter,
better future. Blair said the contest would be tight.

By the end of the day, Howard had clocked up 10,407 miles on the
campaign trail since 11 April, Blair over 5,000 and Kennedy 14,060
miles. Their final journeys before polling day took them to their
constituency homes: Kennedy to his croft in Fort William, Howard
to his house overlooking Romney Marsh and Blair to Myrobella
(named after the plum trees in its garden) in Trimdon, overlooking
a school playing field which had once acted as an impromptu helicopter landing pad for George Bush's *Marine One*. Blair no doubt
cradled one of his endless mugs of tea, or perhaps he indulged in a
bottle of beer; Howard and Kennedy were more likely clutching a
Scotch.

What they all really needed was a good night's sleep. Even Blair.

9
The greasy poll

Thursday 5 May

Polling day, and Carmelia Bond was tidying the bedroom of her bungalow. Mrs Bond, 56, a hairdresser, had offered East Cambridgeshire District Council the use of the bedroom more than 25 years ago after the village hall closed. And ever since, the denizens of Chettisham have trooped to her door to cast their votes.

In Colchester, Oscar Ryland was all set to cast his first general election vote a few weeks after celebrating his eighteenth. But Oscar's opinion, sadly, will not count until at least 2021. He had only just turned eighteen months.

Council officials had sent a polling card by mistake. Father Pete, a 41-year-old car engineer, said: 'He's also had campaign leaflets personally addressed to him by the Lib Dem and Tory candidates.

'We think it's great. We're all in favour of getting the young interested in politics. He's been busy practising drawing crosses with his crayons.'

In Moray, Scotland, the Royal Oak in Urquhart was helping voters enjoy a pint while helping to shape the new government, doubling as the polling station.

Others in the Highlands included the sun lounge of a private house in Ross-shire.

The Monster Raving Loony Party were anxiously awaiting the British people's verdict on their, entirely sensible, policy platform of introducing a 99p coin 'to save on change'.

A performance artist began kissing a photograph of Blair in a bizarre show of support for the PM. Mark McGowan, 37, aimed to plant 100,000 kisses on the lips of a laminated A4 photo of the PM.

Standing outside the gates of Downing Street, Mr McGowan said he wanted to show his appreciation for Blair.

He said: 'I notice he has been getting a lot of abuse and I just wanted to show him some affection today and 100,000 kisses seemed like a lot.

'I haven't heard too many people come out and say good things about him. He has been Prime Minister for eight years and no one has said anything good about the economy. I think he is under-appreciated.'

All part of the patchwork quilt of quirks and quandaries thrown up by the process that begins at 7 a.m. one Thursday of the Prime Minister's choosing and ends at 10 p.m. when the ballot boxes are sealed. And the early hours of tomorrow will see climax, anti-climax, tears, jeers, heckling, howling and for some, triumph.

The final batch of eve-of-poll surveys had again given Labour a lead of between three and six points over the Tories. They tapped straight into the party's anxieties about turnout and tight contests.

There was more poll good news/bad news for Labour during the day. A Mori poll for London's *Evening Standard* put Labour on 38 per cent, the Tories on 33 per cent, and the Liberal Democrats on 23 per cent.

If those figures were replicated at the polls, Tony Blair would be returned to No. 10 Downing Street with a Commons majority of more than 110 seats. Bad news for the complacency factor.

What's more, some 27 per cent of those polled said they might change their minds as they go to cast their votes.

And there was another sting in the tail for Blair.

Those polled were asked, assuming he was returned to power, how long Blair should remain in No. 10 Downing Street. Some 53 per cent said he should step down within two years – including 35 per cent of Labour supporters.

Despite the convention that the parties do not campaign on polling day, Labour today circulated a mass email, in the name of champion cheerleader among party stalwarts, John Prescott, urging the supporters to get out and vote.

Prescott again argued that Labour supporters who failed to cast their vote, or who registered a protest vote with the Liberal Democrats, would effectively be voting for the Conservatives.

Prescott pleaded with the faithful:

> Today you must choose between Labour, under Tony Blair, or the Tories under Michael Howard. A vote for the Liberal Democrats will effectively be a vote for the Tories.
>
> It takes time to design and build new schools, hospitals and town centres and it takes eight years to fully train a doctor. Similarly, it takes time to embed a strong economy and principles of social justice. But it doesn't take long to scrap, cut and destroy! The Tories could wreck many of Labour's achievements in a few short months.
>
> Even though the polls show Labour in front, it doesn't mean we'll win. When I was elected to parliament in 1970, we were sixteen points ahead and everyone assumed Labour had it in the bag. But we lost.
>
> Your vote is vital. Whatever you do today, vote. And if you want Labour, vote Labour.

Blair took his advice. Just after 9 a.m. he strolled across the playing field from Myrobella with Cherie and sons Euan, 21, and Nicky, nineteen, who were voting for the first time in a general election.

The Blairs were among a steady trickle of voters going to Trimdon Colliery Community Centre to mark their X.

Blair, 52 tomorrow, said 'Good morning' to waiting reporters but made no other comment about today's ballot. On a cold and overcast day, the Prime Minister was dressed casually in a dark blue jacket, light blue shirt open at the neck, and dark blue jeans. Cherie wore a white jacket, black top and black trousers. The couple posed for photographs with their two eldest sons on the steps of the polling station before going inside to cast their votes. Howard was also rallying last-minute support. He hit the phones to stiffen the spines of would-be MPs, calling candidates in target seats to offer last-minute encouragement from a Midlands phone centre. Wife Sandra also joined in the ring-round.

Howard said they all agreed the party was 'going great guns'.

He added breathlessly: 'I've just spoken to our candidate in Peterborough where they have every polling station with a teller apart from two. That's the first time that has happened since 1979.'

Turnout was on everybody's minds. The tellers were there to check who had and – more importantly – had not, voted. The no-shows can then be chivvied. In Streatham, south London, there were cheering signs. Up to 10 a.m. officials reported about 50 voters an hour. They calculated this would give a turnout of at least 64 per cent. 2001's turnout of 58.9 per cent had been the lowest since 1918, with troops still returning from the Great War.

And on that turnout, believed Blair, depended at least in part, his place cemented forever in the history of the party he had so success-fully re-created in his own image.

If he achieves a third successive general election victory, he will have achieved something no Labour leader has ever done before. Harold Wilson won four elections, but his time in power was broken by a period of Tory rule. And if Blair sticks to his promise to stay at 10 Downing Street until the next general election, he will become the first Labour leader to serve three full terms as Prime Minister. He had already surpassed the record for longest occupancy of No. 10 by a Labour PM, which previously stood at 2,837 days, totted up by Wilson over two periods in office between 1966–70 and 1974–76.

And in 2003, he overtook post-war PM Clement Attlee's record for an unbroken stretch in power by a Labour leader of six years and 92 days.

If Blair were to win today, and stay on as Prime Minister, he would overhaul Margaret Thatcher's eleven years and 209 days in office in November 2008. By the end of a third term, only a handful of PMs in history – and none for over a century – would have outlasted him.

But he would have to breach his promise to retire at the end of his third term in order to equal Sir Robert Walpole's record of 20 years and 314 days in power (1721–42).

A Labour triumph would be the party's tenth victory in a general election. The first Labour Prime Minister, Ramsay MacDonald, took office in 1924 not through the ballot box, but because George V asked him to form a government after Stanley Baldwin's minority Conservative administration proved unable to govern.

Labour won its first general election under MacDonald in 1929, securing more seats than any other party for the first time, even though it won fewer votes than the Conservatives. Attlee won a historic landslide victory in the post-war election of 1945 and was re-elected by a much smaller majority in 1950.

He called an election the following year in the hope of securing a more comfortable position, but was defeated by Winston Churchill, despite polling more votes than the Tories.

Wilson won a wafer-thin absolute majority of four seats in 1964 and went back to the country in 1966 to secure a healthier margin before losing power to Edward Heath's Tories in 1970.

He returned to office in February 1974 with just four more MPs than the Tories and the smaller parties holding the balance of power. He called another election just eight months later, securing his fourth victory with a small, but workable, absolute majority.

Blair's predecessor as Labour PM, Jim Callaghan, never won a general election. He took office after Wilson's unexpected resignation in 1976 and served three years as PM before being defeated by Mrs Thatcher in 1979. These were the leaves of Labour history into which Blair's name, he hoped, would one day be inserted. And who could say then that he was not a true heir? No longer the 'yuppie' who hijacked 'our' party – but the greatest Labour leader in the party's history.

But it all now depended on all those slips of paper from Carmelia Bond's bungalow, and thousands of other polling stations across the nation. The polls closed at 10 p.m., freeing broadcasters to speculate on the result. At 31 seconds past 10 p.m. a story hit the wires:

PA NEWSFLASH: Tony Blair on course for historic third term with a Labour majority of 66, according to joint BBC/ITV News exit poll.

The Mori/NOP survey gave Labour a comfortable majority with 356 seats, the Conservatives getting 209 seats and the Liberal Democrats 53. The prediction forecast that Labour would win a 37 per cent share of the national vote, with the Tories on 33 per cent and the Lib Dems on 22 per cent. The findings were based on 19,800 voters at 120 polling stations across the UK.

Heads were shaking across the land. Either the TV exit poll – where people who have actually voted had been asked who they supported – had got it badly wrong; or every survey of national opinion had been badly out for not just weeks, but months. And Alastair had been right. Don't believe the national polls. There is something going on 'under the radar'.

Prescott was first to hit the airwaves, telling BBC1: 'We always want a good result. I always want to see a Labour government and there is going to be a Labour government, there is no doubt about that. I'm a little suspicious that it will be as low as you are suggesting.'

Asked about a possible low turnout, he added: 'I think it is a little difficult to tell what is happening around the country.

'But what is clear, and has been all the time, Labour is going to be the next government.'

Tory co-chairman Liam Fox would not concede defeat:

We've known for the last few days that this was going to be an election that was won or lost in those marginal seats.

We've known that a lot of people were very disillusioned with the current government and it remains to be seen exactly who switches across and where they do it.

For politicians this is a time perhaps for a little humility and just to wait and see what the voters deliver to us.

He added: 'I've seen exit polls before being wrong.'

Milburn said the exit poll was 'interesting', but urged caution. 'These polls have been wrong before. I guess they will be wrong again,' he said. 'But it does seem to indicate that there will be a Labour government and that's welcome news.'

Milburn denied that a slashed majority for Labour indicated that without Chancellor Gordon Brown the party's campaign would have been in serious trouble.

'No, I don't think that. I think we really do just have to wait and see. It's very early days.'

He continued: 'As far as our campaign is concerned we ran precisely the campaign we said we would; rooted in our strengths, our leadership, our values, our record on the economy, investment and improvement in the public services.

'There's a health warning on any exit poll, but if this exit poll is right, then Labour would have secured a third term in government for the first time in our party's history.

'Tony Blair would be only the second Prime Minister in history to win three general elections in a row with a mandate and a majority for a New Labour programme of government.

'What also appears clear tonight is that the Conservative Party has stalled. Their failure to change and failure to come to terms with modern Britain will be reflected tonight in their failure to secure any significant increase in their share of the popular vote.'

At 22.45 the first result was declared. Foreign Office minister Chris Mullin held Sunderland South for Labour but with a majority cut to 11,059 from 13,667.

Former Tory leadership contender Michael Portillo said the exit poll indicated 'an amazing result' for Labour. Portillo has his own place in late-night election folklore after Stephen Twigg took his Enfield Southgate seat as Labour swept to power in 1997.

He said: 'I think this is at the lower end of Labour's expectations. It may be at the higher end of Tory expectations.

'It is an amazing result for Labour. They've got 150 seats more than the Tories if this is right – they've won by 66.

'This makes Tony Blair actually a bigger winner in aggregate than Margaret Thatcher.'

Portillo added helpfully: 'But nonetheless on these results I would have thought, not Gordon Brown himself, but the Brown supporters, will be wondering how quickly they can move Tony Blair out of Downing Street. It would be possible, I think, to portray this result as disappointing and that the key factor in the campaign was that this time Tony Blair was not an electoral asset. He was becoming a liability.'

Neil, now Lord, Kinnock, knows all about opinion polls. In 1992 he thought he had been heading for victory, buoyed up by surveys showing Labour ahead of the Tories. The super-confidence culminated in the cringingly over-the-top and now notorious Sheffield Rally featuring a sub-rock star performance from Kinnock.

Tonight, speaking from Chicago, he was confident, too: 'I actually think that the majority will be slightly better than forecast by the exit poll.

'I think it will be in the 80s. The fact is that in a third successive election to get what by any standards is a very substantial majority in the House of Commons is a token of the resilience of Labour and Tony Blair and indeed Gordon Brown and is a secure majority, a very secure majority.' Challenged that the projected majority was 'hardly a token of affection and regard' for Blair, he countered: 'I don't take into account affection. I don't think that general elections are a time for sending Christmas or birthday cards.'

Ripples of anxiety were flowing elsewhere among Labour ranks, though. Education Secretary Ruth Kelly, speaking from her Bolton West constituency, said it looked 'likely' Labour was on course for a third term.

She added: 'I think that is a real vote of confidence in our programme since 1997, investment in schools, the investment in hospitals that we have seen, and actually the British public saying they want that investment to continue.'

Challenged that this was mainly Gordon Brown's achievement, she replied: 'The last eight years has all been Gordon Brown? I don't think so. It's been Gordon Brown, Tony Blair and the rest of the Cabinet and the Labour government working together.'

Asked how long Blair would stay as PM she replied chippily: 'It's a little premature to speculate on the future Labour leadership when the votes aren't yet counted.

'If we are right and we have seen a substantial Labour majority and we have secured a historic third term, Tony Blair has made it absolutely clear he wants to serve a full term.'

So there.

Nerves would have been fraying too in Myrobella. The exit poll, if true, was just the sort of nightmare that had been keeping Campbell, pollster Phillip Gould and David Hill awake at night. Firstly, it would indicate genuine public disenchantment with Blair. Secondly, a majority of the size predicted could lend disproportionate power to rebel backbenchers opposed to precisely the radical reform programme Blair keeps promising; not to mention the air of vulnerability of a man of whom some would quickly observe that the electoral emperor now had no clothes.

Leave aside the simple truth that in 1997 any Labour MP offered a third-term majority of the size the exit poll was predicting would have cheerfully signed away their very soul. Nobody ever accused politicians of having long and graceful memories. In the real world, only four out of 645 seats had been declared by midnight. But plenty of alarm bells were already ringing.

10

Things can only get bitter

Friday 6 May

By the time Blair arrived at Newton Aycliffe Community Centre for his Sedgefield count at 1.45 a.m., he knew that his party's private polling was right, and the national surveys had been wrong. But he didn't know how right, or how wrong.

The handful of Cabinet ministers, fielded on TV or speaking at their own counts, expressed nervous delight at the prospect of a third term. Milburn said Labour expected to have a lower majority, but if the exit poll was correct 'it's a pretty tremendous achievement and vindicates the sort of campaign we have run and what we have done in government'. He said that for the Tories there was 'no short-cut back' and if the projections were right it was a 'disastrous result' for them. Foreign Secretary Straw said that if Labour's majority was in the 60s, he would be 'very sad' for friends and colleagues who lost their seats. 'But a majority of 60 is a working majority,' he stressed. 'It's worked for governments in the past and it's easily workable for what would be a historic third term of a Labour government.'

Prescott claimed unequivocal victory as he celebrated his own re-election in Hull East: 'We clearly will be the government. It's the third term in government. The electorate have given the endorsement; we can get on with that work.'

But ex-Home Secretary Blunkett conceded the government needed to heed the lessons of the campaign. At his count he cautioned: 'There are two lessons: firstly that we should continue building on the economic prosperity and the legacy that Tony Blair and Gordon Brown have created and the investment in public services.

'Secondly, we need to hear the voice of the British people. Over the next five years we will need to be in touch with, listening to, in contact with people in the neighbourhood and the community, building confidence in politics and politicians.'

Brown, victorious in Kirkcaldy, said his win was not just 'a call for renewed work but a summons to even greater commitment'.

He vowed: 'I promise we will listen and we will learn so we can serve our country and communities even better in the years to come.'

The Tories meanwhile did not yet know which way to jump. If a cornerstone of their very strategy was to target relatively small groups of voters in target clusters to exploit volatility in the electorate it would always be, by definition, difficult to call its effect only a few hours after the polls closed.

Co-chairman Fox knew a Labour victory nationally was a foregone conclusion, but like Blair, did not know if he could trust the exit poll.

'It's always been an enormous mountain for us to climb, we knew that, and it was a very difficult task,' he said. But he added, in a classic slip of the tongue:

I think Michael Howard has led the party into that enormous mountain with great gusto and I think the party's campaign has been the most professional and disciplined we have had for a very long

> *time. So we will wait and see what happens now in the marginal*
> *seats. Our candidates' tails are up but we will wait and see.*

He meant 'up that enormous mountain', one assumes.

The Conservatives registered their first gain shortly after midnight, winning back David Mellor's old seat of Putney, south-west London, from Labour.

The Lib Dems were cautiously optimistic. They understood the 'glass ceiling' effect of a first-past-the-post system only too well; parties can garner popular support in ever increasing numbers but that is not necessarily reflected in seats won, until a tipping point is reached, when the reverse effect comes into play and a dispro-portionate number of gains suddenly tumble your way.

Party President Simon Hughes said the exit poll would see the party's best share of the vote since it was formed in 1988.

'If we get a Labour majority but with this share of the vote, they would have lost their authority in terms of who voted for them – barely one in three of the population. The Tories wouldn't have moved and we would have gone up 3 per cent or 4 per cent. So there's not a huge movement except Labour dropping a lot.'

Hughes added: 'My honest judgement is that the Tory core vote has held, and so there is a much tighter contest in the Tory/Liberal Democrat marginals – either where we are defending against Conservatives, or they are defending against us, than there is in the seats we are challenging Labour in. The problem for us is that in the seats we are challenging Labour in, there's a bigger gap for most of them between where we are and where we need to go.'

It was against this backdrop that Blair had left Myrobella for his count. He arrived in Newton Aycliffe with Cherie, sons Euan and Nicky and daughter Kathryn. Cherie's father Tony Booth, the actor, Campbell, and ever-present chief of staff Jonathan Powell.

After being returned with an increased majority, Blair took to the podium: 'I know Iraq has been a divisive issue in this country. But I hope now we can unite again and look to the future.

'If the predictions are right, it looks as if the Labour Party is heading, for the first time in its history, for a historic third term. It's not yet clear, obviously, what the majority is. But it seems as if it is clear that the British people wanted the return of a Labour government, but with a reduced majority. We have to respond to that sensibly and wisely and responsibly.'

Campbell made a rare campaign foray onto the airwaves, saying: 'Tony's probably had more stuff thrown at him than any politician in recent history. He's still standing. It looks like he's still the Prime Minister, and he will carry on doing a very good job for the country.'

But even as he was speaking, there was a poignant moment for the New Labour project. The Conservatives regained Enfield Southgate from a crestfallen Stephen Twigg, whose victory against Michael Portillo on the night of Labour's 1997 landslide had seemed to symbolise the total eclipse of the Tory cause. He was to be one of three junior ministers who lost their seats.

Blair meanwhile was given a tumultuous reception by Labour activists at the Trimdon Labour Club, where 150 supporters had gathered for their traditional election-night party in the smoke-filled function room, made even more crowded by a temporary backdrop, a media scrum and the TV technology. They burst into 'Happy Birthday' as the PM – 52 today – strode in shaking hands, embracing, waving.

Flanked by Cherie and his agent John Burton, Blair told the crowd and those watching on TV:

Thank you, all of you, who have been working in the constituency so hard over these past weeks. It has been difficult sometimes in the past few weeks, and I know you have had quite a lot of to put up with here. It's been a slightly different election from most elections, but the team has been unbelievable.

I feel so proud to have increased my majority, except I have to say I think it is really down to you guys that have done it.

John has put in so much work and become a big star on foreign media, because they have all been following him around on the campaign trail. It's been an amazing few weeks, and we haven't got all the results in yet, obviously, it looks as if we will actually have an historic third term. I know there are lots of lessons to learn but I do feel very proud of the fact that we have managed that historic third-term victory, and I feel proud too, not just of the changes we have made, but of what we can now do with this mandate.

Because one thing is for sure, the Conservative Party people did not want that.

And we managed in the course of the campaign, despite everything that was thrown at us, despite all the problems, we set out an agenda for change in this country and we are now going to take that agenda forward.

For our economy and jobs and living standards, for our NHS and our schools, to give our young people the chance they need in life, on law and order, on bringing back community policing, on making sure we give affordable childcare to people, on reshaping our public services and welfare state for the 21st century, making sure our economy – strong already – can compete in the new world.

I feel a real sense of enthusiasm for that agenda in the third term. When we look back and think now where we were in 1992, some thirteen years ago when after our fourth election defeat in a row people wrote off this party, there were people then who said Labour can never win again.

If we have actually achieved victory this evening, and have got a clear majority, as it seems that we have, that is a huge rebirth of our party. And we did it because we had the courage to change. We did it because we have the courage to take difficult decisions in government.

And yes, of course there will be disagreements and problems – there always are.

But I think we can be very, very proud of what we have done.

I like to think now that we have got the chance as a government, with all the experience behind us but with all the dedication and commitment for the future in front of us, to make the changes this country wants to see.

They want us to take the economy forward. They want us to complete the changes in the health service. They want to make sure that the investment they see in their schools is taken forward and rolled out across the country.

They want us to continue to bring down crime with that visible uniformed presence back on the streets. They want us to deal with the new issues that are coming up – how young couples get their feet on the first rung of the housing ladder, affordable childcare, pensions, making sure that we have in this country a decent, fair society combined with economic prosperity. That is what has happened over these past few years. For the first time, people have been able to vote for a progressive force in politics that combines sensible, tough economic policy, with social compassion, with a conscience, with a belief in helping others.

That is what we have tried to do. That is the party we have tried to create.

And it actually began here in Sedgefield, here where we learnt that we had to reconnect with the lives of people, here where we learnt that our values were fantastic, and the values of the British people, but we had to learn how to apply them in the modern world.

When I think now of what lies ahead of us, it is a tremendous challenge, but it is one we can respond to with an enormous amount of vigour, energy and determination.

It is a great, great thing and a privilege and an honour when the country elects a government.

To be elected once can be difficult, as we found. To be elected twice can be something, in consecutive terms of office, this party never knew before. To be re-elected for a third term is very special.

So it's a tremendous privilege and an honour, and let's make sure we use it now for the good of our country, and the people in it.

As his supporters cheered him to the rafters he shouted back: 'Thank you. I love you. You're wonderful.'

With that, Blair and his entourage sped off for a flight back to Luton, from where they would travel by road to another party in London. A very different plane journey, though, to the one Blair and Campbell had made in 1997 from Teesside Airport. On that occasion they had stared at each other in disbelief as the size of Labour's huge majority became ever more apparent. Howard, arriving at Leas Cliffe Hall in Folkestone with Sandra to hear his result, was all smiles. He increased his personal majority, but he finally conceded national defeat to Blair:

'It looks, from the way in which the national results are going, that Mr Blair is going to win a third term for Labour.

'I congratulate him on that victory. I believe that the time has now come for him to deliver on the things that really matter to the people of our country. If he does, in his third term, then he will have my support.'

He added: 'For the Conservative Party this election marks a real advance towards our recovery. The task which faces us in the next parliament is to complete that recovery and it's a task everyone in the Conservative Party will address with relish.'

So saying, he put his arm supportively around Sandra and they headed home. Howard knew he now had to write the final chapter of his own story as Conservative leader.

Kennedy arrived at his count in Dingwall, in his Ross, Skye and Lochaber constituency with Sarah and, inevitably, baby Donald. He knew in his heart of hearts the Lib Dems would only gain a handful of seats as the evidence became plain the Conservative vote had held up. If there had been a decapitation strategy, it had failed dismally except in one seat. Each senior Tory they had targeted had seen their majority increase, bar shadow Education Secretary Tim Collins who lost his Lake District berth.

All the Scottish seats had seen boundary changes, so Kennedy's seat was a new one. He said:

> But it is also new politics, it strikes me, that we have in our country as we watch these results coming in tonight and there is a long way to go yet.
>
> I think that the era of three-party politics right across the United Kingdom is now with us.
>
> I think it is going to be a very different House of Commons from the one we have had over the past eight years, and I think that is going to be very healthy, whatever people's political views.

As Blair was flying back to London, New Labour was dealt another blow in its political solar plexus.

Former Labour MP George Galloway and his Respect Party took Bethnal Green and Bow from Oona King, a supporter of Blair over Iraq.

Galloway let loose: 'Mr Blair, this defeat is for Iraq and the other defeats New Labour has received are for Iraq. All the people you have killed and all the loss of life have come back to haunt you and the best thing that the Labour Party can do is sack you tomorrow morning.'

The sound and fury of the election-night ordeal over, Blair was back in London now knowing he would enjoy a majority of probably 66 – the precise figure predicted by the TV exit poll.

He went from Luton airport – his plane was too big to land at Heathrow in the early hours – in convoy to the National Portrait Gallery for New Labour's last hurrah. The partying that had begun at the Royal Festival Hall eight years ago had to come to an end sometime.

The PM arrived just after 6 a.m. to join Prescott with wife Pauline, Brown, Milburn and hordes of activists who had been up all night partying with relief once victory at least was assured.

Blair's carefully stage-managed arrival was marred when hunt supporter Otis Ferry once again lunged forward to heckle him, only to be tackled by protection officers, turning the victory stroll into an unsightly scuffle in front of the PM as he swept on, unruffled.

Inside, the enthusiastic staff, who had not read, or had by now forgotten, the anti-triumphalist script, burst into chants of: 'Four more years!'

Blair tried to calm them down as he put the party gloss on his victory. He told them: 'You know how we've done it, we've done it by becoming a party that is true to its values of solidarity and social justice and opportunity for all, but making sure that we never let up on the necessity of applying those values to the modern reality in which we live.'

And speaking in New Labour's punctuation-less language he urged them: 'First time third term. Let's go out and make the most of it for us and for the country. Thank you.' And yes, he loved them too.

With rather less fanfare, Blair returned to No. 10. He was back in the arms of the Civil Service again.

As normal people, who had simply slept through election night, now began to realise over the breakfast table, Labour had taken a battering across the country and suffered some individual shocks. The Conservatives and the Lib Dems between them had squeezed and battered its vote as it won power with just under 37 per cent of the popular vote, the lowest share in modern times. But Tony Blair was still in No. 10.

Howard had failed to deliver. Nobody in their right mind – not even he in his own mind – had ever believed the Tories could possibly overhaul a 161-majority administration in one election. The Conservative leader may have played a heroic role for his party when he could have – as he was so fond of saying – just hung up his boots. He may have defied the campaign opinion polls and helped to start reshaping the political landscape, but he had not won. And he had made it a winner takes all election.

So as he sat at home with Sandra, all he really had to decide was what would be the best manner of his going. Howard may rub some people up the wrong way, but he is a dignified man and – as he had just proved, not only in the campaign itself but in the hits he had delivered consistently against Blair – a canny political operator. The one, possibly final, act of heroism he could do for his party would be somehow to try to avoid a succession battle bloodbath at which – with the exception of his own elevation – his colleagues had become peculiarly adept.

There was a bizarre political symmetry in the fact that this very exercise was now one of the main preoccupations of the bitter campaign rivals – 'liar' Blair and 'unscrupulous' Howard.

When the Conservatives announced he would be going to Roehampton to greet the party's new Putney MP, it hardly seemed like the act of a dispirited and forlorn figure about finally to throw in the towel. There had been stories for months before the election that if the Conservatives could bring Labour's majority down below 100, Howard would stay on for a considerable period. And the constituency was the first he had visited on becoming leader eighteen months ago, saying it was vital for the party to be able to regain such seats.

Howard began by heralding the party's revival. 'Of course I am very sad we didn't do better, sad for our many candidates who came within a whisker of winning a victory,' he said. 'Sad for all of our supporters who worked so hard, and sad for the millions of voters who put their trust in us.

'But today the Conservative Party can hold its head up high. We have begun the process of rebuilding our party, of building a broad and outward-looking party that reflects Britain in the 21st century.'

Then he dropped his bombshell:

As many of you know, as I have mentioned more than once during this campaign, I am 63 years old.

At the time of the next election, I'll be 67 or 68 and I believe that is simply too old to lead a party into government.

So if I can't fight the next election as leader of our party, I believe it is better for me to stand aside sooner rather than later so that the party can choose someone who can.

I want to avoid the uncertainty of prolonged debate about the leadership of the party.

I want the next Conservative leader to have much more time than I had to prepare our party for government.

If we achieved this much in just eighteen months, imagine what we can achieve in the next four to five years.

I have said many times since I became leader, that accountability matters. I have said that if people don't deliver they go, and for me, delivering meant winning the election.

I didn't do that. I didn't do that despite my best efforts and I want to do now what is best for my party and, above all, for my country.

Howard said it was well known that there was 'a good deal of dissatisfaction' with the leadership contest rules brought in under William Hague, whereby MPs whittled contenders down and if two were left standing the party at large voted. It had been Hague's own attempt to avoid leadership squabbles during his time at the top.

'So I intend to stay as leader until the party has had the opportunity to consider whether it wishes the rules to be changed and, if so, how they should be changed. When that process is complete, I will resign as leader.'

Howard added: 'I did not achieve what I set out to achieve, but I hope that over the last eighteen months I have at least given something back, not just for my party, but to my country. A voice for the forgotten majority. A voice for common sense. And above all, a credible opposition that can hold this government to account.'

It was a dignified exit. And the speculation on who would succeed him began within minutes.

Kennedy was the only party leader secure in his tenure, and the Lib Dems' tally of 62 seats in the new parliament was its highest since the old Liberals under Lloyd George. There would be quibbles over the failure to attack the Tories effectively in the south of England. But Lib Dems tend to conduct such affairs as political debate, not a dockyard brawl on liberty boat night. At their party HQ Kennedy signed off his campaign saying: 'In politics and in life in general, probably you can always do better.'

But he insisted: 'This was the very best result we have had for many, many generations.'

Blair had an audience of the Queen just after 11 a.m. at Buckingham Palace where she asked him to form a government. He returned to Downing Street, and abandoned his Jaguar halfway up, just as he had done on 5 April on his return from asking Her Majesty to dissolve parliament. And he strode to the same microphones:

Good morning everyone.

As you know I have just come from Buckingham Palace where the Queen has asked me to form a new government, which I will do.

It is a tremendous honour and privilege to be elected for a third term. And I am acutely conscious of that honour and that privilege. When I stood here first, eight years ago, I was a lot younger but also a lot less experienced. Today as well as having, in our minds, the priorities the people want, we, I, the government has the experience and the knowledge as well as the determination and commitment to deliver them.

Now the great thing about an election is that you go out and you talk to people for week upon week. And I have listened and I have learned. And I think I have a very clear idea of what the British people now expect from this government for a third term.

And I want to say to them very directly, that I, we, the government are going to focus relentlessly now on the priorities the people have set for us. And what are those priorities?

Well, first, they like the strong economy. But life is still a real struggle for many people, many families in this country. And they know that there are new issues – help for first-time buyers to get their feet on the first rungs of the housing ladder; families trying to cope with balancing work and family life; many people struggling to make ends meet; many families on low incomes who desperately need help and support to increase their living standards. Businesses, who whilst they like the economic stability, want us also to focus on stimulating enterprise, on investing in science and skills and technology for the future.

It is very clear what people want us to do, and we will do it.

Secondly, in relation to the public services, health and education, again people like the investment that has gone into public services, they welcome it. I found absolutely no support for any suggestion we cut back on that investment. But people want that money to work better for them. They want higher standards both of care and of education for the investment we are putting in. And so we will focus on delivering not just the investment but the reform and change in those public services.

And I will do so with passion, because I want to keep universal public services but know that the only way of keeping the consent for them is by making the changes necessary for the 21st century.

And third, people welcome the fact that so many more people are in work, and have moved off benefit and into work. But people still know there are too many people economically inactive who should be helped off benefit and into work. And they also know that on pensions today, whatever help we are giving for today's pensioners, tomorrow's pensioners are deeply concerned as to whether they will have the standard of life that they want. People expect us to sort these issues, we will do so.

And fourth, I have also learned that the British people are a tolerant and decent people. They did not want immigration made a divisive issue in the course of the election campaign. But they do believe there are real problems in our immigration and asylum system and they expect us to sort them out. And we will do so.

And fifth, I have been struck again and again in the course of this campaign by people's worries that in our country today, though they like the fact that we have got over the deference of the past, there is a disrespect that people don't like. And whether it is in the classroom or on the street or in town centres on a Friday or Saturday night, I want to focus on this issue. We have done a lot so far, with anti-social behaviour and additional numbers of police, but I want to make this a particular priority for this government: how we bring back a proper sense of respect in our schools, in our communities, in our towns, in our villages.

And arising out of that will be a radical programme of legislation that will focus exactly on those priorities. On education, on health, on welfare reform, on immigration, on law and order.

In addition, I know that Iraq has been a deeply divisive issue in this country. That has been very, very clear.

But I also know and believe that after this election people want to move on. They want to focus on the future in Iraq and here.

And I know too that there are many other issues that concern people in the international agenda. And we will focus on those. On poverty in Africa, on climate change, on making progress in Israel and Palestine.

So there is a very, very big agenda for a third-term Labour government. And as I said to you earlier, even if we don't have quite the same expectations that people had of us in 1997, yet now we do have, I believe, the experience as well as the commitment to see it through.

One final thing, which is that I have also learned something about the British people. That whatever their difficulties and disagreements with us, and whatever issues and challenges confront them, their values of fairness and decency and opportunity for all, and a belief that people should be able to get on, on hard work and merit not class or background, those values are the values I believe in, the values our government will believe in. Thank you.

The humility strategy was back on track. I have listened and I have learned, says Blair. Not so much 'I' and 'me', now it's 'us', now it's 'we' . . . or at least 'I, we, the government' in Blair's latest soundbite of choice.

Cherie, Euan, Nicky and Kathryn joined him on the steps of No. 10, and from the famous front door emerged four-year-old Leo to be scooped into Daddy's arms, and paw at his face in the Downing Street sunshine, to the delight of the massed ranks of photographers. With a final wave, the Blairs walked in for a traditional greeting from staff lined up in the front lobby.

He still had one last election job to do. The Cabinet.

Blair had had plenty of time to make up his mind. Milburn had said publicly he did not wish to remain after his election role, freeing a Cabinet post if needed. The PM was determined to reward his trusted friend Blunkett – who had resigned in the wake of a row connected to his well-publicised affair with the publisher Kimberly Quinn, a matter Blair regarded simply as a personal tragedy. And he wanted to tinker with some of the Whitehall structures. Or remodel the delivery infrastructure machinery, as he might put it.

So all the late afternoon and early evening, ministers traipsed into No. 10 to learn their fate. A curious Westminster tradition.

Blunkett was back as Work and Pensions Secretary. John Reid won the Defence Secretary post he wanted. Patricia Hewitt became Health Secretary. Geoff Hoon switched to Leader of the House as Peter Hain took over the reins at Northern Ireland to continue the intractable peace negotiations. Ed Miliband, rising Blairite star, came in as Minister of Communities and Local Government – a new post taking the bulk of the work from Prescott's department. Prescott was left with his title. Health Minister John Hutton joined as Cabinet Office Minister and Immigration Minister Des Browne was promoted to Chief Secretary to the Treasury. It was almost like a roll-call run on a film credit, explaining what had happened to all those in the movie since it had been filmed. After their performances in the election campaign this is what happened to David, Patricia, John . . .

Blair was determined to use his powers of patronage to the full before they began to wane.

He had begun his first administration in 1997 with a speech to Labour's landslide intake of MPs. They were, he told them, the servants of the people now. They were there not for personal glory but for the common good. To help the many, not the few.

Camelot had come to Westminster. But Blair's loyal court is scattered now, and jealousies and rivalries inevitably flourished, even within it, in the intervening years. The Cabinet table, as he well knows, is not round but coffin-shaped.

His children now have forever the memories and photographs of them bathed in sunshine with their father, as he walked into Labour history the moment he stepped back into No. 10 as the Queen's First Minister once more. It was a nice touch.

But Blair knows that before too long there will be those who seek to usurp him before he is ready to go, and are waiting to see the pictures of him finally walking out of that shiny black door.

His election 2005 majority, though eminently workable, had left him wounded and vulnerable to rebellion, if not open revolt.

That drama has yet to unfold.

But it will. Things can only get bitter.

The complete results

After 645 results out of 646 in the 2005 general election, the state of the parties was as below. The 'Forecast' column anticipates that the by-election in Staffordshire South (see page 314) will return a Conservative MP.

Party	Total seats	Gains	Losses	Total votes	Share %	Change %	Forecast
Labour	356	1	46	9,563,052	35.26	-5.49	356
Conservative	197	40	3	8,772,484	32.34	+0.68	198
Lib Dem	62	15	6	5,981,884	22.06	+3.79	62
UKIP				602,773	2.22	+0.76	
SNP	6	2		412,267	1.52	-0.24	6
Green				282,068	1.04	+0.42	
DUP	9	3	1	241,856	0.89	+0.20	9
BNP				192,746	0.71	+0.53	
Plaid Cymru	3		1	174,838	0.64	-0.10	3
Sinn Fein	5	1		174,530	0.64	-0.02	5
UUP	1		4	127,414	0.47	-0.35	1
SDLP	3	1	1	125,626	0.46	-0.18	3
Respect	1	1		68,094	0.25		1
SSP				43,514	0.16	-0.12	
Veritas				40,471	0.15		
Alliance				28,291	0.10	-0.01	
Ind Lab	1	1		20,505	0.08		1
Socialist Labour				20,027	0.07	-0.13	
KHHC	1			18,739	0.07	-0.04	1
WP				1,669	0.01		
Others			3	229,720	0.85		

Turnout	61.3%						
Total				27,122,568		Labour majority	66

Votes cast for the Speaker Michael Martin and his seat are included under Labour totals.

Collated constituency results

The results do not include that of the Staffordshire South constituency in which the Liberal Democrat candidate, Jo Harrison, died five days before the election, requiring that the constituency be fought in a by-election after parliament is reconvened.

Key to results table

#	Notional hold in a redrawn Scottish constituency
*	A sitting MP in that constituency
+	A sitting MP in a boundary change seat

Constituency	Result	Majority	Vote Share %	Swing %	MP
Aberavon	Lab Hold	13,937	60.05	-3.09	Dr Hywel Francis*
Aberdeen North	Lab Win#	6,795	42.47		Frank Doran+
Aberdeen South	Lab Win#	1,348	36.69		Anne Begg+
Aberd'nshire W & Kin	LD Win#	7,471	46.30		Sir Robert Smith+
Airdrie & Shotts	Lab Win#	14,084	59.01		Dr John Reid+
Aldershot	Con Hold	5,334	42.73	+0.55	Gerald Howarth*
Aldridge-Brownhills	Con Hold	5,507	47.39	-2.80	Richard Shepherd*
Altrincham & Sale W	Con Hold	7,159	46.42	+0.26	Graham Brady*
Alyn & Deeside	Lab Hold	8,378	48.83	-3.47	Mark Tami+
Amber Valley	Lab Hold	5,275	45.56	-6.33	Judy Mallaber*
Angus	SNP Win#	1,590	33.65		Mike Weir*
Antrim East	DUP Gain From UUP	7,304	49.63	+13.59	Sammy Wilson
Antrim North	DUP Hold	17,965	54.78	+4.92	Rev Ian Paisley*
Antrim South	DUP Gain From UUP	3,448	38.22	+3.45	Rev. William McCrea
Argyll & Bute	LD Win#	5,636	36.52		Alan Reid+

Constituency	Result	Majority	Vote Share %	Swing %	MP
Arundel & S Downs	Con Gain From Ind Con	11,309	49.81	-2.42	Nick Herbert
Ashfield	Lab Hold	10,213	48.59	-9.54	Geoff Hoon*
Ashford	Con Hold	13,298	51.56	+4.13	Damian Green*
Ashton-under-Lyne	Lab Hold	13,952	57.38	-5.09	David Heyes*
Aylesbury	Con Hold	11,066	49.07	+1.75	David Lidington*
Ayr, Carrick & Cum	Lab Win#	9,997	45.36		Sandra Osborne+
Ayrshire Central	Lab Win#	10,423	46.43		Brian Donohoe+
Ayrshire N & Arran	Lab Win#	11,296	43.92		Katy Clark
Banbury	Con Hold	10,797	46.94	+1.77	Tony Baldry*
Banff & Buchan	SNP Win#	11,837	51.17		Alex Salmond*
Barking	Lab Hold	8,883	47.83	-13.07	Margaret Hodge*
Barnsley Central	Lab Hold	12,732	61.08	-8.56	Eric Illsley*
Barnsley E & Mexboro	Lab Hold	14,125	62.921	-4.59	Jeff Ennis*
Barnsley W & Pen	Lab Hold	11,314	55.28	-3.29	Michael Clapham*
Barrow & Furness	Lab Hold	6,037	47.57	-8.10	John Hutton*
Basildon	Lab Coop Hold	3,142	43.39	-9.33	Angela Smith*
Basingstoke	Con Gain From DUP	4,680	41.47	-1.23	Maria Miller*
Bassetlaw	Lab Hold	10,837	56.63	+1.34	John Mann*
Bath	LD Hold	4,638	43.85	-6.63	Don Foster*
Batley & Spen	Lab Hold	5,788	48.54	-4.04	Mike Wood*
Battersea	Lab Hold	163	40.36	-9.90	Martin Linton*
Beaconsfield	Con Hold	15,253	55.43	+2.68	Dominic Grieve*
Beckenham	Con Hold	8,401	45.30	+0.05	Jacqui Lait*
Bedford	Lab Hold	3,383	41.73	-6.21	Patrick Hall*
Bedfordshire Mid	Con Gain From Ind Con	11,355	46.30	-3.62	Nadine Dorries
Bedfordshire NE	Con Hold	12,251	49.94	+2.54	Alistair Burt*
Bedfordshire SW	Con Hold	8,277	48.27	+6.14	Andrew Selous*
Belfast East	DUP Hold	5,877	49.15	+6.61	Peter Robinson*
Belfast North	DUP Hold	5,188	45.63	+4.79	Nigel Dodds*
Belfast South	SDLP Gain From UUP	1,235	32.28	+1.69	Dr Alasdair McDonnell

Election 2005

Constituency	Result	Majority	Vote Share %	Swing %	MP
Belfast West	SF Hold	19,315	70.48	+4.37	Gerry Adams*
Berw'shire, Rox & Sel	LD Win#	5,901	41.85		Michael Moore+
Berwick-upon-Tweed	LD Hold	8,632	52.79	+1.42	Alan Beith
Bethnal Green & Bow	Respect Gain From Lab	823	35.91		George Galloway+
Beverley & Holderness	Con Hold	2,580	40.70	-0.63	Graham Stuart
Bexhill & Battle	Con Hold	13,449	52.59	+4.46	Greg Barker*
Bexleyheath & Cray	Con Gain From Lab	4,551	46.32	+6.39	David Evennett
Billericay	Con Hold	11,206	52.17	+4.78	John Baron*
Birkenhead	Lab Hold	12,934	64.99	-5.49	Frank Field*
Birm'ham Edgbaston	Lab Hold	2,349	43.75	-5.30	Gisela Stuart*
Birm'ham Erdington	Lab Hold	9,575	52.95	-3.82	Siôn Simon*
Birm'ham Hall Green	Lab Hold	5,714	47.21	-7.35	Stephen McCabe*
Birm'ham Hodge Hill	Lab Hold	5,449	48.64	-15.22	Liam Byrne*
Birm'ham Ladywood	Lab Hold	6,801	51.92	-16.96	Clare Short*
Birm'ham Northfield	Lab Hold	6,454	49.65	-6.31	Richard Burden*
Birm'ham Perry Barr	Lab Hold	7,948	46.95	+0.41	Khalid Mahmood*
Birm'ham Selly Oak	Lab Hold	8,851	46.06	-6.35	Dr Lynne Jones*
Birm Spark & Sm Heath	Lab Hold	3,289	36.10	-21.44	Roger Godsiff*
Birm'ham Yardley	LD Gain From Lab	2,672	46.37	+8.03	John Hemming
Bishop Auckland	Lab Hold	10,047	50.00	-8.82	Helen Goodman
Blaby	Con Hold	7,873	45.53	-0.86	Andrew Robathan*
Blackburn	Lab Hold	8,009	42.01	-12.13	Jack Straw*
Bl'kpool N & Fleetw'd	Lab Hold	5,062	47.63	-3.12	Joan Humble*
Blackpool South	Lab Hold	7,922	50.53	-3.76	Gordon Marsden*
Blaenau Gwent	Ind Lab Gain From Lab	9,121	58.17		Peter Law
Blaydon	Lab Hold	5,335	51.52	-3.33	David Anderson
Blyth Valley	Lab Hold	8,527	54.95	-4.75	Ronnie Campbell*
Bognor R & Littleh'ton	Con Hold	7,822	44.62	-0.55	Nick Gibb*
Bolsover	Lab Hold	18,437	65.16	-3.43	Dennis Skinner*

Constituency	Result	Majority	Vote Share %	Swing %	MP
Bolton North East	Lab Hold	4,103	45.72	-8.63	David Crausby*
Bolton South East	Lab Hold	11,638	56.92	-4.94	Dr Brian Iddon*
Bolton West	Lab Hold	2,064	42.52	-4.50	Ruth Kelly*
Bootle	Lab Hold	16,357	75.50	-2.05	Joe Benton*
Boston & Skegness	Con Hold	5,907	46.17	+3.26	Mark Simmonds*
Bosworth	Con Hold	5,319	42.55	-1.85	David Tredinnick*
Bournemouth East	Con Hold	5,244	45.01	+1.71	Tobias Ellwood
Bournemouth West	Con Hold	4,031	41.44	-1.41	Sir John Butterfill*
Bracknell	Con Hold	12,036	49.69	+3.05	Andrew Mackay*
Bradford North	Lab Hold	3,511	42.51	-7.23	Terry Rooney*
Bradford South	Lab Hold	9,167	49.05	-6.74	Gerry Sutcliffe*
Bradford West	Lab Hold	3,026	40.06	-7.90	Marsha Singh*
Braintree	Con Gain From Lab	3,893	44.48	+3.21	Brooks Newmark
Brecon & Radnorshire	LD Hold	3,905	44.81	+7.97	Roger Williams*
Brent East	LD Hold	2,712	47.52	+36.95	Sarah Teather*
Brent North	Lab Hold	5,641	48.82	-10.55	Barry Gardiner*
Brent South	Lab Hold	11,326	58.80	-14.48	Dawn Butler
Brentford & Isleworth	Lab Hold	4,411	39.83	-12.46	Ann Keen*
Brentwood & Ongar	Con Hold	11,612	53.48	+15.45	Eric Pickles*
Bridgend	Lab Hold	6,523	43.35	-9.14	Madeleine Moon
Bridgwater	Con Hold	8,469	44.15	+3.70	Ian Liddell-Grainger*
Brigg & Goole	Lab Hold	2,894	45.23	-3.65	Ian Cawsey*
Brighton Kemptown	Lab Hold	2,737	39.93	-7.89	Dr Desmond Turner*
Brighton Pavilion	Lab Coop Hold	5,030	35.52	-13.22	David Lepper*
Bristol East	Lab Hold	8,621	45.91	-9.08	Kerry McCarthy
Bristol North West	Lab Coop Hold	8,962	46.73	-5.41	Dr Doug Naysmith*
Bristol South	Lab Hold	11,142	49.09	-7.78	Dawn Primarolo*
Bristol West	LD Gain From Lab	5,128	38.31	+9.42	Stephen Williams
Bromley & Chislehurst	Con Hold	13,342	51.12	+1.59	Eric Forth*
Bromsgrove	Con Hold	10,080	51.01	-0.74	Julie Kirkbride*
Broxbourne	Con Hold	11,509	53.85	-0.28	Charles Walker

Election 2005

Constituency	Result	Majority	Vote Share %	Swing %	MP
Broxtowe	Lab Hold	2,296	41.91	-6.73	Dr Nick Palmer*
Buckingham	Con Hold	18,129	57.44	+3.77	John Bercow*
Burnley	Lab Hold	5,778	38.48	-10.85	Kitty Ussher
Burton	Lab Hold	1,421	41.14	-7.90	Janet Dean*
Bury North	Lab Hold	2,926	43.11	-8.12	David Chaytor*
Bury South	Lab Hold	8,912	50.42	-8.78	Ivan Lewis*
Bury St Edmunds	Con Hold	9,930	46.24	+2.77	David Ruffley*
Caernarfon	PC Hold	5,209	45.53	+1.15	Hywel Williams*
Caerphilly	Lab Hold	15,359	56.57	-1.62	Wayne David*
Caithness, S'land & E R	LD Win#	8,168	50.45		John Thurso+
Calder Valley	Lab Hold	1,367	38.57	-4.11	Christine McCafferty*
Camb'well & Peckham	Lab Hold	13,483	65.31	-4.30	Harriet Harman*
Cambridge	LD Gain From Lab	4,339	43.93	+18.87	David Howarth
Cambridgeshire NE	Con Hold	8,901	47.53	-0.61	Malcolm Moss*
Cambridgeshire NW	Con Hold	9,833	45.84	-3.97	Shailesh Vara
Cambridgeshire S	Con Hold	8,001	44.97	+0.73	Andrew Lansley*
Cambridgeshire SE	Con Hold	8,624	47.05	+2.86	James Paice*
Cannock Chase	Lab Hold	9,227	51.30	-4.83	Dr Tony Wright*
Canterbury	Con Hold	7,471	44.37	+2.91	Julian Brazier*
Cardiff Central	LD Gain From Lab	5,593	49.79	+13.08	Jenny Willott
Cardiff North	Lab Hold	1,146	39.04	-6.86	Julie Morgan*
Cardiff S & Penarth	Lab Coop Hold	9,334	47.40	-8.80	Alun Michael*
Cardiff West	Lab Hold	8,167	45.51	-9.04	Kevin Brennan*
Carlisle	Lab Hold	5,695	48.08	-3.07	Eric Martlew*
Carmarthen E & Din	PC Hold	6,718	45.86	+3.47	Adam Price*
Carmarth'n W&Pem S	Lab Hold	1,910	36.85	-4.73	Nick Ainger*
Carshalton & Wall	LD Hold	1,068	40.31	-4.73	Tom Brake*
Castle Point	Con Hold	8,201	48.29	+3.68	Bob Spink*
Ceredigion	LD Gain From PC	219	36.53	+9.66	Mark Williams
Charnwood	Con Hold	8,809	46.57	-1.67	Stephen Dorrell*

Constituency	Result	Majority	Vote Share %	Swing %	MP
Chatham & Aylesford	Lab Hold	2,332	43.70	-4.57	Jonathan Shaw*
Cheadle	LD Hold	4,020	48.88	+6.51	Patsy Calton*
Chelmsford West	Con Hold	9,620	44.95	+2.48	Simon Burns*
Cheltenham	LD Hold	2,303	41.54	-6.19	Martin Horwood
Chesham & Amersham	Con Hold	13,798	54.40	+3.90	Cheryl Gillan*
Chester, City of	Lab Hold	915	38.88	-9.61	Christine Russell*
Chesterfield	LD Hold	3,045	47.31	-0.50	Paul Holmes*
Chichester	Con Hold	10,860	48.29	+1.25	Andrew Tyrie*
Ch'gford & Wdfd Grn	Con Hold	10,641	53.19	+4.96	Iain Duncan Smith*
Chipping Barnet	Con Hold	5,960	46.59	+0.18	Theresa Villiers
Chorley	Lab Hold	7,625	50.70	-1.62	Lindsay Hoyle*
Christchurch	Con Hold	15,559	54.70	-0.39	Christopher Chope*
C of Lon & Westm'ster	Con Hold	8,095	47.30	+0.99	Mark Field*
Cleethorpes	Lab Hold	2,642	43.33	-6.25	Shona McIsaac*
Clwyd South	Lab Hold	6,348	44.97	-6.43	Martyn Jones*
Clwyd West	Con Gain From Lab	133	36.25	+0.67	David Jones
Coatbridge, Chr's & B	Lab Win#	19,519	64.48		Thomas Clarke+
Colchester	LD Hold	6,277	47.09	+4.50	Bob Russell*
Colne Valley	Lab Hold	1,501	35.85	-4.52	Kali Mountford*
Congleton	Con Hold	8,246	45.39	-0.91	Lady Ann Winterton*
Conwy	Lab Hold	3,081	37.08	-4.73	Betty Williams*
Copeland	Lab Hold	6,320	50.46	-1.31	Jamie Reed
Corby	Lab Coop Hold	1,517	43.10	-6.21	Phil Hope*
Cornwall North	LD Hold	3,076	42.59	-9.43	Dan Rogerson
Cornwall SE	LD Hold	6,507	46.74	+0.84	Colin Breed*
Cotswold	Con Hold	9,688	49.26	-1.05	Geoffrey Clifton-Brown*
Coventry NE	Lab Hold	14,222	56.94	-4.08	Bob Ainsworth*
Coventry NW	Lab Hold	9,315	48.21	-3.24	Geoffrey Robinson*
Coventry South	Lab Hold	6,255	45.84	-4.35	Jim Cunningham*
Crawley	Lab Hold	37	39.10	-10.22	Laura Moffatt*
Crewe & Nantwich	Lab Hold	7,078	48.84	-5.45	Gwyneth Dunwoody*
Crosby	Lab Hold	5,840	48.25	-6.89	Claire Curtis-Thomas*

Election 2005

Constituency	Result	Majority	Vote Share %	Swing %	MP
Croydon Central	Con Gain From Lab	75	40.80	+2.29	Andrew Pelling
Croydon North	Lab Hold	13,888	53.72	-9.81	Malcolm Wicks*
Croydon South	Con Hold	13,528	51.78	+2.58	Richard Ottaway*
Cumbernauld, Kilsyth	Lab Win#	11,562	51.81		Rosemary McKenna+
Cynon Valley	Lab Hold	13,259	64.07	-1.53	Ann Clwyd*
Dagenham	Lab Hold	7,605	50.08	-7.15	Jonathan Cruddas*
Darlington	Lab Hold	10,404	52.41	-3.93	Alan Milburn*
Dartford	Lab Hold	706	42.56	-5.42	Dr Howard Stoate*
Daventry	Con Hold	14,686	51.63	+2.39	Tim Boswell*
Delyn	Lab Hold	6,644	45.70	-5.76	David Hanson*
Denton & Reddish	Lab Hold	13,498	57.39	-7.84	Andrew Gwynne
Derby North	Lab Hold	3,757	43.98	-6.90	Bob Laxton*
Derby South	Lab Hold	5,657	45.38	-11.06	Margaret Beckett*
Derbyshire NE	Lab Hold	10,065	49.31	-6.33	Natascha Engel
Derbyshire South	Lab Hold	4,495	44.47	-6.23	Mark Todd*
Derbyshire West	Con Hold	10,753	47.67	-0.33	Patrick McLoughlin*
Devizes	Con Hold	13,194	48.54	+1.29	Michael Ancram*
Devon East	Con Hold	7,936	46.86	-0.56	Hugo Swire*
Devon North	LD Hold	4,972	45.91	+1.68	Nick Harvey*
Devon South West	Con Hold	10,141	44.81	-2.03	Gary Streete*
Devon West & Torridge	Con Gain From LD	3,236	42.70	+2.68	Geoffrey Cox
Dewsbury	Lab Hold	4,615	40.96	-9.59	Shahid Malik
Don Valley	Lab Hold	8,598	52.67	-1.95	Caroline Flint*
Doncaster Central	Lab Hold	9,802	51.29	-7.81	Rosie Winterton*
Doncaster North	Lab Hold	12,656	55.52	-7.58	Ed Miliband
Dorset Mid & Poole N	LD Hold	5,482	48.72	+6.72	Annette Brooke*
Dorset North	Con Hold	2,244	44.90	-1.76	Robert Walter*
Dorset South	Lab Hold	1,812	41.64	-0.32	Jim Knight*
Dorset West	Con Hold	2,461	46.53	+1.89	Oliver Letwin*
Dover	Lab Hold	4,941	45.28	-3.53	Gwyn Prosser*
Down North	UUP Hold	4,944	50.38	-5.64	Lady Sylvia Hermon*

Constituency	Result	Majority	Vote Share %	Swing %	MP
Down South	SDLP Hold	9,140	44.75	-1.60	Eddie McGrady*
Dudley North	Lab Hold	5,432	44.21	-7.90	Ian Austin
Dudley South	Lab Hold	4,244	45.32	-4.51	Ian Pearson*
Dulwich & W N'wood	Lab Hold	8,807	45.39	-9.51	Tessa Jowell*
Dumfries & Galloway	Lab Win#	2,922	41.12		Russell Brown+
Dumfriessh, Cl'dale&T	Con Win Notional Gain From Lab	1,738	36.18		David Mundell
Dunbartonshire E	LD Win Notional Gain From Lab	4,061	41.81		Jo Swinson
Dunbartonshire W	Lab Coop Win#	12,553	51.94		John McFall+
Dundee East	SNP Win Notional Gain From Lab	383	37.20		Stewart Hosie
Dundee West	Lab Win#	5,379	44.59		James McGovern
Dunfermline & Fife W	Lab Win#	11,562	47.44		Rachel Squire+
Durham North	Lab Hold	16,781	64.09	-3.12	Kevan Jones*
Durham NW	Lab Hold	13,443	53.94	-8.58	Hilary Armstrong*
Durham, City of	Lab Hold	3,274	47.17	-8.88	Roberta Blackman-Woods
Ealing Acton&Shep B	Lab Hold	5,520	41.84	-12.31	Andrew Slaughter
Ealing North	Lab Hold	7,059	45.06	-10.60	Stephen Pound*
Ealing Southall	Lab Hold	11,440	48.76	+1.26	Piara Khabra*
Easington	Lab Hold	18,636	71.36	-5.46	John Cummings*
East Ham	Lab Hold	13,155	53.90	-19.18	Stephen Timms*
East Kilbride, S & L	Lab Win#	14,723	48.74		Adam Ingram+
East Lothian	Lab Win#	7,620	41.47		Anne Picking*
Eastbourne	Con Hold	1,124	43.46	-0.62	Nigel Waterson*
Eastleigh	LD Hold	568	38.61	-2.09	Christopher Huhne
Eccles	Lab Hold	12,886	56.89	-7.59	Ian Stewart*
Eddisbury	Con Hold	6,195	46.37	+0.06	Stephen O'Brien*
Edinburgh East	Lab Win#	6,202	40.04		Gavin Strang+
Edinburgh N & Leith	Lab Coop Win#	2,153	34.23		Mark Lazarowicz+
Edinburgh South	Lab Win#	405	33.23		Nigel Griffiths+
Edinburgh SW	Lab Win#	7,242	39.79		Alistair Darling+
Edinburgh West	LD Win#	13,600	49.52		John Barrett+

321

Election 2005

Constituency	Result	Majority	Vote Share %	Swing %	MP
Edmonton	Lab Coop Hold	8,075	53.18	-5.71	Andy Love*
Ellesmere Port & N	Lab Hold	6,486	48.42	-6.87	Andrew Miller*
Elmet	Lab Hold	4,528	47.22	-0.76	Colin Burgon*
Eltham	Lab Hold	3,276	43.57	-9.27	Clive Efford*
Enfield North	Lab Hold	1,920	44.31	-2.37	Joan Ryan*
Enfield Southgate	Con Gain From Lab	1,747	44.61	+6.00	David Burrowes
Epping Forest	Con Hold	14,358	53.02	+3.90	Eleanor Laing*
Epsom & Ewell	Con Hold	16,447	54.42	+6.34	Chris Grayling*
Erewash	Lab Hold	7,084	44.45	-4.76	Liz Blackman*
Erith & Thamesmead	Lab Hold	11,500	54.40	-4.87	John Austin*
Esher & Walton	Con Hold	7,727	45.70	-3.27	Ian Taylor*
Essex North	Con Hold	10,903	47.56	+0.12	Bernard Jenkin*
Exeter	Lab Hold	7,665	41.07	-8.71	Ben Bradshaw*
Falkirk	Lab Win#	13,475	50.85		Eric Joyce+
Falmouth & Camb	LD Gain From Lab	1,886	34.88	+10.42	Julia Goldsworthy
Fareham	Con Hold	11,702	49.72	+2.65	Mark Hoban*
Faversham & Mid K	Con Hold	8,720	49.72	+4.07	Hugh Robertson*
Feltham & Heston	Lab Coop Hold	6,820	47.59	-11.58	Alan Keen*
Fermanagh & S Tyrone	SF Hold	4,582	38.20	+4.07	Michelle Gildernew*
Fife North East	LD Win#	12,571	52.10		Sir Menzies Campbell+
Finchley & G'ders Grn	Lab Hold	741	40.47	-5.80	Rudi Vis*
Folkestone & Hythe	Con Hold	11,680	53.94	+8.91	Michael Howard*
Forest of Dean	Con Gain From Lab	2,049	40.88	+2.09	Mark Harper
Foyle	SDLP Hold	5,957	46.30	-3.90	Mark Durkan
Fylde	Con Hold	12,459	53.37	+1.10	Michael Jack*
Gainsborough	Con Hold	8,003	43.87	-2.34	Edward Leigh*
Gatesh'd E & Wash W	Lab Hold	13,407	60.57	-7.57	Sharon Hodgson
Gedling	Lab Hold	3,811	46.13	-4.95	Vernon Coaker*
Gillingham	Lab Hold	254	41.23	-3.27	Paul Clark*
Glasgow Central	Lab Win#	8,531	48.21		Mohammad Sarwar+

Constituency	Result	Majority	Vote Share %	Swing %	MP
Glasgow East	Lab Win#	13,507	60.68		David Marshall+
Glasgow North	Lab Win#	3,338	39.40		Ann McKechin+
Glasgow North East	Speaker Win#	10,134	53.32		Michael Martin+
Glasgow North West	Lab Win#	10,093	49.17		John Robertson+
Glasgow South	Lab Win#	10,832	47.24		Tom Harris+
Glasgow South West	Lab Coop Win#	13,896	60.22		Ian Davidson+
Glenrothes	Lab Win#	10,664	51.91		John MacDougall+
Gloucester	Lab Hold	4,271	44.67	-1.09	Parmjit Dhanda*
Gordon	LD Win#	11,026	45.02		Malcolm Bruce+
Gosport	Con Hold	5,730	44.77	+1.13	Peter Viggers+
Gower	Lab Hold	6,703	42.45	-4.87	Martin Caton*
Grantham & Stamford	Con Hold	7,445	46.89	+0.82	Quentin Davies*
Gravesham	Con Gain From Lab	654	43.69	+4.94	Adam Holloway
Great Grimsby	Lab Hold	7,654	47.06	-10.85	Austin Mitchell*
Great Yarmouth	Lab Hold	3,055	45.56	-4.84	Anthony Wright*
Greenwich & Wool'ch	Lab Hold	10,146	49.21	-11.31	Nick Raynsford*
Guildford	Con Gain From LD	347	43.76	+2.33	Anne Milton
Hackney N & Stoke N	Lab Hold	7,427	48.56	-12.48	Diane Abbott*
Hackney S & Shored	Lab Coop Hold	10,204	52.88	-11.28	Meg Hillier
Halesowen & R'ley R	Lab Hold	4,337	46.56	-6.41	Sylvia Heal*
Halifax	Lab Coop Hold	3,417	41.80	-7.22	Linda Riordan
Halt'price & Howden	Con Hold	5,116	47.45	+4.22	David Davis*
Halton	Lab Hold	14,606	62.78	-6.38	Derek Twigg*
Ham'smith & Fulham	Con Gain From Lab	5,029	45.43	+5.64	Greg Hands
Hampshire East	Con Hold	5,509	45.68	-1.95	Michael Mates*
Hampshire NE	Con Hold	12,549	53.73	+0.53	James Arbuthnot*
Hampshire NW	Con Hold	13,264	50.73	+0.61	Sir George Young*
Hampstead & Highgate	Lab Hold	3,742	38.31	-8.58	Glenda Jackson*
Harborough	Con Hold	3,892	42.85	-1.84	Edward Garnier*
Harlow	Lab Hold	97	41.41	-6.38	Bill Rammell*

Election 2005

Constituency	Result	Majority	Vote Share %	Swing %	MP
Harrogate & Knaresbro	LD Hold	10,429	56.26	+0.68	Phil Willis*
Harrow East	Lab Hold	4,730	46.13	-9.18	Tony McNulty*
Harrow West	Lab Coop Hold	2,028	42.50	-7.11	Gareth Thomas*
Hartlepool	Lab Hold	7,478	51.50	-7.64	Iain Wright*
Harwich	Con Gain From Lab	920	42.13	+1.90	Douglas Carswell
Hastings & Rye	Lab Hold	2,026	42.11	-4.97	Michael Foster*
Havant	Con Hold	6,508	44.42	+0.48	David Willetts*
Hayes & Harlington	Lab Hold	10,847	58.69	-6.98	John McDonnell*
Hazel Grove	LD Hold	7,748	49.48	-2.55	Andrew Stunell*
Hemel Hempstead	Con Gain From Lab	499	40.33	+1.87	Michael Penning
Hemsworth	Lab Hold	13,481	58.79	-6.60	Jon Trickett*
Hendon	Lab Hold	2,699	44.45	-8.02	Andrew Dismore*
Henley	Con Hold	12,793	53.49	+7.40	Boris Johnson*
Hereford	LD Hold	962	43.26	+2.37	Paul Keetch*
Hertford & Stortford	Con Hold	13,097	50.46	+5.79	Mark Prisk*
Hertfordshire NE	Con Hold	9,138	47.29	+3.17	Oliver Heald*
Hertfordshire SW	Con Hold	8,473	46.91	+2.62	David Gauke
Hertsmere	Con Hold	11,093	53.24	+5.40	James Clappison*
Hexham	Con Hold	5,020	42.41	-2.19	Peter Atkinson*
Heywood & Mid'ton	Lab Coop Hold	11,083	49.77	-7.93	Jim Dobbin*
High Peak	Lab Hold	735	39.63	-6.99	Tom Levitt*
Hitchin & Harpenden	Con Hold	11,393	49.86	+2.51	Peter Lilley*
Holborn & St Pancras	Lab Hold	4,787	43.24	-10.63	Frank Dobson*
Hornchurch	Con Gain From Lab	480	42.85	+0.57	James Brokenshire
Hornsey & Wood G	LD Gain From Lab	2,395	43.34	+17.57	Lynne Featherstone
Horsham	Con Hold	12,627	49.99	-1.49	Francis Maude*
Houghton & Wash E	Lab Hold	16,065	64.31	-8.90	Fraser Kemp*
Hove	Lab Hold	420	37.47	-8.38	Celia Barlow
Huddersfield	Lab Coop Hold	8,351	46.77	-6.48	Barry Sheerman*

Constituency	Result	Majority	Vote Share %	Swing %	MP
Hull East	Lab Hold	11,747	56.76	-7.81	John Prescott*
Hull North	Lab Hold	7,351	51.93	-5.22	Diana Johnson
Hull West & Hessle	Lab Hold	9,450	55.02	-3.36	Alan Johnson*
Huntingdon	Con Hold	12,847	50.83	+0.91	Jonathan Djanogly*
Hyndburn	Lab Hold	5,587	45.97	-8.68	Greg Pope*
Ilford North	Con Gain From Lab	1,653	43.68	+3.13	Lee Scott
Ilford South	Lab Coop Hold	9,228	48.85	-10.77	Mike Gapes*
Inverclyde	Lab Win#	11,259	50.75		David Cairns+
Inverness, Nairn	LD Win Notional Gain From Lab	4,148	40.29		Danny Alexander
Ipswich	Lab Hold	5,332	43.78	-7.54	Chris Mole*
Isle of Wight	Con Hold	12,978	48.95	+9.21	Andrew Turner*
Islington North	Lab Hold	6,716	51.18	-10.71	Jeremy Corbyn*
Islington S & Finsbury	Lab Hold	484	39.87	-14.06	Emily Thornberry
Islwyn	Lab Coop Hold	15,740	63.78	+2.24	Don Touhig*
Jarrow	Lab Hold	13,904	60.49	-5.57	Stephen Hepburn*
Keighley	Lab Hold	4,852	44.74	-3.46	Ann Cryer*
Kensington & Chelsea	Con Hold	12,418	57.90	+3.44	Sir Malcolm Rifkind
Kettering	Con Gain From Lab	3,301	45.65	+2.17	Philip Hollobone
Kilmarnock & Loud	Lab Win#	8,703	47.26		Des Browne+
Kingston & Surbiton	LD Hold	8,966	51.05	-9.13	Edward Davey*
Kingswood	Lab Hold	7,873	47.04	-7.83	Roger Berry*
Kirkcaldy & Cowdnbth	Lab Win#	18,216	58.09		Gordon Brown+
Knowsley N & Sefton E	Lab Hold	16,269	63.32	-3.41	George Howarth*
Knowsley South	Lab Hold	17,688	68.10	-3.15	Eddie O'Hara*
Lagan Valley	DUP Hold	14,117	54.70	+41.29	Jeffrey Donaldson*
Lanark & Hamilton E	Lab Win#	11,947	46.05		Jimmy Hood+
Lancashire West	Lab Hold	6,084	48.07	-6.39	Rosie Cooper
Lancaster & Wyre	Con Gain From Lab	4,171	42.77	+0.60	Ben Wallace
Leeds Central	Lab Hold	11,866	60.05	-6.88	Hilary Benn*

Election 2005

Constituency	Result	Majority	Vote Share %	Swing %	MP
Leeds East	Lab Hold	11,578	59.18	-3.77	George Mudie*
Leeds North East	Lab Hold	5,262	44.93	-4.20	Fabian Hamilton*
Leeds North West	LD Gain From Lab	1,877	37.15	+10.23	Greg Mulholland
Leeds West	Lab Hold	12,810	55.47	-6.67	John Battle*
Leicester East	Lab Hold	15,876	58.14	+0.59	Keith Vaz*
Leicester South	Lab Gain From LD	3,717	39.35	-15.13	Peter Soulsby
Leicester West	Lab Hold	9,070	51.72	-2.51	Patricia Hewitt*
Leicestershire NW	Lab Coop Hold	4,477	45.50	-6.56	David Taylor*
Leigh	Lab Hold	17,272	63.30	-1.24	Andy Burnham*
Leominster	Con Hold	13,187	52.07	+3.11	Bill Wiggin*
Lewes	LD Hold	8,474	52.36	-3.96	Norman Baker*
Lewisham Deptford	Lab Hold	11,811	55.61	-9.37	Joan Ruddock*
Lewisham East	Lab Hold	6,751	45.82	-7.89	Bridget Prentice*
Lewisham West	Lab Hold	9,932	52.03	-9.03	Jim Dowd*
Leyton & Wanstead	Lab Hold	6,857	45.78	-12.22	Harry Cohen*
Lichfield	Con Hold	7,080	48.63	-0.50	Michael Fabricant*
Lincoln	Lab Hold	4,614	45.38	-8.50	Gillian Merron*
Linlithgow & Falk E	Lab Win#	11,202	47.69		Michael Connarty+
Liverpool Garston	Lab Hold	7,193	54.04	-7.35	Maria Eagle*
Liverpool Riverside	Lab Coop Hold	10,214	57.55	-13.82	Louise Ellman*
Liverpool Walton	Lab Hold	15,957	72.76	-5.05	Peter Kilfoyle*
Liverpool Wavertree	Lab Hold	5,173	52.43	-10.28	Jane Kennedy*
Liverpool W Derby	Lab Hold	15,225	62.83	-3.35	Robert Wareing*
Livingston	Lab Win#	13,097	51.10		Robin Cook+
Llanelli	Lab Hold	7,234	46.94	-1.64	Nia Griffith
Londonderry East	DUP Hold	7,727	42.88	+10.74	Gregory Campbell*
Loughborough	Lab Coop Hold	1,996	41.39	-8.36	Andy Reed*
Louth & Horncastle	Con Hold	9,896	46.58	-1.88	Sir Peter Tapsell*
Ludlow	Con Gain From LD	2,027	45.08	+5.68	Philip Dunne
Luton North	Lab Hold	6,487	48.72	-7.98	Kelvin Hopkins*

Constituency	Result	Majority	Vote Share %	Swing %	MP
Luton South	Lab Hold	5,650	42.68	-12.51	Margaret Moran*
Macclesfield	Con Hold	9,401	49.60	+0.72	Sir Nicholas Winterton*
Maidenhead	Con Hold	6,231	50.84	+5.81	Theresa May*
Maidstone & Weald	Con Hold	14,856	52.65	+3.02	Ann Widdecombe*
Makerfield	Lab Hold	18,149	63.22	-5.29	Ian McCartney*
Maldon & Chel'ford E	Con Hold	12,573	51.49	+2.24	John Whittingdale*
Manchester Blackley	Lab Hold	12,027	62.29	-6.65	Graham Stringer*
Manchester Central	Lab Hold	9,776	58.07	-10.63	Tony Lloyd*
Manchester Gorton	Lab Hold	5,808	53.15	-9.64	Sir Gerald Kaufman*
Manchester Withington	LD Gain From Lab	667	42.37	+20.36	John Leech
Mansfield	Lab Hold	11,365	48.07	-9.05	Alan Meale*
Medway	Lab Hold	213	42.18	-6.81	Bob Marshall-Andrews*
Meirionnydd NC	PC Hold	6,614	51.34	+1.70	Elfyn Llwyd*
Meriden	Con Hold	7,009	48.20	+0.52	Caroline Spelman*
Merthyr Tydfil & Rh	Lab Hold	13,934	60.48	-1.30	Dai Havard*
Middlesbrough	Lab Hold	12,567	57.75	-9.82	Sir Stuart Bell*
Midbh S & ClevelandE	Lab Hold	8,000	50.22	-5.06	Dr Ashok Kumar*
Midlothian	Lab Win#	7,265	45.49		David Hamilton+
Milton Keynes NE	Con Gain From Lab	1,665	39.27	+1.19	Mark Lancaster
Milton Keynes SW	Lab Hold	4,010	42.83	-6.71	Phyllis Starkey*
Mitcham & Morden	Lab Hold	12,560	56.41	-4.01	Siobhan McDonagh*
Mole Valley	Con Hold	11,997	54.76	+4.22	Sir Paul Beresford*
Monmouth	Con Gain From Lab	4,527	46.87	+4.95	David Davis
Montgomeryshire	LD Hold	7,173	51.23	+1.83	Lembit Öpik*
Moray	SNP Win#	5,676	36.59		Angus Robertson+
Morecambe & L'dale	Lab Hold	4,768	48.83	-0.73	Geraldine Smith*
Morley & Rothwell	Lab Hold	12,343	48.41	-8.61	Colin Challen*
Motherwell & Wishaw	Lab Win#	15,222	57.47		Frank Roy+
Na h-Eileanan an Iar	SNP Gain From Lab	1,441	44.90	+8.05	Angus MacNeil
Neath	Lab Hold	12,710	52.59	-8.10	Peter Hain*

Election 2005

Constituency	Result	Majority	Vote Share %	Swing %	MP
New Forest East	Con Hold	6,551	48.58	+6.14	Dr Julian Lewis*
New Forest West	Con Hold	17,285	56.45	+0.71	Desmond Swayne*
Newark	Con Hold	6,464	48.03	+1.55	Patrick Mercer*
Newbury	Con Gain From LD	3,460	48.97	+5.48	Richard Benyon
Newcastle-under-Lyme	Lab Hold	8,108	45.37	-8.02	Paul Farrelly*
Newcastle Central	Lab Hold	3,982	45.13	-9.84	Jim Cousins*
Newcastle E & Wallsend	Lab Hold	7,565	55.12	-8.01	Nick Brown*
Newcastle North	Lab Hold	7,023	50.01	-10.14	Doug Henderson*
Newport East	Lab Hold	6,838	45.21	-9.52	Jessica Morden
Newport West	Lab Hold	5,458	44.84	-7.89	Paul Flynn*
Newry & Armagh	SF Gain From SDLP	8,195	41.35	+10.41	Conor Murphy
Norfolk Mid	Con Hold	7,560	43.05	-1.71	Keith Simpson*
Norfolk North	LD Hold	10,606	53.45	+10.80	Norman Lamb*
Norfolk North West	Con Hold	9,180	50.29	+1.76	Henry Bellingham*
Norfolk South	Con Hold	8,782	44.76	+2.59	Richard Bacon*
Norfolk South West	Con Hold	10,086	46.95	-5.24	Christopher Fraser
Normanton	Lab Coop Hold	10,002	51.20	-4.87	Ed Balls
Northampton North	Lab Hold	3,960	40.20	-9.22	Sally Keeble*
Northampton South	Con Gain From Lab	4,419	43.72	+2.57	Brian Binley
Northavon	LD Hold	11,033	52.28	-0.12	Steve Webb*
Norwich North	Lab Hold	5,459	44.86	-2.55	Dr Ian Gibson*
Norwich South	Lab Hold	3,653	37.70	-7.77	Charles Clarke*
Nottingham East	Lab Hold	6,939	45.82	-13.14	John Heppell*
Nottingham North	Lab Hold	12,171	58.72	-5.83	Graham Allen*
Nottingham South	Lab Hold	7,486	47.38	-7.12	Alan Simpson*
Nuneaton	Lab Hold	2,280	44.05	-8.08	Bill Olner*
Ochil & Perthshire S	Lab Win#	688	31.36		Gordon Banks
Ogmore	Lab Hold	13,703	60.42	-1.62	Huw Irranca-Davies*
Old Bexley & Sidcup	Con Hold	9,920	49.79	+4.38	Derek Conway*
Oldham E & Sadd	Lab Hold	3,590	41.43	+2.82	Phil Woolas*

Constituency	Result	Majority	Vote Share %	Swing %	MP
Oldham W & Royton	Lab Hold	10,459	49.13	-2.02	Michael Meacher*
Orkney & Shetland	LD Hold	6,627	51.50	+10.16	Alistair Carmichael*
Orpington	Con Hold	4,947	48.81	+4.95	John Horam*
Oxford East	Lab Hold	963	36.86	-12.53	Andrew Smith*
Oxford West & Abingdn	LD Hold	7,683	46.27	-1.57	Evan Harris*
Paisley & Renfr'w N	Lab Win#	11,001	45.73		James Sheridan+
Paisley & Renfr'w S	Lab Win#	13,232	52.57		Douglas Alexander+
Pendle	Lab Hold	2,180	37.08	-7.55	Gordon Prentice*
Penrith & Border	Con Hold	11,904	51.29	-3.63	David Maclean*
Perth & Perthshire N	SNP Win#	1,521	33.68		Peter Wishart+
Peterborough	Con Gain From Lab	2,740	42.14	+4.16	Stewart Jackson
Plymouth Devonport	Lab Hold	8,103	44.30	-14.00	Alison Seabeck
Plymouth Sutton	Lab Coop Hold	4,109	40.58	-10.17	Linda Gilroy*
Pontefract & Castleford	Lab Hold	15,246	63.66	-6.08	Yvette Cooper*
Pontypridd	Lab Hold	13,191	52.78	-7.16	Kim Howells*
Poole	Con Hold	5,988	43.37	-1.77	Robert Syms*
Poplar & Canning T	Lab Hold	7,129	40.06	-21.13	Jim Fitzpatrick*
Portsmouth North	Lab Coop Hold	1,139	40.86	-9.80	Sarah McCarthy-Fry
Portsmouth South	LD Hold	3,362	42.22	-2.38	Mike Hancock*
Preseli Pembrokeshire	Con Gain From Lab	607	35.56	+3.22	Stephen Crabb
Preston	Lab Coop Hold	9,407	50.50	-6.49	Mark Hendrick*
Pudsey	Lab Hold	5,870	45.78	-2.30	Paul Truswell*
Putney	Con Gain From Lab	1,766	42.37	+4.01	Justine Greening
Rayleigh	Con Hold	14,726	55.44	+5.33	Mark Francois*
Reading East	Con Gain From Lab	475	35.43	+3.47	Rob Wilson
Reading West	Lab Hold	4,682	44.98	-8.13	Martin Salter*
Redcar	Lab Hold	12,116	51.38	-8.90	Vera Baird*
Redditch	Lab Hold	2,716	44.70	-0.93	Jacqui Smith*
Regent's P'k & Ken N	Lab Hold	6,131	44.73	-9.92	Karen Buck*
Reigate	Con Hold	10,988	49.02	+1.20	Crispin Blunt*

Election 2005

Constituency	Result	Majority	Vote Share %	Swing %	MP
Renfrewshire East	Lab Hold	6,657	43.91	-3.72	Jim Murphy*
Rhondda	Lab Hold	16,242	68.06	-0.26	Chris Bryant*
Ribble South	Lab Hold	2,184	43.00	-3.37	David Borrow*
Ribble Valley	Con Hold	14,171	51.91	+0.44	Nigel Evans*
Richmond (Yorks)	Con Hold	17,807	59.12	+0.19	William Hague*
Richmond Park	LD Hold	3,731	46.74	-0.96	Susan Kramer
Rochdale	LD Gain From Lab	442	41.12	+6.23	Paul Rowen
Rochford & S'thend E	Con Hold	5,494	45.29	-8.26	James Duddridge
Romford	Con Hold	11,589	59.10	+6.07	Andrew Rosindell*
Romsey	LD Hold	125	44.65	-2.31	Sandra Gidley*
Ross, Skye & Loch	LD Win#	14,249	58.70		Charles Kennedy+
Rossendale & Darwen	Lab Hold	3,676	42.92	-5.75	Janet Anderson*
Rother Valley	Lab Hold	14,224	55.38	-6.71	Kevin Barron*
Rotherham	Lab Hold	10,681	52.84	-11.07	Dennis MacShane*
Rugby & Kenilworth	Con Gain From Lab	1,556	41.17	+1.50	Jeremy Wright
Ruislip-Northwood	Con Hold	8,910	47.74	-1.03	Nick Hurd
Runnymede & Weyb	Con Hold	12,349	51.39	+2.72	Philip Hammond*
Rushcliffe	Con Hold	12,974	49.54	+2.03	Kenneth Clarke*
Rutherglen & H'tn W	Lab Coop Win#	16,112	55.60		Tommy McAvoy+
Rutland & Melton	Con Hold	12,930	51.21	+3.13	Alan Duncan*
Ryedale	Con Hold	10,469	48.17	+0.99	John Greenway*
Saffron Walden	Con Hold	13,008	51.42	+2.49	Sir Alan Haselhurst*
St Albans	Con Gain From Lab	1,361	37.29	+2.05	Anne Main
St Helens North	Lab Hold	13,962	56.86	-4.25	Dave Watts*
St Helens South	Lab Hold	9,309	54.53	+4.84	Shaun Woodward*
St Ives	LD Hold	11,609	50.73	-0.85	Andrew George*
Salford	Lab Hold	7,945	57.55	-7.51	Hazel Blears*
Salisbury	Con Hold	11,142	47.79	+1.16	Robert Key*
Scarborough & Whitby	Con Gain From Lab	1,245	41.03	+1.38	Robert Godwill

Constituency	Result	Majority	Vote Share %	Swing %	MP
Scunthorpe	Lab Hold	8,963	53.13	-6.63	Elliot Morley*
Sedgefield	Lab Hold	18,457	58.59	-5.97	Tony Blair*
Selby	Lab Hold	467	43.05	-2.01	John Grogan*
Sevenoaks	Con Hold	12,970	51.82	+2.42	Michael Fallon*
Sheffield Attercliffe	Lab Hold	15,967	60.10	-7.69	Clive Betts*
Sheffield Brightside	Lab Hold	13,644	68.52	-8.38	David Blunkett*
Sheffield Central	Lab Hold	7,055	49.86	-11.59	Richard Caborn*
Sheffield Hallam	LD Hold	8,682	51.23	-4.21	Nick Clegg
Sheffield Heeley	Lab Coop Hold	11,370	53.98	-2.99	Meg Munn*
Sheffield Hillsborough	Lab Hold	11,243	51.17	-5.66	Angela Smith
Sherwood	Lab Hold	6,652	48.44	-5.81	Paddy Tipping*
Shipley	Con Gain From Lab	422	39.04	-1.85	Philip Davies
Shrewsbury & Atcham	Con Gain From Ind	1,808	37.70	+0.28	Daniel Kawczynski
Shropshire North	Con Hold	11,020	49.58	+0.93	Owen Paterson*
Sittingbourne & Shep	Lab Hold	79	41.79	-4.01	Derek Wyatt*
Skipton & Ripon	Con Hold	11,620	49.68	-2.71	David Curry*
Sleaford & N Hykeham	Con Hold	12,705	50.29	+0.64	Douglas Hogg*
Slough	Lab Hold	7,851	47.22	-11.03	Fiona Mactaggart*
Solihull	LD Gain From Con	279	39.94	+13.99	Lorely Burt
Somerton & Frome	LD Hold	812	44.06	+0.44	David Heath*
S Holland & Deepings	Con Hold	15,780	57.09	+1.65	John Hayes*
South Shields	Lab Hold	12,312	60.48	-2.68	David Miliband*
Southampton Itchen	Lab Hold	9,302	48.28	-6.23	John Denham*
Southampton Test	Lab Hold	7,018	42.71	-9.78	Dr Alan Whitehead*
Southend West	Con Hold	8,959	46.22	-0.11	David Amess*
Southport	LD Hold	3,838	46.34	+2.58	John Pugh*
Southwark N & B'dsy	LD Hold	5,406	47.09	-9.86	Simon Hughes*
Spelthorne	Con Hold	9,936	50.48	+5.38	David Wilshire*
Stafford	Lab Hold	2,121	43.66	-4.32	David Kidney*
Staffordshire Moorlands	Lab Hold	2,438	40.96	-8.04	Charlotte Atkins*

Election 2005

Constituency	Result	Majority	Vote Share %	Swing %	MP
Stalybridge & Hyde	Lab Hold	8,348	49.65	-5.83	James Purnell*
Stevenage	Lab Hold	3,139	42.93	-8.95	Barbara Follett*
Stirling	Lab Win#	4,767	36.00		Anne McGuire+
Stockport	Lab Hold	9,163	50.51	-8.08	Ann Coffey*
Stockton North	Lab Hold	12,437	54.94	-8.49	Frank Cook*
Stockton South	Lab Hold	6,139	47.82	-5.15	Dari Taylor*
Stoke-on-Trent C	Lab Hold	9,774	52.89	-7.78	Mark Fisher*
Stoke-on-Trent N	Lab Hold	10,036	52.64	-5.34	Joan Walley*
Stoke-on-Trent S	Lab Hold	8,681	46.87	-6.88	Robert Flello
Stone	Con Hold	9,089	48.33	-0.74	Bill Cash*
Stourbridge	Lab Hold	407	40.97	-6.17	Lynda Waltho
Strangford	DUP Hold	13,049	56.49	+13.65	Iris Robinson*
Stratford-on-Avon	Con Hold	12,184	49.20	-1.07	John Maples*
Streatham	Lab Hold	7,466	46.66	-10.21	Keith Hill*
Stretford & Urmston	Lab Hold	7,851	50.96	-10.15	Beverley Hughes*
Stroud	Lab Coop Hold	350	39.61	-6.94	David Drew*
Suffolk C & Ipswich N	Con Hold	7,856	43.91	-0.52	Sir Michael Lord*
Suffolk Coastal	Con Hold	9,685	44.55	+1.21	John Gummer*
Suffolk South	Con Hold	6,606	42.03	+0.64	Tim Yeo*
Suffolk West	Con Hold	8,909	49.05	+1.46	Richard Spring*
Sunderland North	Lab Hold	9,995	54.37	-8.29	Bill Etherington*
Sunderland South	Lab Hold	11,059	58.55	-5.33	Chris Mullin*
Surrey East	Con Hold	15.921	56.16	+3.65	Peter Ainsworth*
Surrey Heath	Con Hold	10,845	51.49	+1.82	Michael Gove
Surrey South West	Con Hold	5,711	50.41	+5.12	Jeremy Hunt
Sussex Mid	Con Hold	·5,890	48.02	+1.86	Nicholas Soames*
Sutton & Cheam	LD Hold	2,846	47.14	-1.65	Paul Burstow*
Sutton Coldfield	Con Hold	12,283	52.48	+2.06	Andrew Mitchell*
Swansea East	Lab Hold	11,249	56.62	-8.60	Sian James
Swansea West	Lab Hold	4,269	41.81	-6.93	Alan Williams*
Swindon North	Lab Hold	2,571	43.69	-9.16	Michael Wills*
Swindon South	Lab Hold	1,353	40.33	-10.98	Anne Snelgrove
Tamworth	Lab Hold	2,569	42.98	-6.02	Brian Jenkins*

Constituency	Result	Majority	Vote Share %	Swing %	MP
Tatton	Con Hold	11,731	51.79	+3.67	George Osborne*
Taunton	LD Gain From Con	573	43.28	+2.00	Jeremy Browne
Teignbridge	LD Hold	6,215	45.66	+1.25	Richard Younger-Ross*
Telford	Lab Hold	5,406	48.25	-6.33	David Wright*
Tewkesbury	Con Hold	9,892	49.15	+3.06	Laurence Robertson*
Thanet North	Con Hold	7,634	49.62	-0.66	Roger Gale*
Thanet South	Lab Hold	664	40.40	-5.26	Dr Stephen Ladyman*
Thurrock	Lab Hold	6,375	47.23	-9.30	Andrew Mackinlay*
Tiverton & Honiton	Con Hold	11,051	47.86	+0.79	Angela Browning*
Tonbridge & Malling	Con Hold	13,352	52.88	+3.49	Sir John Stanley*
Tooting	Lab Hold	5,381	43.10	-10.99	Sadiq Khan
Torbay	LD Hold	2,029	40.84	-9.65	Adrian Sanders*
Torfaen	Lab Hold	14,791	56.90	-5.19	Paul Murphy*
Totnes	Con Hold	1,947	41.74	-2.76	Anthony Steen*
Tottenham	Lab Hold	13,034	57.93	-9.53	David Lammy*
Truro & St Austell	LD Hold	7,403	46.72	-1.59	Matthew Taylor*
Tunbridge Wells	Con Hold	9,988	49.60	+0.74	Greg Clark
Twickenham	LD Hold	9,965	51.65	+2.90	Vincent Cable*
Tyne Bridge	Lab Hold	10,390	61.19	-9.28	David Clelland*
Tynemouth	Lab Hold	4,143	47.00	-6.22	Alan Campbell*
Tyneside North	Lab Hold	15,037	61.95	-7.52	Stephen Byers*
Tyrone West	SF Hold	5,005	38.89	-1.94	Pat Doherty*
Ulster Mid	SF Hold	10,976	47.64	-3.43	Martin McGuinness*
Upminster	Con Hold	6,042	48.50	+2.98	Angela Watkinson*
Upper Bann	DUP Gain From UUP	5,298	37.55	+8.08	David Simpson
Uxbridge	Con Hold	6,171	48.98	+1.85	John Randall*
Vale of Clwyd	Lab Hold	4,669	46.03	-3.98	Chris Ruane*
Vale of Glamorgan	Lab Hold	1,808	41.17	-4.26	John Smith*
Vale of York	Con Hold	13,712	51.66	+0.03	Anne McIntosh
Vauxhall	Lab Hold	9,977	52.86	-6.25	Kate Hoey*
Wakefield	Lab Hold	5,154	43.34	-6.57	Mary Creagh

Election 2005

Constituency	Result	Majority	Vote Share %	Swing %	MP
Wallasey	Lab Hold	9,109	54.77	-6.06	Angela Eagle*
Walsall North	Lab Hold	6,640	47.83	-10.28	David Winnick*
Walsall South	Lab Hold	7,946	49.93	-9.02	Bruce George*
Walthamstow	Lab Hold	7,993	50.29	-11.87	Neil Gerrard*
Wansbeck	Lab Hold	10,581	55.19	-2.58	Denis Murphy*
Wansdyke	Lab Hold	1,839	40.61	-6.22	Dan Norris*
Wantage	Con Gain From Lab	8,017	43.05	+3.41	Ed Vaizey
Warley	Lab Hold	10,147	54.42	-6.08	John Spellar*
Warrington North	Lab Hold	12,204	53.52	-8.23	Helen Jones*
Warrington South	Lab Hold	3,515	40.54	-8.73	Helen Southworth*
Warwick & Leam'ton	Lab Hold	266	40.59	-8.17	James Plaskitt*
Warwickshire North	Lab Hold	7,553	48.06	-6.03	Mike O'Brien*
Watford	Lab Hold	1,148	33.56	-11.71	Claire Ward*
Waveney	Lab Hold	5,915	45.32	-5.38	Bob Blizzard*
Wealden	Con Hold	15,921	52.06	+2.25	Charles Hendry*
Weaver Vale	Lab Hold	6,855	47.59	-4.90	Mike Hall*
Wellingborough	Con Gain From Lab	687	42.78	+0.06	Peter Bone
Wells	Con Hold	3,040	43.56	-0.21	David Heathcoat-Amory*
Welwyn Hatfield	Con Gain From Lab	5,946	49.58	+9.21	Grant Shapps
Wentworth	Lab Hold	15,056	59.63	-7.87	John Healey*
West Bromwich E	Lab Hold	11,652	55.59	-0.28	Tom Watson*
West Bromwich W	Lab Coop Hold	10,894	54.27	-6.50	Adrian Bailey*
West Ham	Lab Hold	9,801	51.15	-18.70	Lyn Brown
Westbury	Con Hold	5,349	44.51	+2.44	Dr Andrew Murrison*
Westmorland & Lons	LD Gain From Con	267	45.47	+5.10	Tim Farron
Weston-super-Mare	Con Gain From LD	2,079	40.34	+1.59	John Penrose
Wigan	Lab Hold	11,767	55.14	-6.60	Neil Turner*
Wiltshire North	Con Hold	5,303	46.88	+1.38	James Gray*

The complete results

Constituency	Result	Majority	Vote Share %	Swing %	MP
Wimbledon	Con Gain From Lab	2,301	41.21	+4.57	Stephen Hammond
Winchester	LD Hold	7,476	50.64	-3.93	Mark Oaten*
Windsor	Con Hold	10,292	49.54	+2.28	Adam Afriyie
Wirral South	Lab Hold	3,724	42.54	-4.90	Ben Chapman*
Wirral West	Lab Hold	1,097	42.55	-4.66	Stephen Hesford*
Witney	Con Hold	14,756	49.33	+4.30	David Cameron*
Woking	Con Hold	6,612	47.43	+1.41	Humfrey Malins*
Wokingham	Con Hold	7,240	48.13	+2.02	John Redwood*
Wolverhampton NE	Lab Coop Hold	8,156	54.46	-5.82	Ken Purchase*
Wolverhampton SE	Lab Hold	10,495	59.43	-8.01	Pat McFadden
Wolverhampton SW	Lab Hold	2,879	44.36	-3.89	Rob Marris*
Woodspring	Con Hold	6,016	41.82	-1.86	Dr Liam Fox*
Worcester	Lab Hold	3,144	41.87	-6.72	Michael Foster*
Worcestershire Mid	Con Hold	13,327	51.50	+0.41	Peter Luff*
Worcestershire W	Con Hold	2,475	45.39	-0.58	Sir Michael Spicer*
Workington	Lab Hold	6,895	49.21	-6.29	Tony Cunningham*
Worsley	Lab Hold	9,368	51.04	-6.06	Barbara Keeley
Worthing E & Shor'm	Con Hold	8,183	43.89	+0.68	Tim Loughton*
Worthing West	Con Hold	9,379	47.58	+0.12	Peter Bottomley*
The Wrekin	Con Gain From Lab	942	41.95	+3.52	Mark Pritchard
Wrexham	Lab Hold	6,819	46.05	-6.98	Ian Lucas*
Wycombe	Con Hold	7,051	45.76	+3.37	Paul Goodman*
Wyre Forest	KHHC Hold	5,250	39.88	-18.18	Dr Richard Taylor*
Wythenshawe & Sale E	Lab Hold	10,827	52.17	-7.82	Paul Goggins*
Yeovil	LD Hold	8,562	51.41	+7.22	David Laws*
Ynys Mon	Lab Hold	1,242	34.62	-0.38	Albert Owen*
York, City of	Lab Hold	10,472	46.86	-5.39	Hugh Bayley*
Yorkshire East	Con Hold	6,283	45.21	-0.64	Greg Knight*

Highs and lows

HIGHEST majority: Labour's Thomas Clarke in the redrawn Scottish seat of Coatbridge, Chryston and Bellshill, with a winning margin of 19,519, 50.9 per cent of the vote, over Duncan Ross of the SNP.

LOWEST majority: Labour's Laura Moffat, with a breathing space of just 37, or 0.09 per cent of the vote, over Tory Henry Smith.

OLDEST MP: Ealing Southall returned Labour's Piara Khabra, 80, with a majority of 11,440.

YOUNGEST MP: The Liberal Democrats' Jo Swinson, 25, who won East Dunbartonshire, a redrawn seat, on a notional swing from Labour of 7.49 per cent.

HIGHEST NUMBER OF WOMEN MPs: The 2005 election saw the highest number of female MPs elected to the House of Commons – 125 – since women got the vote. The previous record was in 1997 when 120 were elected. It fell back to 118 in 2001.

MOST RELIEVED MP: Labour's Jim Knight who held the party's most marginal seat at the 2001 general election, increasing his majority from 153 to 1,812 after Tony Blair made his first campaign stop of the 2005 contest to back him.

MOST DISAPPOINTED CANDIDATE: Schools Minister Stephen Twigg who lost the Enfield Southgate seat, symbol of New Labour election power in 1997 when he captured it from Michael Portillo, back to the Tories.

HIGHEST NUMBER OF CANDIDATES: There were fifteen candidates in Tony Blair's Sedgefield seat, but he saw his fourteen opponents off, increasing his majority to 18,457.

FIRST: The MP who comes first alphabetically in the list of the new parliament is Labour's Diane Abbott, Hackney North and Stoke Newington.

LAST: The MP who comes last alphabetically is the Liberal Democrat Richard Younger-Ross, Teignbridge.